D0194935

Serenity in the Storm

ALSO BY KAYLEIGH MCENANY

For Such a Time as This

The New American Revolution

Serenity in the Storm

LIVING THROUGH CHAOS
BY LEANING ON CHRIST

KAYLEIGH MCENANY

Liberatio
Protocol

A LIBERATIO PROTOCOL BOOK
An Imprint of Post Hill Press
ISBN: 978-1-63758-729-4
ISBN (eBook): 978-1-63758-730-0

Serenity in the Storm:
Living Through Chaos by Leaning on Christ
© 2023 by Kayleigh McEnany
All Rights Reserved

Cover Design by Cody Corcoran

Cover Photography by Angelina Oliva

Interior Design by Yoni Limor, www.YoniLimor.com

Scripture quotations taken from the Holy Bible, New International Version®, NIV®: Copyright ©1973, 1978, 1984, 2011 by Biblica, Inc.™ Used by permission of Zondervan. All rights reserved worldwide. www.zondervan.com The "NIV" and "New International Version" are trademarks registered in the United States Patent and Trademark Office by Biblica, Inc.™

Scripture quotations taken from The ESV® Bible (The Holy Bible, English Standard Version®): Copyright © 2001 by Crossway, a publishing ministry of Good News Publishers. Used by permission. All rights reserved.

This is a work of nonfiction. All people, locations, events, and situation are portrayed to the best of the author's memory.

No part of this book may be reproduced, stored in a retrieval system, or transmitted by any means without the written permission of the author and publisher.

Post Hill Press
New York • Nashville
posthillpress.com

Published in the United States of America
1 2 3 4 5 6 7 8 9 10

To my newborn son, Nash.

You were nestled inside my belly as I wrote every word of this book.

May you always know that He is walking beside you through every trial you face.

Be strong, look up, and know you are a child of Christ.

To my daughter, Blake, and husband, Sean.

You were both by my side as I penned Serenity in the Storm.

You inspire me every single day.

I love you.

TABLE OF CONTENTS

EDUCATION

LIBERTY

SOCIETY

A BROKEN COUNTRY,
BUT A GREATER GOD

What is happening to our country? It's a question I find myself asking almost daily. Something has changed in the United States of America, and it transcends politics.

God has been exiled.

Hate proliferates.

Society perverted.

Truth rejected.

American symbols desecrated.

What has become of the country I love so dearly? This cultural shift is far more insidious than the election of any one president or the dominance of any one political party in Washington, DC. All of that is very important, no doubt, but I am speaking of a dangerous tectonic eruption in the American conscience that is upending us from the inside out, making our country virtually unrecognizable.

At the center of this cultural shift is the eradication of God from American society. Look no further than famous atheist Richard Dawkins's assessment: "It is fashionable to wax apocalyptic about the threat to humanity posed by the AIDS virus, 'mad cow' disease, and many others, but I think a case can be made that *faith* is one of the world's great evils, comparable to the smallpox virus but harder to eradicate."[1]

We have seen this shocking, callous attitude manifested in everyday life, in our schools, and in our government. In Bremerton, Washington, a high school sought to stop a football coach from kneeling in silent prayer alone at the 50-yard line.[2] In Nevada, during the COVID-19 outbreak, the directive was clear: open the casinos, close the churches.[3] And in Kentucky, drive-through liquor stores were no problem at all. But drive-in church services? Well, that was criminal activity.[4]

And yet faith was at the very center of America's founding. Our Declaration of Independence was written "with a firm reliance on the protection of divine Providence...."[5] At the first presidential inauguration, before swearing the oath, George Washington opened the Bible to Psalm 121:1: "I raise my eyes toward the hills. Whence shall my help come."[6] Subsequent presidents also swore the presidential oath of office with one hand on a Bible while reciting the words "so help me God."[7] During some of America's most exigent moments from the Civil War and World War I to the Great Depression and World War II, presidents have appealed to God, the very being our country now seeks to ostracize.

Meanwhile, there is a new quest to cancel the symbols that bind us together as Americans: our flag, our anthem, our Pledge of Allegiance, even our Founding Fathers. A *New York Times* editorial board member announced that she was "disturbed" to see the American flag.[8] Singer Macy Gray called the flag "tattered, dated, divisive, and incorrect."[9] And an Olympic alternate said she dreamed of winning a medal so that she could stand on the podium and burn the American flag, not drape it over her shoulders in appreciation of our magnificent country. "My goal is to win the Olympics so I can burn a US flag on the podium," the athlete said in no uncertain terms.[10]

Far too many schools are pushing these radical ideas on our children. We are told that parents have no role in their children's education, that elementary-aged school children can change their pronouns while their parents remain in the dark. Critical race theory and critical gender theory divide our children. Even preschoolers have racist tendencies, they say![11] All this as drag queen shows at American schools have become in vogue, with New York City schools spending more than $200,000 taxpayer dollars to bring these provocative performances to elementary, middle, and high schools.[12]

The media, for its part, continues to stoke division with furious and fallacious headlines meant to divide us at a time when we already walk on eggshells around one another, concealing our political opinions in fear that we might be canceled. Social media, meanwhile, is a swirling cesspool, poisoning the minds of our children. Inciting competition among young girls in a quest for unattainable perfection, these platforms provoke body image issues, depression, and at times even self-harm. Drug dealers have seized on the newfound power of social media, preying on innocent teenagers, offering fentanyl-laced prescription drugs that prove deadly, and making overdose deaths the number one killer of young people ages eighteen to forty-five.[13]

Senseless, shocking criminal activity has taken over American streets. A woman shoved into the subway tracks, falling to her death in Times Square.[14] An innocent, little one-year-old boy shot and killed at a barbeque.[15] A man sucker-punched out of nowhere and beaten into a coma.[16] The stories of these victims are endless while the repercussions for the criminals are too often minimal.

At its core, it seems some have totally lost sight of the value of human life. That became very clear when I woke up to this headline in June of 2022: "US abortions rise: 1 in 5 pregnancies terminated in 2020."[17] One in five! Overall, sixty-three million children have been lost to the scourge of abortion—sixty-three million little ones created by God, who we will never come to know in this life.[18]

All of this as the world is spiraling out of control. In soul-crushing agony, America watched as Afghanistan fell to the Taliban, leaving countless Americans behind and thirteen fallen heroes in the wake. Russia invaded Ukraine, bringing us as close to World War III as we have ever been. North Korea is firing off missiles as China circles Taiwan, and Iran awaits another cushy nuclear deal.

It is safe to say that America is not just enduring a storm but a raging hurricane. Society has rejected truth and common sense and opted instead for moral relativism.

Up is down.

Right is wrong.

None of it makes sense.

But as dim as the future may seem and as hopeless as it may feel, I am here to bring you a message of hope and optimism. While we are up against formidable foes and much adversity, our God is greater.

In Afghanistan, even amid despair and human atrocity, the underground church is at work for Christ. We've seen just the same in Syria and Iran—oppressive countries, where the Christian community is nevertheless growing. Who would have thought that "Iran has the fastest growing church in the world" and "there's a revival in northern Syria," according to Joel Richardson of Global Catalytic Ministries?[19]

Even though God has been removed from our schools, and churches were targeted for closure during COVID-19, the Supreme Court has delivered steady victories for men and women of faith. Furthermore, the *Dobbs* decision overturning *Roe v. Wade* proved to be the most consequential Supreme Court decision of my lifetime. In deciding to return power to the people, some jurisdictions in this country have now chosen to protect innocent life.

Our God is bigger than the challenges we face, and make no mistake, He is at work!

In the pages that follow, I will walk you through several global, political, and cultural challenges: the fall of Afghanistan, the war in Ukraine, education, life, liberty, and societal decay. Most of these chapters are accompanied by a subsequent one that highlights how God is moving even now. These are the stories and insights that you will never see on the news and are rarely discussed. It is my hope that these pages will give you encouragement at a time when it is in short supply.

Among these chapters are two that stand out: "An All-Powerful God and a Suffering World" and "A Proven Savior." These portions of the book raise some of the most challenging questions in life. How can a perfect, all-loving God tolerate a world full of evil, pain, and suffering? And how do we know that God is real? That Jesus Christ is Savior? In these chapters, I survey scholarly literature and biblical text in an effort to provide answers.

As you flip through the pages of this book, it may be tempting to focus on the many troubles our country faces. These are rocky, tumultuous, uncertain times indeed. As Christians, though, we have cause for hope, even amid despair. Why?

Because, as Pastor Rick Warren aptly observed, our all-powerful "God has already written the end of the story."[20]

AFGHANISTAN

CHAPTER 1

THE UNFATHOMABLE FALL

It was a warm, sunny Friday in August as I hugged my daughter and rushed out the door, down the yellow, glossy steps and toward a large van waiting in my driveway. I grabbed the hefty black handle on the right side of the vehicle and pulled the door toward me with a firm jerk. Climbing up the steps, I rushed to the wooden chair and table, placed just in front of a television monitor displaying vibrant tones of yellow, red, and white. Today, this nondescript, rather ordinary-looking van would function as a television studio, permitting me to broadcast from my driveway in Florida and into millions of homes across the country. While my setup was certainly different from the flashy, blazing television sets of New York City, it would get the job done.

Noon was approaching, and that meant we were moments away from broadcasting on Fox News's *Outnumbered* and discussing an increasingly frightening situation halfway across the globe. Though the day in Florida was bright and glimmering with the sun's rays piercing through the palm trees, a far different scene was transpiring just under eight thousand miles away in Kabul, Afghanistan.

Back in April, President Biden had announced his plan for a complete withdrawal of the remaining 2,500 American troops from Afghanistan by September 11, the war's 20th anniversary.[21] "We will not conduct a hasty rush to the exit," Biden promised. "We'll do it responsibly, deliberately, and safely."[22]

On the contrary, by that Friday afternoon in August, the Taliban had overtaken the majority of Afghanistan with striking rapidity.[23] American troops and countless citizens remained in harm's way, and the US intelligence assessment suggested the fall of Afghanistan could occur within three months.[24] The projection was an abrupt turnaround from what our commander in chief had assured the American public just over a month earlier. "[T]he likelihood there's going to be the Taliban overrunning everything and owning the whole country is highly unlikely," President Biden told the nation.[25] But the prospects of the Afghan government retaining control of the country appeared far bleaker on the afternoon of Friday, August 13, 2021.

Even so, I never imagined leaving my *Outnumbered* studio van on Friday and returning on Monday to find a newly declared state: the Islamic Emirate of Afghanistan—a murderous and gruesome terrorist safe haven, Americans trapped within. After all, in June, Secretary of State Antony Blinken assured us that the fall of Afghanistan would not "be something that happens from a Friday to a Monday."[26] That, however, is exactly what transpired.

By Sunday, Taliban fighters overtook the streets of Kabul. Afghan president Ashraf Ghani fled amid allegations that he escaped with more than $150 million in US dollars intended for the Afghan people.[27] Shortly thereafter, the Taliban was "handed" the presidential palace. Armed Taliban militants were seen posing behind President Ghani's wooden desk, clad in their weaponry. Ironically, one such Taliban militant claimed to have been previously detained in Guantanamo Bay, only to be released by President Obama in the infamous swap of five terrorist prisoners for Bowe Bergdahl, the American deserter.[28]

As Afghanistan's capital descended into anarchy, prisoners were released en masse from the Kabul jail, fleeing on foot.[29] And less than a month later—on the twentieth anniversary of the September 11, 2001, attacks—the Taliban raised their black-and-white flag over Afghanistan, a country where 2,448 American soldiers lost their lives.[30]

While the Taliban entered Kabul, a United States Chinook helicopter was photographed descending parallel to a cloud of billowing, black smoke and into the American embassy. The image immediately drew comparisons to the infamous image from the 1975 fall of Saigon, when the United States evacuated a CIA safe house in Saigon after exiting the Vietnam War.[31] That image defined a controversial and tumultuous war in American history, depicting a helicopter perched on top of an evacuation point as throngs of Americans climbed stairs trying to flee.

Now, America watched the chaotic final chapter of a war that had defined the twenty-first century of American history. In the case of Afghanistan, Chairman of the Joint Chiefs Mark Milley told the nation two months prior to Kabul's fall, "You can't predict the future. But, I don't see Saigon 1975 in Afghanistan.... The Taliban just aren't the North Vietnamese army. It's not that kind of situation."[32] Even more brazenly, one month later, President Biden echoed the assessment in blunt terms: "There's going to be no circumstance where you're going to see people being lifted off the roof of a embassy of the United States from Afghanistan," he said.[33] And while the administration dismissed parallels to Saigon, noting that the Afghan evacuation was "very deliberate," the comparison was unavoidable to a watching world.[34]

The "highly unlikely" fall of Kabul—as predicted by the commander in chief—on the contrary, proved highly *likely*.

Biden's ill-fated prediction of an orderly withdrawal from Afghanistan turned out to be about as accurate as President Barack Obama calling ISIS the "jayvee team" just before the ruthless terrorist group declared a caliphate and took over vast swathes of Syria and Iraq.[35]

Grievously wrong.

Terribly naïve.

Worse than any naïve predictions, though, were the actions of the Biden administration in the aftermath. As Afghanistan fell, our president was not in the White House Situation Room surrounded by military leaders; rather, our president was at the presidential retreat, Camp David, pictured alone at a table video conferencing government officials about the impending disaster in Afghanistan.[36] The timeline of the president's movements leading up to the fall of Afghanistan tells the story of a country rapidly on the brink of collapse and an administration that did not see it coming.

ON WEDNESDAY EVENING, August 11, 2021—days before Afghanistan's Sunday collapse—President Biden met with his team about the gradually worsening conditions in Afghanistan. Based on interviews with thirty-three US officials and lawmakers, *Politico* recounted this meeting and several others leading up to Afghanistan's collapse.[37] Ahead of that Wednesday evening meeting, described by an official as a "serious moment," *Politico* characterized the mood in the White House as "ebullient." Earlier in the day, President Biden and Vice President Kamala Harris had celebrated "back-to-back legislative wins…pump[ing] their fists in triumph" in the president's private dining room, but the mood was very different that Wednesday night, as the president requested that his top military brass draw up plans for sending American troops back into the increasingly threatened Afghanistan.[38]

On Thursday, a "sobering" meeting took place at 7:30 a.m. in the Situation Room among top national security advisors, where it was determined that Kabul could fall in "weeks or days." This was described by a US official as the "oh, shit" moment. The stunning news ultimately prompted President Biden to send three thousand troops to Afghanistan. And as these troops traveled back into the country they were supposed to depart, President Biden left for vacation in Delaware after spending only two days in Washington, DC—yes, vacation.[39] "Biden was looking forward to his summer vacation," *Politico* reported.[40] Neither the shocking developments in Afghanistan nor the sending of more US troops prompted President Biden to change his vacation plans. Predictably, he took no questions on his way out the door.[41] It was not until the fall of Afghanistan was imminent that President Biden relocated, not to the White House, but to Camp David—a strategic blunder no doubt.

As White House press secretary, I had been in both the Situation Room and Camp David. The Situation Room—a five-thousand-square-foot secure area in the West Wing—served as the location for the Trump-era daily coronavirus task force meetings. I distinctly remember my first time entering the "Sit Room" as we called it. Leaving my phone at the entry point of the complex, I walked into the main conference room. With a large mahogany table in the center and wood paneling outlining the room, the center point of the Sit Room was the large monitor equipped with secure conferencing capabilities and couched by neon red and green clocks with times from across the globe.

During the first coronavirus task force meeting I attended, I took my seat along the wall of the room, reflecting on all of the major, consequential operations that had been monitored from this very location—the Cuban Missile Crisis, the Tet Offensive in Vietnam, the death of Osama bin Laden, and so much more.[42]

Now, though, as Afghanistan fell after a two-decade-long war, where was President Biden?

Approximately seventy miles away, President Biden sat—almost as a spectator—at "the president's country residence" tucked away in Catoctin Mountain Park. Offering "an opportunity for solitude and tranquility"—as described by the official White House website—Camp David was truly a getaway.[43] I would know. I visited the woody retreat the weekend after my first press briefing.

Huddled around a fire with my husband in early May of 2020, an intimate group of guests and I enjoyed cocktails, reflecting on my very first briefing before retiring to the dining room for dinner situated just off the quaint and rather cozy living room where several presidents celebrated Christmas with their families. The quiet maze of intimate cabins—also known as Shangri-La—indeed offered an escape. Though many presidents hosted foreign leaders at the venue, providing a chance for a more personal interaction, Camp David hardly seemed like the ideal place for observing the fall of a country—a country Americans had fought to liberate from the Taliban for twenty years.

As Afghanistan fell during that weekend in August of 2021, I hustled through John F. Kennedy International Airport in New York with my mother, intent on making it to a potential Fox News appearance to react to the jarring images crossing our television screens. The world watched and Americans took a collective breath in utter disbelief while our president appeared woefully aloof. On that Sunday, the Taliban overwhelmed the streets of Afghanistan's capital, but there was no presidential address to the nation. No questions were taken. Americans were left in the dark.

In fact, we had not heard from our so-called "commander in chief" in six days—yes, six days![44] Not only that, an attempt to contact the White House press secretary was met with an automated reply that she would be out of the office until the 22nd of

August—nearly a week from the day Kabul fell.[45] When the White House press secretary finally turned off the auto-reply (earlier than denoted in her auto-response) and held a briefing, we learned from National Security Advisor Jake Sullivan that forty-eight hours after the fall of Afghanistan, the president still had not even picked up the phone to call a single world leader.

"He has not yet spoken to any other world leaders," Sullivan admitted. "Myself, Secretary Blinken, several other senior members of the team have been engaged on a regular basis with foreign counterparts, and we intend to do so in the coming days."[46]

Wow.

After not speaking to a single world leader or the American public for nearly a week, President Biden announced on Monday, "I will be addressing the nation on Afghanistan at 3:45 PM ET today."[47]

Too little too late.

Afghanistan had fallen, and an undetermined number of US citizens were stranded behind enemy lines. Meanwhile, our nation watched a hurried evacuation effort and the horrific images of Afghans falling from a US aircraft.[48] Desperate Afghans rushed onto a US C-17 aircraft intended for US embassy personnel; in one case, 640 people crowded into a jet meant to carry 150.[49]

Video images showed hundreds of Afghan men and women chasing an aircraft during takeoff, trying to escape the Taliban hellhole behind them. The Associated Press describes the moment this way: "As the C-17 transporter gains altitude, shaky mobile phone video captures two tiny dots dropping from the plane…. The dots, it turns out, were desperate Afghans hidden in the wheel well. As the wheels folded into the body of the plane, the stowaways faced the choice of being crushed to death or letting go and plunging to the ground."[50] Gruesomely, human remains were later discovered in the wheel well of that C-17 military plane.[51] All of this, as we waited to hear from our president.

When President Biden finally addressed the nation from the East Room of the White House, he used the moment to place blame for the fall of Afghanistan at the foot of his predecessor. "When I came into office, I inherited a deal that President Trump negotiated with the Taliban," Biden complained. "Under his agreement, U.S. forces would be out of Afghanistan by May 1, 2021—just a little over three months after I took office. U.S. forces had already drawn down during the Trump administration from roughly 15,500 American forces to 2,500 troops in country...."[52]

The remark echoed President Biden's previous attempt to blame President Trump. "When I came to office, I inherited a deal cut by my predecessor," Biden said in a Saturday night statement, one of the only presidential communications during his six-day period of silence. Now, he was using his first public, on-camera remarks to do just the same. Biden quickly moved from blaming Trump to blaming the Afghans, noting that "[w]e gave them every tool they could need. We paid their salaries, provided for the maintenance of their air force.... We gave them every chance to determine their own future. What we could not provide them was the will to fight for that future."[53]

After using much of his speech to point fingers, President Biden then had the audacity to declare, "I am President of the United States of America, and the buck stops with me."[54]

And all of those whom he chose to blame, of course.

The "buck stops with me" empty promise—contradicted by his effort to place blame—reflected a similar vow that then-candidate Joe Biden had made on the campaign trail. "It's hard to believe this has to be said, but unlike this president, I'll do my job and take responsibility. I won't blame others. And I'll never forget that the job isn't about me—it's about you."[55]

Right.

Predictably, some in the media—like MSNBC's Nicolle Wallace and Brian Williams—chose to cover for the president following his disaster of a speech. Wallace praised Biden as being "unapologetic" and "confident" with "resolve"—only to be outdone by Williams.[56] "I'm curious to hear your reaction [to]…this consequential speech by the American president," Williams said on his show to US Army veteran Matt Zeller. "Didn't run from it. He owned it. He owned his decision. He owned the fact that—as he put it—the buck stops with him."

"Did I watch a different speech?" I wondered. It appears that I was not the only one with that thought.

Zeller, the veteran, replied, "I hope he gets to own their deaths too. I feel like I watched a different speech than the rest of you guys. I was appalled. There was such a profound bold-faced lie in that speech. The idea that we planned for every contingency. I have been personally trying to tell this administration since it took office…that this was coming. We sent them plan after plan about how to evacuate these people. Nobody listened to us."[57]

Despite the delusional defenses of some in the media, by Tuesday, the list of critics of Biden's Afghanistan policy was long and bipartisan.

"The debacle in Afghanistan is the worst kind: Avoidable," read the *Washington Post* Editorial Board headline.[58]

"Biden's Betrayal of Afghans Will Live in Infamy," noted the typically liberal *Atlantic*.[59]

And the *New York Times*'s David Sanger wrote, "Biden will go down in history, fairly or unfairly, as the president who presided over a long-brewing, humiliating final act in the American experiment in Afghanistan."[60]

Obama officials far and wide from former secretary of homeland security Jeh Johnson and ambassador to Afghanistan Ryan Crocker to former senior advisor to the president David

Axelrod and CIA directors Leon Panetta, David Petraeus, and John Brennan all criticized the Biden administration to varying degrees.[61]

"I'm left with some grave questions in my mind about his ability to lead our nation as commander in chief...to have read this so wrong—or, even worse, to have understood what was likely to happen and not care," remarked Crocker.[62]

"They clearly were caught off guard by the events of the last seventy-two hours," Brennan said.[63]

"In many ways, I think of John Kennedy and the Bay of Pigs," Panetta offered, analogizing the fall of Afghanistan to the failed Bay of Pigs invasion.[64]

Nevertheless, the predictable cheerleaders still did their cheerleading.

"The President is to be commended for his strong leadership and exceptional focus," House Speaker Nancy Pelosi said in a statement.[65]

But the bad just kept getting worse for the Biden administration. As the week progressed, the administration suffered from catastrophic communications failures—first from the White House spokespeople and next from the president himself. For example, one of the pointed questions from the press was just how many American citizens remained stranded in Afghanistan.

On Tuesday morning, Department of Defense press secretary John Kirby told us approximately five thousand to ten thousand Americans were in Afghanistan.[66] By the afternoon, White House press secretary Jen Psaki had the number at eleven thousand before the State Department and Pentagon officials estimated that the number was actually somewhere between ten thousand and fifteen thousand Americans.[67] No one seemed to have an accurate count.

Then came President Biden's disastrous interview with George Stephanopoulos. "[W]e've all seen the pictures. We've seen those hundreds of people packed into a C-17. We've seen Afghans falling,"

Stephanopoulos said, leading Biden to quickly and callously quip, "That was four days ago, five days ago."[68]

Four or five days ago? As if the loss of human life had an expiration date.

Then, Stephanopoulos remarked, "Still a lot of pandemonium at the airport." Biden replied with foreboding words as he knocked on the wooden table beside him, "But no one's being killed right now. God forgive me if I'm wrong about that, but no one's being killed right now."[69]

It was an ill-fated prediction that would unfortunately prove untrue in time.

President Biden's sit-down interview with Stephanopoulos came as chaos and mayhem began to unfold at the Kabul airport. American citizens attempted to make their way to evacuation flights only to encounter tens of thousands of local Afghans blocking the gates.[70] Stun grenades flashed in an effort to disperse the crowd as Taliban militants shot into the air.[71]

Taliban beat and whipped innocent Afghans, some of whom were pictured holding their babies over the gates trying to offer their own flesh and blood to an American soldier in hopes that their little ones would escape life under the Taliban. A British officer told *The Independent*, "The mothers were desperate, they were getting beaten by the Taliban. They shouted, 'Save my baby' and threw the babies at us, some of the babies fell on the barbed wire. It was awful what happened. By the end of the night there wasn't one man among us who was not crying."[72]

But, to President Biden, the Taliban was being cooperative—to some degree. "I think they're going through sort of an existential crisis about do they want to be recognized by the international community as being a legitimate government," Biden told Stephanopoulos.[73]

Really? As they took young women into forced marriages and beat innocent civilians, they were calculating the odds of their acceptance into the international community? Hardly.

Biden went on to say, "I'm not sure I would've predicted, George, nor would you or anyone else, that when we decided to leave, that they'd provide safe passage for Americans to get out."[74]

The havoc and turmoil at the gates of the Kabul airport surely were not the picture of "safe passage," but here was our president telling the American people otherwise.

The day following President Biden's indefensible interview, the White House press shop—in a rare move—did not schedule the daily briefing that they vowed to have each weekday. Indeed, during Press Secretary Jen Psaki's very first White House briefing, she assured the press that she would usher in a "return [to] these daily briefings, Monday through Friday...."[75] But apparently not on Thursday, August 19, 2021, when the going got tough.[76]

The Department of Defense and the State Department, however, did hold a briefing. When John Kirby was asked the million-dollar question about how many American citizens were in Afghanistan, he replied, "I don't know," and then referred the reporter to the State Department.[77]

Later, a reporter asked State Department spokesperson Ned Price, "How many more Americans [are] left in Afghanistan? This was raised in Pentagon, and they referred them to the State [Department]—."[78]

Price, like Kirby, had no answer.[79]

The days that followed provided little clarity on this point as troops at Kabul airport rushed to evacuate Americans from Afghanistan ahead of the August 31 deadline to withdraw American forces—a date that the Taliban called a "red line."[80] The images at Kabul airport grew more dire despite Biden assuring us that there was "no circumstance" where Americans could not get to the airport.[81]

Jen Psaki, for her part, said, "I think it's irresponsible to say Americans are stranded. They are not."[82] Never mind the reports that the "ISIS terror threat forces US military to establish alternate routes to Kabul airport" and "U.S. Embassy tells Americans to stay away from airport."[83]

"The scenes are apocalyptic," *PBS NewsHour* correspondent Jane Ferguson reported. "People are fainting and dying. Children are going missing."[84]

And then there was the warning from President Biden: "I want to say again just how difficult this mission is, and the dangers it poses to our troops on the ground. The security environment is changing rapidly. There are civilians crowded at the airport.... We know that terrorists may seek to exploit the situation and target innocent Afghans or American troops."[85]

It was an admonition from the president of the United States that would come to tragic fruition.

WHILE THE BIDEN administration failed to foresee "a Friday to a Monday" fall of Afghanistan, the Trump administration saw just such a scenario. The American public would learn this in the days following Thursday, August 26, 2021—a date so many Americans, including myself, will never forget.

On that harrowing Thursday morning, I began my daily routine, which could be quite chaotic! Rushing to get ready for *Outnumbered* and studying the variety of topics in my inbox amid shouts and contagious giggles from my almost two-year-old daughter was the norm on weekdays.

It seemed like just another workday on that Thursday until a tweet from *Politico* reporter Daniel Lippman hit my inbox at 9:42 a.m.: "JUST IN: Sources tell @laraseligman, @alexbward and me that there has been a large explosion at Abbey Gate at the Kabul airport." My heart sunk. For weeks, ever since the fall of Kabul, America worried for our Afghan allies, for Americans trying to escape, and especially for our US servicemen and women. I hoped and prayed that no innocents were among the fallen.

America's fears were substantiated when Fox News reported just after 10:00 a.m. that American troops were injured in the suicide bombing.[86] Tragically, more casualties were expected.

Like a vicious spiral, the news broke rapidly that fateful Thursday as I prepared for the fast-approaching noon hour when I would broadcast *Outnumbered* from the studio van waiting in my driveway. Endeavoring to keep up with every new bit of reporting, I collected as much information as I could on this fast-moving story. Sitting on the edge of my bathtub, I quickly typed each new detail into my notes. At this point, we knew that there were two explosions, both outside of the Kabul airport with the total number of casualties still unknown.

Unfortunately, that news would become tragically worse. Just six minutes before the end of our program, the *Wall Street Journal* reported the heartbreaking news: "The U.S. ambassador in Kabul has told staff there that four U.S. Marines were killed in an explosion at the city's airport and three wounded, a U.S. official with knowledge of the briefing said."[87] With a shattered heart, I walked back into my home just after 1:00 p.m., reflecting on the loss of four of America's best. Sadly, that number continued to grow as the day progressed—from ten to twelve and then finally thirteen.

Thirteen fallen American heroes, thirteen American families about to experience unspeakable pain.

America collectively mourned on Thursday, August 26, 2021, hour by hour learning of more and more fatalities. It was the deadliest twenty-four hours for our servicemen and women since 2011, and on that somber day in August, we waited to hear from our commander in chief.[88] Learning of the explosion in the 9:00 a.m.

hour, it seemed like an eternity before President Biden addressed the nation just after 5:00 p.m.

"Where is our president?" I wondered as the hours ticked by.

"We will hunt you down and make you pay!" President Biden said in his first remarks to the nation.[89] A fine message delivered far too late. These tough words should have been the White House message to the Taliban days ago.

Instead, America was treated to a litany of denials about the failures in Afghanistan. Now, in the wake of an attack leaving Americans dead, the message from the White House was finally shifting, though still accompanied by President Biden's trademark statement of blaming his predecessor. "I bear responsibility for all that's happened," President Biden said, moments before blaming Trump for all that had transpired—of course. "But here's the deal.... You know as well as I do that the former president made a deal with the Taliban that he would get all American forces out of Afghanistan by May 1."[90]

President Biden's version of events left out some key points. While no one wanted to get out of Afghanistan more than President Trump—of course, he ran on the issue and desperately wanted to bring our American troops home—President Trump would never have pulled out without a firm peace accord and a strong, solid government in place. Moreover, the condition-based withdrawal that President Trump had negotiated included a number of conditions that must be met ahead of a withdrawal, including a small, stay-behind special-operations force that would remain in Afghanistan among other necessary benchmarks.[91] These facts were all rather inconvenient for President Biden's "blame Trump" narrative.

Another condition was the strongly worded warning from President Trump that no Americans would be harmed in Afghanistan. In March of 2020, President Trump spoke with the head of the Taliban, Abdul Ghani Baradar. During the call, President

Trump secured a promise from Baradar that there would be "no violence."[92] He also issued a warning, according to former director of national intelligence John Ratcliffe: "[I]f a single American is harmed at the hands of the Taliban, I will take you out the way I took out Qasem Soleimani and the way I took out [Abu Bakr] Al-Baghdadi."[93] As a former colleague pointed out to me, President Trump's first call with Baradar occurred one month after the United States killed Qasem Soleimani, a top Iranian general considered "the second-most-powerful leader in Iran," who was responsible for the deaths of an estimated six hundred US service-members in Iraq.[94] The Taliban got the message.

Following President Trump's signing of a conditions-based withdrawal and his unequivocally firm phone call, not a single American was killed in Afghanistan during the remainder of Trump's presidency.[95] But the status quo changed when President Biden set a symbolic date for withdrawing from Afghanistan: September 11, 2021, the twentieth anniversary of 9/11—regardless of whether any conditions had actually been met.

There was perhaps no greater example of the failure to plan than the way in which President Biden departed Bagram Airfield, America's largest airfield in Afghanistan.[96] Rather than having a methodical departure from Bagram, the Biden administration shut off the lights in July without giving the Afghan military advance notice. Overnight, looters took over the US airbase, plundering buildings and "loading anything that was not nailed down into trucks," according to the Associated Press.[97]

"The sudden darkness was like a signal to looters," an Afghan soldier noted.[98] "Why was Bagram closed? And the Secretary of State Antony Blinken and the Deputy Secretary of State Wendy Sherman, why were they not screaming to say you cannot close Bagram and remove U.S. troops when we have an embassy in harm's way in a warzone?" former director of national intelligence Richard Grenell asked.[99]

Why would you shut down America's largest airfield, leaving the Kabul airport as the only escape route for thousands of stranded Americans? Moreover, why would you evacuate the military before the civilians? It all defied common sense.

The familiar quote from former secretary of defense Bob Gates comes to mind: Biden has "been wrong on nearly every major foreign policy and national security issue over the past four decades."[100] This one included!

To make matters worse, President Biden had ample warning about the dangers of a quick, messy Afghanistan withdrawal. Ratcliffe said it best: "Let me be clear, it was not an intelligence failure. It was a failure to listen to intelligence…When I was the DNI (Director of National Intelligence), we correctly assessed that this is precisely what would happen if we didn't have a conditioned-based withdrawal, which is exactly the way this plan was put together."[101]

Echoing Ratcliffe, Grenell noted, "This was not an intelligence failure. This was a failure of politicians in Washington D.C.… [The] intelligence community, State Department officials, a whole bunch of people started briefing in May, telling them [the Biden administration] that the Taliban was on the march."[102]

"Wow," I thought to myself. "Then why didn't Biden listen to the intelligence?"

But the dangers of a quick pullout seemed to have been lost upon President Biden. In the ABC interview, Stephanopoulos said to Biden, "[Y]our top military advisors warned against withdrawing on this timeline. They wanted you to keep about 2,500 troops."

President Biden protested, "No, they didn't. It was split. That wasn't true. That wasn't true."

"They didn't tell you that they wanted troops to stay?" Stephanopoulos countered.

"No. Not at a—not in terms of whether we were going to get out in a timeframe all troops. They didn't argue against that," Biden assured him.[103]

On the contrary, though, the *New York Times* reported that "classified assessments by American spy agencies over the summer painted an increasingly grim picture of the prospect of a Taliban takeover of Afghanistan and warned of the rapid collapse of the Afghan military, even as President Biden and his advisers said publicly that was unlikely to happen as quickly, according to current and former American government officials."[104]

Meanwhile, the *Wall Street Journal* reported that "[a]n internal State Department memo…warned top agency officials of the potential collapse of Kabul soon after the U.S.'s Aug. 31 troop withdrawal deadline in Afghanistan…represent[ing] the clearest evidence yet that the administration had been warned by its own officials on the ground that the Taliban's advance was imminent and Afghanistan's military may be unable to stop it."[105]

Indeed, just over a month later, General Frank McKenzie, the head of Central Command, directly contradicted Biden's assertion to Stephanopoulos during a Senate hearing. "I recommended that we maintain 2,500 troops in Afghanistan, and I also recommended early in the fall of 2020 that we maintain 4,500 at that time, those were my personal views. I also had a view that the withdrawal of those forces would lead inevitably to the collapse of the Afghan military forces and eventually the Afghan government," McKenzie said.[106]

A former colleague of mine in the Trump administration summed up the collapse of Afghanistan well: "When we walked out of the White House on January 20, 2021, ISIS was obliterated. Baghdadi was gone. There were less than two hundred al-Qaeda. Our focus shifted away from terrorism and to China-related matters. How—in eight months—do you go from no American deaths, no problem with ISIS anywhere in the world, al-Qaeda decimated, to now this?"

The day after the attack at Kabul airport, I boarded a flight to Houston, Texas, where I was set to speak to an audience of nearly two thousand people at the Texas Youth Summit. Upon landing in Houston, I traveled to Mims Baptist Church in Conroe, Texas, where I talked with a small group of community leaders before taking photos with a few hundred attendees.

Between the photo line and my speech, I had about an hour to sit in a room off to the side of the main worship facility and reflect on my remarks. Perusing the news, I came across an article with the names and personal details of several of the thirteen fallen servicemen and women in Afghanistan. "These are the US service members killed in the Kabul airport attack," the *New York Post* headline read.[107] It occurred to me in that moment that I needed to end my speech in a very specific way: honoring our fallen heroes.

I opened my white three-ring binder and quickly pulled my prepared remarks out of the plastic slipcover, scribbling down the names and personal details I could find about the American troops who had lost their lives just one day prior. As I read about these young patriots, it was crushing to learn that most of these heroes were in their young twenties, the full breadth of their life on earth cut so short. At the end of my speech, I told the crowd that we must remember these names—heroes of our military who made the ultimate sacrifice:

"Maxton Soviak, twenty-two
Kareem Nikoui, twenty
David Lee Espinoza, twenty
Rylee McCollum, twenty
Jared Schmitz, twenty
Hunter Lopez, twenty-two

Daegan Page, twenty-three
Ryan Knauss, twenty-three
Darin Taylor Hoover Jr., thirty-one
And four others whose names we'll learn."

As I read the names of the fallen on that Friday evening before a crowd, packed into green church pews going up into the rafters, the audience stood up instinctually to applaud passionately for each and every young hero. When I read the name of Rylee McCollum, a twenty-year-old marine, I shared that he was expecting a beautiful baby in three weeks.

I could barely get the words out as I thought about my own daughter, Blake, and how excruciatingly painful it must be for a young mother to become a young widow just weeks before the birth of her first child. Overcome with emotion, I began to tear up on stage before taking a deep breath and completing the reading of names. The hurt I felt was the pain being felt by an entire nation.

In the days that followed, we learned the identities of the four servicemen and women whose names we did not know on that Friday night:

Johanny Rosario Pichardo, twenty-five
Nicole Gee, twenty-three
Humberto Sanchez, twenty-two
Dylan Merola, twenty
May we always remember their names!

On Monday, September 13, 2021, Levi "Rylee" Rose was born. Swaddled in a white blanket with blue and pink stripes, Marine Lance Cpl. Rylee McCollum's little girl laid beneath a sign that read, "Naval Hospital Camp Pendleton welcomes baby girl Levi Rylee Rose 8lb 10oz."[108] Beside her sat a picture of her brave, heroic father, whom Levi will not meet in this life.

At just twenty years old, Rylee McCollum intrepidly did what scripture describes as the greatest example of love. John 15:13 says, "Greater love has no one than this: to lay down one's life for one's friends."[109] This verse exactly describes the actions of Rylee McCollum and twelve other patriots on that fateful day at the Kabul airport.

When duty called, the thirteen rose to the occasion, entering a war-torn country and caring for the vulnerable along the way. The world saw this depicted vividly when twenty-three-year-old marine Nicole Gee posted an image, depicting her gallantry and compassion just days before she was killed. With her weapon by her side and dressed in military camouflage, Nicole held a baby in her arms as she gently gazed down at the Afghan child. Beneath the picture, Nicole wrote a simple caption: "I love my job."

The lives of Rylee and Nicole are the embodiment of love and sacrifice. Their stories are the stories of the best among us: our American servicemen and women. Each time darkness attempts to rear its ugly head in our world, our servicemembers bring light, and their stories never cease to amaze.

In February, I traveled to Hernando, Mississippi, to give a talk to the County Seat Club, an organization that hosts various business and political leaders from around the country. On that rather chilly Saturday night, I made my way into a 1930s cottonseed warehouse-turned-event venue called 1 Memphis Street. I began taking pictures with the attendees before a very special guest was escorted toward me.

"Meet Olin Pickens," a man said. "He's a one-hundred-year-old World War II veteran and two-time POW."

"Two-time POW!?" I replied in bewilderment. "Thank you for your service, sir."

Mr. Pickens, smiling from ear to ear, shook my hand and began to tell me about his service in World War II. Captured the

SERENITY IN THE STORM

first time in North Africa, he eventually escaped, only to be recaptured in Czechoslovakia.[110] Olin Pickens spent twenty-six months in the hands of the enemy. He lost one-third of his body weight during his time in prison, part of which he spent in a dark hole in solitary confinement. Reflecting on his time in solitary confinement, Mr. Pickens's eyes filled up with tears as he spoke to me; however, they were not tears of sadness but of joy.

"I saw Jesus there," Mr. Pickens said to me. "He was there with me."

I felt moisture fill my eyes as Mr. Pickens recounted to me that he only made it through imprisonment because of his savior. "I lost my freedom, my dignity, and my pride, right there, but I didn't lose my faith," Mr. Pickens told his local news station. "As bad as it was, we would do it again for freedom."[111]

A hero. That is what Mr. Olin Pickens is—in every sense of the word.

In Genesis, we learn the story of Joseph, the son of Jacob. Joseph's eleven brothers, consumed with jealousy, threw Joseph in a deep pit before selling him into slavery. For more than a decade, Joseph spent his life in servitude in Egypt, including some time in prison. Like Olin Pickens sitting in that German prison, the future seemed dim for Joseph in an Egyptian prison. But, similar to Mr. Pickens, God had other plans for Joseph. Scripture reassures us more than once that, despite Joseph's hardship, "the Lord was with him."[112]

After a thirteen-year journey, Joseph was freed from prison, and—in a remarkable turn of events—went from prisoner to the close confidant of Pharaoh. As fate would have it, Joseph's brothers, failing to recognize him, came to him amid a famine seeking food. Later, upon the death of their father and after learning of Joseph's identity, the brothers asked, "'What if Joseph holds a grudge against us and pays us back for all the wrongs we did to him?'"[113] They even "threw themselves down before him" and proclaimed, "'We are your slaves....'"[114] But Joseph replied with infinite wisdom: "'Don't be afraid. Am I in the place of God? You intended to harm me, but God intended it for good to accomplish what is now being done, the saving of many lives.'"[115] Indeed, it was through Joseph's suffering that he was identified by Pharaoh and ultimately placed in a role where Joseph would help to prepare Egypt for many years of famine. God used evil to bring about good—something we are seeing now in Afghanistan. While the loss of the thirteen is indeed the last dreadful chapter in our Afghanistan nightmare, it is not where the story of Afghanistan ends.

CHAPTER 2

THE UNDERGROUND CHURCH

As the Taliban took over Afghanistan, seeking to restore their murderous reign of terror, hundreds of thousands of Afghans left the country, leaving behind their homes in hopes of a better life. Asmaan—as I will call her for the purposes of anonymity—did not. "I was extremely scared, for sure," Asmaan told me during our hour-and-a-half-long conversation, recounting her decision to stay in Afghanistan and live under Taliban rule. "Fear was not controlling my heart; the Holy Spirit was controlling my heart."

Asmaan shared one encounter she had with an older lady who was leaving the country after experiencing the Taliban's treacherous rule the first time prior to the United States toppling the evil regime after the September 11, 2001 attacks. "Why, my daughter? Why are you staying here?" the woman asked Asmaan. "This country is not good anymore."

"Because of that encounter, it became stronger in my heart that I did the right thing staying in Afghanistan," Asmaan reflected before passionately telling me about her love for her fellow Afghans and her desire to share Jesus with them. As Asmaan and I talked via video, I watched a woman who radiated with joy. She smiled as she spoke, exuding a very evident internal peace and happiness. From halfway across the world in Afghanistan, I could see the love of Jesus Christ pouring out of Asmaan.

"To be a Christian in Afghanistan, now is a good time," she said. "It is hard. There are many times that I want to give up, but at the same time, I see how thirsty people are here. It is an excellent time to be a Christian here."

"Good" and "excellent" are hardly two words you would think to use in characterizing what it is like to be a believer in one of the most hostile countries to Christianity in the entire world, but here was Asmaan saying just that. She explained to me that the church is growing in Afghanistan despite the Taliban's persecution of Christian men and women.

When I asked her if the Afghan people have shown an openness toward Christ after the fall of Afghanistan, Asmaan replied, "Now, much more than before…. They see the darkness and the light. For twenty years, during the war in Afghanistan, Afghans were able to go to universities, to have hope, and then, suddenly, all of that was gone. It's gone because the Taliban came."

Afghans contrast the brutal reign of the Taliban with the acts of generosity from Christians. "They see the Christians helping most. They have love and respect," Asmaan said. "Many American soldiers died in the explosion at Kabul airport. Why did they die? Because they were trying to help people get out of the country. They didn't have to be here. Afghans see these people as Christian, so when we go to their houses and tell them about Jesus, they are very open. They just want to find that peace and hope."

But finding peace and hope in Christ comes at great personal cost for believers in Afghanistan. Asmaan described this cost: "People just disappear. No one hears about them. The Taliban is trying to get credibility from other countries, so they persecute quietly."

"Do you know anyone who has disappeared?" I asked Asmaan.

In this moment, Asmaan's demeanor changed. She took on a more somber tone, slightly looking down as she replied, "Yes, I have friends who have disappeared. They have been imprisoned. That is what I mean when I say that I have joy every day, but there is such pain when we lose someone."

When the Taliban took over Afghanistan in the mid-1990s, "Taliban Supreme Leader Mullah Omar ordered his men to raze churches to the ground, to lynch Afghan Christians and to kill or drive out foreigners who followed Jesus Christ," according to *Der Spiegel*.[116] Hashim Kabar, a Christian in Afghanistan, interviewed with the publication and described exactly how Taliban rule worked: "They tortured prisoners until they got them to tell them the names of other Christians. Then the Taliban would kill them and go in search of new victims."[117]

During the twenty-year period when the Taliban no longer ruled Afghanistan, there was indeed Christian persecution, yet "[w]ith church numbers growing, in 2019 some church leaders agreed to change their religious affiliation on national identity cards all Afghans are required to carry. The reason: They wanted their children and future generations to be able to publicly own a Christian identity," according to *World*.[118] Even so, Open Doors, which ranks countries for Christian persecution, reported that "Afghanistan had been No. 2 on the Open Doors World Watch List for several years" during this time period.

When the Taliban regained control of the country in August of 2021, prospects for Christians became just as dire as they had been prior to the United States toppling the Taliban. Open Doors notes, "This is the first time Afghanistan has been No. 1 on the World Watch List."[119] Asmaan says that, while the persecution is quieter this time, it is worse now than before.

As I was covering the fall of Afghanistan, I came across Global Catalytic Ministries (GCM), a ministry in touch with various members of the underground church in Afghanistan. In a "first-hand ground report" from Kabul, Afghanistan, GCM reported that "[t]he Taliban has a hit list of known Christians they are targeting to pursue and kill."[120] Saad, a secret Christian in Afghanistan, told Open Doors, "The list has been circulated with our names on it. Some [of us] have been killed. Some have been kidnapped, some have disappeared. It feels like the morning after a massive cataclysmic explosion."[121]

Dr. Rex Rogers, North American president of SAT-7, a Christian television network that broadcasts across the Middle East, reported that "the Taliban demand people's phones, and if they find a downloaded Bible on your device, they will kill you immediately…. It's incredibly dangerous right now for Afghans to have anything Christian on their phones. The Taliban have spies and informants everywhere."[122]

Will Stark, South Asia regional manager for International Christian Concern, told the *Washington Times*, "I've heard reports from people I know on the ground, that they're receiving phone calls from unknown [telephone] numbers in which they're being told, 'We know who you are, and we are going to come for you.' And that's a direct threat and likely coming from Taliban fighters or maybe the Taliban itself, that they will be targeted, because of their faith identity."[123]

And yet, amazingly, defying every natural inclination of self-preservation, some Christians like Asmaan chose to stay in the country to share the good news of Jesus. But they must do so with caution. "In the past, we could worship in groups, but, now, we must worship low, not loud. Sometimes this means listening from a computer in silence together. If you are stopped in the streets, you cannot have the Bible on your phone," Asmaan described.

"Do you see God at work?" I asked.

"I see that all the time," Asmaan quickly replied. "I see it every day in the simple things, and it is so sweet—to meet a fellow believer in the street. 'I'm so glad to see you. You are my sister,' I will say." Asmaan proceeded to make a very important, salient point. In countries like America, where we do not experience persecution like in Afghanistan, we tend to say hello and goodbye to fellow Christians and think little of it. "It's too normal," Asmaan said. "We lose the value of this interaction. Here, it is precious— the joy of knowing we are the same, we are of the same blood. We see the joy of the kingdom of God in the simple things. When I meet a new believer and we have the opportunity to pray together for ten minutes, it is so precious because I can't always have that. Everything has become so precious. The Bible is a treasure. Or when I take communion, it is not something so simple as, 'Oh yes, I had communion today.' For us, it is precious."

Baptism, in particular, takes on a whole new level of importance. Asmaan explained: "I love baptism. It is the best. In Afghanistan, though, baptism means that you are accepting to be killed, to suffer for Jesus. When you get baptized, it's not just committing to church, it is saying, 'Yes, I accept to die, to suffer, to be tortured because I follow Jesus.'"

How incredible is that statement? Here, in America when we commit to follow Jesus, we do so in a free society, where we can go to church every Sunday, pray with our friends and family in peace, and openly speak about our faith—things we all too regularly take for granted. For the American believer, the extent of persecution is being ostracized from a group or perhaps being fired from your job, a situation that happened recently but was rectified at the Supreme Court.[124] For the Afghan believer, the consequences of faith can be torture and death.

Despite this terrifying reality, the church is growing in Afghanistan. Anywhere between one thousand to twelve thousand Christians lived in Afghanistan prior to the United States' withdrawal and the Taliban's takeover.[125] Given that the church operates almost entirely underground, finding an exact number is difficult.[126] While many Christians left the country, some—like Asmaan—chose to stay, and because of their sacrifice, Asmaan told me that the church is indeed growing. Asmaan said, "When I bring food to people, they start to cry. 'How can it be that you are here?' they say. They see believers who chose to stay here."

GCM shared with me the thoughts of a leader of the underground church who did not flee Afghanistan but instead chose to stay at great personal risk. Here is what they said about the fall of Afghanistan: "Everyone is in despair; doesn't matter Muslims... Pashto, Christian; all are very afraid.... The despair is very visible, but at the same time, today I went out to walk around and sing songs and visit my friends.... When the people saw me they were so happy to see me. 'So glad you are here and didn't leave,' they said. It gives them hope.... God will do great things through the believers that stayed."

Singing through despair as the murderous Taliban regime took hold? Staying despite every human instinct telling you to flee? It is an almost incomprehensible decision, and yet selfless Christians set on spreading the Gospel message did just that.

One Christian told GCM, "There is no need to fear what the Taliban is doing, yes bad things may happen to us, but God will do something and glorify His name. If something bad happens to me, I will remember God and how he works miracles.... I trust God...."[127]

One Christian mentioned Psalm 2 as a source of inspiration. The Psalm reads, in part, "Why do the nations conspire and the peoples plot in vain? The kings of the earth rise up and the rulers band together against the Lord and against his anointed, saying, 'Let us break their chains and throw off their shackles.' The One enthroned in heaven laughs...."[128] The Christian in Afghanistan marveled at God laughing at the enemy, who seeks to harm. "God is still in control," he or she wrote. "Yes, things are hard and we have been afraid but to see the hands of God and to meet the believers...I feel lucky. This has been the hardest time of my life but also the best. It is a privilege to see that nothing can stop the word of God in Afghanistan, not the Taliban, not anything."[129]

"*I feel lucky.*" Can you imagine writing those words as a hostile invader has taken over your country, threatened your life, and even killed your fellow believers?

And yet another testimony provided to GCM recounts an interaction a Christian had with an Afghan driver. "I've never seen anyone like you," the driver said. Reflecting on the comment, the Christian wrote, "I find it funny. Being a Christian matters and impacts the life of people no matter where you are. I have the privilege to be in Afghanistan. I definitely think that is a privilege. Just being a Christian should impact the lives around us.... Despite me feeling like I'm inside of a fire, I am at peace in my spirit."[130]

"*A privilege.*" Amazing. A privilege to be in the number one most dangerous country in the world for Christian men and women.

Despite the danger, the work of Christian men and women in Afghanistan is making an enormous difference for the kingdom of God. One Christian in Afghanistan told GCM the story of a man who was angry at God, having been through so much war and devastation. The Christians suggested to the man that he express his feelings to God and "ask God to show him if he was real."

"After two months," they reported. "[H]e was touched by God." As he shared his newfound faith with his family, he experienced rejection. He specifically started to pray for his brother, who "was angry and wanted to kill and kidnap Christians and foreigners and sell them to the Taliban."[131] The Christian sharing the story said, "The brother is the worst person I knew. He killed many people. When I would hear about the things he would do I would become ill and feel like I was going to vomit."[132]

After much prayer, the brother gave his life to Christ. Writing of their conversion, the Christian said, "These brothers are like diamonds. If you look at them some will see stones, but they are so valuable. They are diamonds, they just don't know it yet. They need to be polished. Their faith is incredible to me. We are so excited to see what God is doing in their lives."[133] And this only happened because there were Christians who chose to stay, putting the lives of others above their own.

Asmaan said that stories like these are not uncommon. In fact, she has met many Afghan converts whose stories are very similar. "They've killed many, many people, and then they are totally changed. I think to myself that it is not possible to change this much without Jesus."

"Have you even seen Taliban come to Christ?" I asked Asmaan.

"Yes," she confirmed. "And then they realize all of the bad that they did in the past." Asmaan said that she shares Romans 5:20 with them, which reads, "Now the law came in to increase the trespass, but where sin increased, grace abounded all the more, so that, as sin reigned in death, grace also might reign through righteousness leading to eternal life through Jesus Christ our Lord."[134]

How powerful is that verse? The thought that *none* of our sin is too big for the grace of Christ Jesus. The Jeremiah Study Bible explains it this way: "The abundance of grace available through the work of Christ far surpasses the quantity of Adam's sin. No one can out-sin God's infinite grace."[135] With this in mind, Asmaan tells these repentant sinners, "You may have killed hundreds, but you can now lead double to Christ. You have received the grace of God, and that is more powerful than the things that you did."

The story of the two transformed brothers in Afghanistan reminds me of the story of Saul of Tarsus. Saul was a Pharisee, a member of the elite religious sect during the time of Jesus. In Acts, we first learn of Saul during the stoning of Stephen, the first Christian martyr. Acts 8 tells us not only that "Saul approved of his execution," but that "Saul was ravaging the church, and entering house after house, he dragged off men and women and committed them to prison."[136] The Jeremiah Study Bible (JSB) points out that "[t]he Greek word translating ravaging is rare; it was used in secular Greek literature to refer to the destruction of a wild boar."[137] Ravaging, in other words, is meant to communicate a rather intense form of destruction. The "destruction of a wild boar" analogy almost evokes similar imagery to some of the tactics used today by the Taliban.

The JSB notes that while Saul did not actively stone Stephen himself, he clearly approved and was a "self-confessed leader in the great persecution against the church, which was so intense that people fled Jerusalem for safety to towns in Judea and Sumaria and beyond."[138] Acts 9 depicts Paul as "breathing threats and murder against the disciples of the Lord...."[139] Once again, the thought invokes an immediate comparison to Christians who fled Afghanistan.

But like the brothers in Afghanistan described above, Saul of Tarsus has a dramatic encounter with Christ, in his case, on the road to Damascus. Saul leaves Damascus forever changed, becoming Paul the Apostle, who authored much of the New Testament. Not only that, this "great persecution against the church... was the beginning of the missionary movement," according to the JSB. "God used the persecution that people intended for evil to evangelize the world."[140] Once again, we come back to the words of Joseph, "You mean evil against me, but God used it for good."

Even so, as a human, it is difficult to rationalize how so much evil, pain, and suffering can seem to dominate on earth. Asmaan told me the story of a young, middle school-aged girl in Afghanistan whom the Taliban forced into marriage. When she refused to be intimate, many Taliban men raped her before returning this broken young girl to her family. Remarking on this tragedy and so many others, Asmaan noted, "I can feel the pain in the heart of God when these tragedies occur. It was not his desire to see Afghanistan get worse."

While I explore this question of pain and suffering more in depth in chapter four, I wanted to pose this quandary to Asmaan, who has seen more suffering than most of us—Christian brothers and sisters who have disappeared, young girls abused by the Taliban, and untold human anguish. She replied almost instantly, "We cannot see the whole picture" before ticking through several examples of God using evil for good—whether it be an earthquake in Afghanistan, COVID-19, or the Taliban takeover. "People are more open to faith because they see light and darkness in these situations. When COVID-19 came in 2020, I never saw so many people die, but because people were so afraid of death, their hearts were open. Because of fear, they found peace."

Asmaan said that she has seen a difference in how people die—some in agony and others in complete peace. She gave an example of a woman who allowed Asmaan to pray with her just before she passed. As the woman struggled with COVID-19, Asmaan offered to gently massage her back to alleviate some pressure on her lungs. The lady sat up, and Asmaan began to rub her back. By the end of the massage, much to Asmaan's surprise, the lady had passed—peacefully.

"She asked God to come into her heart, and she died in such peace," Asmaan revealed. "Their soul is so much more important than tragedy. I know that this lady is in heaven. How many people are going to be touched by her story and saved because of her death? There is pain now, but we cannot see how our pain is used for good. The soul of people is so much more important than anything here on earth."

As I did so many times during my hour with Asmaan, I paused to tell her how incredibly profound her statement was. Her words displayed such wisdom. But Asmaan's wisdom was matched by her humility. She explained to me that she had a difficult upbringing. Her father passed away when she was young. Her mother battled severe alcoholism. Asmaan was the youngest among many children, and she grew up in unfathomable poverty and destitution. She felt unwanted.

At the age of twelve, Asmaan became a Christian after a friend invited her to church. When she met this Christian community, she was amazed by the love that they showed and how they received her so openly. "They told me that God loves you, but then I would go back to my house and see this mess of my family, so it was hard for me to believe in the love of God until my pastor and his wife showed that love to me and opened the door for me to believe in the love of God."

Asmaan said that 1 Corinthians 13 changed her life. Among this chapter are the beautiful words many of us know so well, "Love is patient and kind; love does not envy or boast; it is not arrogant or rude. It does not insist on its own way; it is not irritable or resentful; it does not rejoice at wrongdoing, but rejoices with truth. Love bears all things, believes all things, hopes all things, endures all things."[141]

A loving community of Christian believers truly living out the vows of 1 Corinthians 13 changed Asmaan's life. At this point in her young life, Asmaan said, "Only God wanted me," but she began to pray for her family, and after many years, Jesus Christ completely transformed her family—her mother and her siblings.

Now God is using both Asmaan and her family to be a light in this world to others in a very dark place.

"God chose a weak one," Asmaan said, as she humbly described herself—a woman who clearly exhibited untold strength and grace. "He used me, someone who should not even have been born, who did not feel wanted by her family and who was among the poorest of people…. When I look at this mess in Afghanistan, I know that God can change things because I see what Jesus did in my family and in my personal life. I can see the hands of God at work when a child is born and not wanted. This is what he did with me. He chose to use me."

God has used humble servants like Asmaan to further his kingdom. The phenomenon of using Christians to change lives in oppressive countries is not a phenomenon unique to Afghanistan. Joel Richardson of GCM told CBN News, "Iran has the fastest growing Church in the world. Seven years after the ISIS blitzkrieg, there's a revival in northern Syria…the establishment of Islamic government provides ripe soil for the Church to grow."[142]

Meanwhile, in Afghanistan, a spokesman for the Taliban declared in May of 2022, "There are no Christians in Afghanistan. Christian minority has never been known or registered here."[143] Richardson told CBN otherwise, noting that the church in Afghanistan is still similarly strong. "We actually have a report from one of our leaders who has been sharing the gospel with Taliban members that came into their village, and they've actually been engaging in Bible studies and prayer."[144] Richardson explained to me, "Wherever people are broken, that's where the Gospel thrives…. This is where people come to faith. It is only in Jesus that people can find genuine hope in the midst of such incredible suffering."

GROWING UP AS a young teenage girl, there was a book that always intrigued me called *Jesus Freaks*.[145] The book was named after a song by DC Talk called "Jesus Freak" that described having a passionate love for Jesus Christ that put you at odds with the self-serving norms of society. The book told the stories of Christian martyrs from around the world who lost their lives after refusing to denounce Christ.

Martyrdom has been embedded in Christianity from the very beginning. Of course, our savior, Jesus Christ, suffered death on a cross to save humanity. The twelve apostles spread the message of Christianity far and wide after Jesus's death and resurrection, but they did so at great personal cost. Eleven of the twelve apostles died a martyr's death.[146] Clubbing, stabbing, burning, beheading, and even crucifixion upside down were among the brutal ways in which the apostles met their tortuous fate on this earth before entering heaven in glory.[147]

Martyrdom, though, is not just an atrocity of the past. *Jesus Freaks*, published in 1997, described the suffering of the modern-day martyr. "It is said that there are more Christian martyrs today than there were in 100 AD—in the days of the Roman Empire," it reads. "According to a study done at Regent University, there were close to 156,000 Christians martyred around the world in 1998. An estimated 164,000 will be martyred in 1999."[148] Today, Christian martyrdom is a bit less prevalent than it was in the 1990s and 2000s, but, even so, the Center for the Study of Global Christianity (CSGC) estimates that approximately ninety thousand Christians were killed each year in the last decade—about "one [Christian] every six minutes."[149] Christians, according to CSGC, are "the most persecuted religious group in the world...."[150]

The sacrifices of Christians in heavily oppressive countries are paying off. Iran, for example, has seen an explosion in Christianity—from an estimated five hundred believers of Muslim background in 1979 to perhaps now more than one million, according to Operation World, an organization that tracks Christian growth in countries worldwide.[151] "The Church in Persia has not grown this fast since the 7th century," Operation World reports.[152] The growth is happening despite death being among the punishments for so-called "apostasy" or forsaking Muslim faith.[153]

I spoke to Pastor X, a pastor at the forefront of the underground church in Iran, and he told me that when Jesus is shared with Iranians, "Eight out of ten would come to Christ right then and there. Jesus has come to people through dreams, visions, and powerful encounters." This is happening despite a very high level of persecution in Iran, where believing in Christ can cost you your life, and secret informants work with the government in exposing believers. In keeping with what Pastor X has seen on the ground, Open Doors notes, "[M]ore Iranians have become Christians in the last 20 years than in the previous 13 centuries put together since Islam came to Iran."[154]

In war-torn Syria, Christianity is likewise growing. A Reuters headline reads, "Christianity grows in Syrian town once besieged by Islamic State," referring to the Northern Syria town of Kobani, located on the Syrian-Turkish border.[155] Ironically, Richardson told me, "This is a nation that is deeply traumatized. For ten years, Syrian children have known nothing but war and devastation.... [Nevertheless], there has been a sudden surge of evangelical Christianity in Afghanistan. This is blowback as people saw the brutal evil of ISIS and rejected it. Christ used this for his own redemptive purposes."

A similar trend is happening in China. In 2021, Open Doors ranked China among the top twenty most oppressive countries for Christians.[156] As one source told Open Doors, Christians "are simply snatched away only to appear months later in a kind of house arrest, where they get re-educated."[157] Nevertheless, even amid government suppression, Christianity is flourishing. Operation World writes, "2.7 million evangelicals in 1975 grew to over 75 million in just 35 years!"[158]

Emphasizing this phenomenon, the Council on Foreign Relations described China as having something of a "religious revival" over a four-decade period with a particular increase in Christians.[159] "The number of Chinese Protestants has grown by an average of 10 percent annually since 1979," Eleanor Albert wrote. "By some estimates, China is on track to have the world's largest population of Christians by 2030."[160]

In America, the opposite is happening. Despite relative freedom of worship compared to Iran and China, Pew found a 12 percent decrease in Americans self-describing as Christian over the last ten years.[161] Conversely, those describing as non-religious have increased over the same time period by 11 percent.[162] Where oppression reigns, Christianity flourishes, but where materialism and underappreciated freedom coexist, faith is diminishing.

As brothers and sisters in Christ, we are instructed to pray for the persecuted. Hebrews 13:3 tells us: "Continue to remember those in prison as if you were together with them in prison, and those who are mistreated as if you yourselves were suffering."[163] Each night in my home, my three-year-old daughter, husband, and I get on our knees beside her crib and, among the many items on our prayer list, is Afghanistan and those suffering.

While a great policy failure led to human detriment in a country that has already experienced far too much devastation, God can use human failure to bring about eternal success.

While the atrocities of the Taliban are great, our God is greater.

While pain and loss on this earth are real, the hope of eternity can overcome.

And while the fall of Afghanistan marred the American conscience, we have a God who can make "beauty instead of ashes."[164] On the night that Kabul fell to the Taliban, He did just that for Saad and Fatimah, two Christians living in Afghanistan. As the nightmare of a Taliban takeover became a reality, a little girl was born—the daughter of Saad and Fatimah.[165] "A baby girl born to a Christian family on such a fateful night," Saad reflected.[166] Saad told Open Doors that his father read Psalm 20:7-8 over their new little girl: "Some trust in chariots and some in horses, but we trust in the name of the Lord our God. They are brought to their knees and fall, but we rise up and stand firm. Lord, give victory to the king! Answer us when we call!"[167]

As I mentioned at the end of the last chapter, Levi Rylee Rose was born on September 13, 2021, in Camp Pendleton on US soil. Levi is the daughter of a fallen hero, Rylee McCollum, one of the thirteen whose sacrifice will never be forgotten. Just about one month after Levi's birth, this new little girl was born to two Christian parents in Afghanistan—an incredible gift during a very dark time. From the ashes came beauty, from suffering came new life. Rest assured, God is at work, even in the most dire of circumstances.

Asmaan, too, remarked on this beautiful, redemptive biblical concept. "We see evil coming to destroy and then God changes everything for his blessing. We see the mess of people in Afghanistan, and then God changes things for good. God is using past experiences to bless many people. We saw this in the book of Acts, and then we see this happening now because God did not change. The Holy Spirit has changed hearts. Nothing can stop the word of God from growing, not my weakness, my fears, my struggles, my anxieties, my insecurity. Nothing can stop the Gospel here in Afghanistan. Not the Taliban. Not ISIS."

Asmaan realizes the importance of her mission in Afghanistan. She told me that when you're a Christian in a country like America, you have churches everywhere. But that is not the case in Afghanistan. "How do we have hope here? Hope comes from Jesus. There is no other way," Asmaan emphasized. "But people can't find Jesus because they don't even know He's here." That's where Asmaan and the community of Christian believers who chose to stay come in, sharing the love of Christ in a country where His word is suppressed.

Remarking on her decision to remain in the country, Asmaan said, "It can change the nation—not just things on earth now but for eternity. One person and their children can change a generation. They may die, but they then have eternity. It's not a small thing. Eternity is the most important thing in life, and becoming a Christian is priceless, because it is not just one person. It is an entire country that can be changed."

Even though Asmaan knows this deep in her heart, it does not change the struggle here on earth in the depths of Afghanistan. "I cry almost every day," she said. "But then I find strength in the morning, and I keep going. I turn my eyes to Jesus, and then I can keep going. 'Lord, I just want your joy to be my joy,' I pray. 'I want to see the kingdom keep growing.'"

Asmaan continues to keep her eyes firmly focused on eternity. Reflecting on the friends she has lost, Asmaan said, "One day, we will all be together in heaven. Christians from all nations free forever. We won't have to sing low anymore, and we won't have to worship low anymore. We can sing together. At some point you see so much pain that death—eternity—is welcome. We will be free forever."

UKRAINE

CHAPTER 3

ON THE VERGE OF
WORLD WAR III

The camera shot was ubiquitous across the airwaves on that Wednesday afternoon in January. The navy blue and brown podium with the presidential seal stood prominently beneath a large crystal chandelier. A row of gold curtains lined the wall as an American flag and a flag with the presidential seal couched either side of the podium's backdrop. America waited as President Joe Biden prepared to take to the lectern. In some ways, the empty lectern was a metaphor for the Biden presidency—carefully crafted, cautiously teleprompted, and noticeably short on meaningful questions and answers between the press and the president. That Wednesday, January 19, 2022, would mark only the second formal press conference of President Biden's presidency, and the press conference came only after much clamoring from the press.

Then-president of the White House Correspondents' Association (WHCA), Steve Portnoy, observed ten days earlier, "Eisenhower—who championed democracy versus totalitarian communism, built the interstates, and sent troops to integrate schools—made a point of holding news conferences 2x a month. The historical record of a presidency requires more than fleeting Q&A."[168] After the president refused to take questions following an event on January 13, the president-elect of WHCA, Kelly O'Donnell, shouted, "Maybe a press conference soon, Mr. President? We would look forward to that," to which the president responded, "Me too."[169] Only after the prodding, and just one day after O'Donnell's question, came the announcement: "Another little bit of news for all of you," Press Secretary Jen Psaki informed the press corps from the podium. "[N]ext Wednesday, the President will hold a formal press conference at 4:00 p.m. in the afternoon. So, we look forward to seeing you there and...the President looks forward to speaking directly to the American people."[170]

America eagerly awaited the president's entrance into the East Room of the White House ahead of that second presidential press conference. The East Room—perhaps the most elaborate room in the White House—was truly something to behold. I will never forget entering the East Room for the first time as an intern in President George W. Bush's administration. It was my first time in the Executive Residence portion of the White House, where I was to attend a Medal of Honor ceremony. The East Room, just to the left of the main entrance into the White House, took my breath away. Three "massive Bohemian glass chandeliers" from President Theodore Roosevelt's administration—as described by the White House Historical Association—glistened brightly as the centerpiece of the room.[171] Off to the right is a massive portrait of President George Washington, rescued from the White House after British troops lit the People's House ablaze in 1814. Now, in 2022, the portrait has been "in the White House collection longer than any other item."[172] The East Room was stunning, coming quite a long way from the days of President John Adams when it was used for drying washed clothes on a clothesline.[173] During my tenure as White House press secretary, President Trump and the administration had used the East Room often—for events, for celebrations, and for the delicious food buffet during the White House Christmas Party. Now, President Biden would add to the history of the East Room in addressing the press on that January afternoon.

Just after 4:00 p.m., President Biden approached the podium, removing his black mask and commencing the high-stakes event. During President Biden's first press conference, only ten reporters received questions in an event that lasted just over one hour.[174] I wondered how the second press conference of Biden's tenure would compare. "It's been a year of challenges, but it's also been a year of enormous progress," the president declared before announcing a litany of perceived economic achievements. Touting economic progress and achievement seemed a bit tone deaf given that just 38 percent of those polled approved of Biden's handling of the economy, but the unusually rosy portrayal of the US economy would be just a footnote to a press conference on the verge of taking a seriously wrong turn.[175]

In addition to the presidential press conference being a rather rare occurrence during the Biden presidency, this press conference carried added importance given the events transpiring on the world stage. According to a Ukrainian intelligence assessment on the same day as Biden's press conference, Russia had amassed 127,000 troops near Ukraine and had "almost completed" deploying its military forces.[176] Additionally, the Wednesday press conference came on the heels of a Friday report from the *Washington Post* that "[t]he Russian government has sent operatives into eastern Ukraine in preparation for potential sabotage efforts that could serve as a pretext for a renewed Russian invasion...."[177] With tensions building in Ukraine, the entire world was watching the commander in chief that Wednesday. You can be certain one key player was keenly taking notes: Russian president Vladimir Putin.

The pivotal moment came a short way into the press conference when a reporter asked President Biden about the efficacy of sanctions in deterring Putin. The president briefly addressed sanctions before assuring the public that "Russia will be held accountable if it invades." In the next breath, however, Biden said the line for which the press conference would become known: "And it depends on what it does. It's one thing if it's a minor incursion and then we end up having a fight about what to do and not do, et cetera."[178]

"It's one thing if it's a *minor incursion....*"

It was a line no one expected. What, after all, was a "minor incursion?" It sounded an awful lot like making an excuse for Russia's dictator exiling just a small piece of a sovereign country rather than engaging in a full-scale invasion. The statement was truly shocking, especially from the mouth of the president of the United States.

Without a doubt, the question merited follow-up from reporters. To be sure, if President Trump had made a similar statement, there would have been a collective, ferocious roar from the White House press corps—likely an interruption, but certainly a follow-up. In the Biden era, though, the press corps had largely lost their voice. Ten questions followed—yes, ten—but not a single one pushed the president on his "minor incursion" comment. Reporters asked about the economy, midterms, vaccines, voting rights, and Build Back Better (part of the president's domestic agenda in Congress) but nothing about his flamboyant remark.[179] The lack of follow-up was truly incomprehensible.

Finally, eleven questions later, a reporter asked, "Are you saying that a minor incursion by Russia into Ukrainian territory would not lead to the sanctions that you have threatened? Or are you effectively giving Putin permission to make a small incursion into the country?"[180]

"Good question," President Biden replied with a laugh. "That's how it did sound like, didn't it?… If it's a—something significantly short of a significant invasion—or not even significant, just major military forces coming across—for example, it's one thing to determine that if they continue to use cyber efforts, well, we can respond the same way, with cyber…I think we will, if there's something that is—that—where there's Russian forces crossing the border, killing Ukrainian fighters, et cetera—I think that changes everything."[181]

The answer hardly cleared anything up, which is why Press Secretary Jen Psaki had to put out a statement cleaning up the mess just one hour after the press conference. "President Biden has been clear with the Russian President: If any Russian military forces move across the Ukrainian border, that's a renewed invasion, and it will be met with swift, severe, and united response from the United States and our allies," the statement read in part.[182] Issuing a statement one hour after a presidential press conference is a quick turnaround, considering the press secretary's office would likely need buy-in from the chief of staff's office and probably the president's as well. After all, the press secretary was fixing the president's blunder.

As press secretary, I accompanied the president to most of his events and almost all of his press conferences. The president opted to do most of his coronavirus task force briefings from the James S. Brady Press Briefing Room. At these briefings, you could often find me sitting along the wall in a blue chair just to the left of the president. In the rare event that I was not sitting in the room, I would be watching the briefing from the press secretary's office. I don't know where Psaki was on the day of President Biden's second presidential press conference, but it occurred to me that, given the swift timing in issuing a clean-up statement, she might very well have been drafting it in real time as the president was speaking. Imagine that—having to clean up the president's words on a major foreign policy issue as he's mid-sentence!

I suppose it's no wonder that Psaki told former senior advisor to President Obama David Axelrod during a podcast that her press shop wished that Biden would refrain from impromptu questions. "That is not something we recommend," Psaki said. "In fact, a lot of times we say 'Don't take questions,' you know, but he's going to do what he wants to do because he's the president."[183]

The media's reaction to Biden's "minor incursion" remark was unusually critical.

NBC's Richard Engel said that Ukrainian officials were likely pondering whether Biden had given Putin "a greenlight to launch an invasion."[184] Margaret Brennan of CBS predicted, "Russia is going to pounce on that."[185] A CNN reporter said that officials watched his remarks with "horror" and were "shocked" at Biden's green-lighting a Putin invasion.[186] And CNN's Dana Bash succinctly noted, "Clean up on aisle State Department."[187] The State Department indeed followed the press shop in trying to undo the president's mess with Secretary of State Antony Blinken rushing to give remarks the next morning.

In August of 2022, a *Washington Post* article was published that sheds even more light on just how irresponsible the "minor incursion" remark truly was. The *Post* wrote about an Oval Office meeting "on a sunny October morning," during which President Biden was shown "newly obtained satellite images, intercepted communications and human sources, that amounted to Russian President Vladimir Putin's war plans for a full-scale invasion of Ukraine."[188] The article detailed that "Biden pressed his advisers" about whether they thought a full-scale invasion was likely. "Yes, they affirmed. This is real." The *Post* continued, "Although the administration would publicly insist over the next several months that it did not believe Putin had made a final decision, the only thing his team couldn't tell the president that autumn day was exactly when the Russian president would pull the trigger."[189]

A truly remarkable revelation! Nearly four months before the invasion, Biden knew that Putin's attack was on the horizon. Rather than taking strong action, Biden instead gave Putin license to invade by saying a minor incursion would somehow be treated as a lesser matter!

Biden's "minor incursion" moment was a rather significant departure from President Trump's strategy not to broadcast America's playbook to its enemies. During the 2016 campaign, President Trump was mocked by the media for refusing to share his plans to defeat ISIS. His reason? "I have a substantial chance of winning. If I win, I don't want to broadcast to the enemy exactly what my plan is."[190] Common sense, right? Well, President Biden took the exact opposite approach.

In December, President Biden said that sending US troops to Ukraine was "not on the table."[191] Though Americans widely agreed, why broadcast this to Russia? In January, the *New York Times* reported that "[t]he Biden administration and its allies are assembling a punishing set of financial, technology and military sanctions against Russia that they say would go into effect within hours of an invasion...."[192] *After*, not *before*. "In interviews, officials described details of those plans for the first time...." the *Times* continued. "Such moves are rarely telegraphed in advance." Why telegraph sanctions in advance? Moreover, why signal exactly when they would come—"within hours of an invasion"?[193]

Now, in his January press conference, the president seemed to all but green-light a "minor incursion"—laying out specific gradations of how certain attacks will be met with certain responses, for example, a "minor incursion" incurring less blowback and a full-scale invasion meriting a tougher response.

Not only that, President Biden made another strategic blunder in that January press conference that got far less attention. "My guess is he will move in," Biden said of Putin. "He has to do something."[194]

He has to do something? So much for deterrence.

A follow-up question on this point later led Biden to underscore his initial sentiment. "Look, the only thing I'm confident of is that decision is totally, solely, completely a Putin decision. Nobody else is going to make that decision; no one else is going to impact that decision. He's making that decision."[195]

No one else is going to impact that decision? Gone were the days of peace through strength. "Peace through strength" had been a foreign policy doctrine embraced by President Ronald Reagan and included in the Republican Party's platform going back to 1980.[196] President Trump put the doctrine to good use. With Russia, peace through strength meant aggressive deterrence. President Trump closed Russian consulates in San Francisco and Seattle, leaving Russia with no diplomatic presence on the west coast.[197] He threw out sixty Russian intelligence officers, withdrew from the Intermediate-Range Nuclear Forces (INF) Treaty because of Russian violations, and leveled onerous sanctions.[198] As National Security Advisor Robert O'Brien put it, "No administration has been tougher on the Russians. We sanctioned hundreds of Russian entities…. There's almost nothing we can sanction left of the Russians. We put so many sanctions on the Russians that, by the way, the prior administration didn't do."[199]

In stark contrast, the Biden administration not only broadcast its strategy but also gave the Russians a much-sought-after goal: a pipeline. After just a few months in office, President Biden opted to waive sanctions on Nord Stream 2—a pipeline between Russia and Germany. President Trump had imposed sanctions on Nord Stream 2 and its CEO, but the Biden administration essentially greenlit the project.[200] This naïve action came despite Biden's own press secretary, Jen Psaki, calling the pipeline "a bad deal for Europe" and State Department spokesperson Ned Price calling it a "Kremlin geopolitical project that is intended to expand Russia's influence...."[201] Now, after just paving the way for the pipeline a few months earlier and with Russia on the brink of invading Ukraine, Biden warned that if an invasion occurred "there will no longer be a Nord Stream 2. We will bring an end to it." A curious reversal. Why did he ever give birth to it?

A year into the Biden presidency, it was clear that Vladimir Putin was taking notes and altering his calculus as he watched the new commander in chief. While Putin amassed troops on the Ukrainian border in December, President Biden had a virtual meeting with the Russian president. Putin sat at the end of a peculiarly long black polished table. President Biden, meanwhile, was at the head of the brown wooden table in the Situation Room surrounded by top advisors. Following the meeting, Putin described the call as "very open, substantive, and I would say constructive," emphasizing the likelihood of working "professionally" with the United States.[202]

But Putin's actions told a different story. ABC's Martha Raddatz reported, "After the call with President Biden, they [Russia] added at least 10,000 more troops. If he's bluffing, it's a very good bluff."[203] But Putin wasn't bluffing. The days that followed would make that abundantly clear.

IN THE DAYS after Biden's disastrous press conference, Russia continued to engage in what *The Economist* called "the largest military build-up in Europe since the cold war."[204] Enemies across the world flexed their muscles alongside Russia. The *Washington Post* listed several examples.[205] Houthi rebels, supported by Iran, shot off ballistic missiles dangerously close to US troops; North Korean dictator Kim Jong Un tested what he claimed were hypersonic missiles; and China flew more than three dozen warplanes near Taiwan.[206]

President Biden seemed to be taking it all in stride. On Tuesday, January 25, 2022, President Biden visited a Capitol Hill gift shop to highlight "the tremendous growth in new small business applications since the start of the Biden-Harris administration."[207] It was yet another "the economy is better than you think" moment for the administration. While at the gift shop, Biden veered toward reporters with a coffee cup in hand that he had selected. The mug featured a painted portrayal of Vice President Kamala Harris smiling in front of a light blue background with white stars.

"Do you guys have any questions? I know you guys never have questions," Biden quipped to the reporters.

Reporters asked about Ukraine and the announcement that 8,500 American troops were placed on high alert. Holding his newly acquired Kamala mug, Biden answered questions before observing that if Russia invaded, it would be "the largest invasion since World War Two. It would change the world."[208] After raising this alarming prospect, Biden departed the gift shop for Jeni's ice cream shop to purchase an ice cream cone.[209]

Many months later—and following a Russian invasion—Biden made a similar wild statement, asserting that Putin was "not joking when he talks about the use of tactical nuclear weapons or biological or chemical weapons…. We have not faced the prospect of Armageddon since Kennedy and the Cuban Missile Crisis."[210] This time, he refrained from making the statement with an ice cream cone.

By February, Putin had 70 percent of troops in place necessary for a full-scale assault on Ukraine.[211] Evoking memories of Afghanistan, the United States evacuated most of its embassy personnel from Kyiv, the Ukrainian capital.[212] That meant the United States had evacuated two American embassies in the span of a few months—one from Kabul and another from Kyiv. Amid the heightened tensions in Europe, Vice President Kamala Harris traveled to Germany for the Munich Security Conference. As I said at the time, sending Kamala to stop a war instilled little confidence in anyone.[213] Indeed, the trip did nothing meaningful to assuage the situation.

On Friday, February 18, President Biden told the world, "As of this moment, I am convinced he [Putin] has made the decision" to invade.[214] Echoing this assessment, a US official told CBS news that "[t]he U.S. has intelligence that Russian commanders have received orders to proceed with an invasion of Ukraine...."[215] At this point, the United States had still not issued any deterrent sanctions. Why? With certainty of an invasion, why not go ahead and sanction? By Monday, Putin had declared two eastern portions of Ukraine as independent, ordering Russian troops to "maintain peace."[216] On Tuesday, the United States issued "limited sanctions," which Reuters noted "only scratch [the] surface."[217] All of this setting the stage for a full-scale Russian invasion of Ukraine.

On Wednesday, February 23, I traveled with my daughter, Blake, to Florida for the Conservative Political Action Conference (CPAC) in Orlando. Along with *Fox & Friends* weekend co-host Pete Hegseth, I would be broadcasting for Fox Nation from the nation's largest gathering of conservatives.[218] The CPAC event was intended to be more than just a work function for me. My mom, aunt, sister, daughter, and I had planned a girls' weekend alongside the event—a chance for us all to reunite and enjoy some relaxation between my broadcasts. Arriving in Florida late on Wednesday evening, my mom and I began to discuss the days ahead and to prepare Blake for bedtime when the news took an abrupt turn just after 10:00 p.m. (ET).

"This is a CBS News Special Report.... We are coming on the air because the war in Ukraine has begun. Just minutes after Russian president Vladimir Putin announced a special military operation in eastern Ukraine, explosions were heard in Kyiv," Norah O'Donnell reported.[219] The CBS foreign correspondent announced that five large explosions had been heard before he abruptly turned around to the sound of what appeared to be fighter jets flying overhead.[220]

In an instant, everything changed.

Lighthearted conversation with my mother turned to taking in the violent sounds of war. Anticipated broadcasts about CPAC and politics shifted to wartime reporting about casualties and destruction. The mood of what would typically be a jubilant political gathering was overtaken by a rather grim news cycle.

On Friday, I hosted *Outnumbered* live from CPAC. Attendees of the conservative rally surrounded the set wearing American flags and political paraphernalia as I shared Russia-Ukraine war updates with the audience. "Make Molotov cocktails and take down the occupier," the Ukrainian Defense Ministry had tweeted in a dire warning that citizens would have to become citizen soldiers should they remain in Ukraine.[221] "Ukrainian parents brace their children for a Russian invasion, sending them to school with stickers identifying their blood type," read a *Business Insider* headline.[222]

The devastating new reality for Ukrainian families had already become so vivid less than forty-eight hours into the war. One video depicted a tearful Ukrainian girl in a pink jacket with a gray fur hood standing just in front of a train.[223] Her father kisses her on the cheek, places a white snow cap on her head, and takes a knee. The father, clearly trying to stay strong for his daughter, gently grabs her hands, knowing that this might be the last time that he sees her. The little girl was about to board a train out of Ukraine while the father—like so many Ukrainian men—prepared to stay and fight the Russians. As the father looks into his daughter's eyes, he begins to cry loudly, audibly, and painfully. So, too, does his sweet little girl.

And then there were the heartbreaking images of another little girl in a pink jacket that emerged just a few days later.[224] A six-year-old girl wearing a pink jacket, gray sweatpants with unicorns, and purple socks is placed on a stretcher. Her dark hair and tiny body are covered in blood from injuries caused by Russian shelling in the heavily hit city of Mariupol. Her father—also wounded—stays near his child as her mother sheds tears just outside the ambulance.

"Take her out! Take her out! We can make it!" a medical professional shouts, trying to speed along the process of the six-year-old being rushed into the hospital.

Soon after, the pale young girl's body appears lifeless, the frustrated team of hospital workers unable to save her.

"Show this to Putin," the doctor said to an Associated Press video journalist. "The eyes of this child and crying doctors."[225]

Watching the videos and images of these young girls, I could not help but think of my own daughter. There with me at CPAC, Blake, my family, and I enjoyed wonderful dinners, an inspiring event, and a beautiful hotel room overlooking a massive resort-style pool with glimmering colors and a nighttime light show. Amid all of the comforts America had to offer, it was difficult to fathom the somber realities of war-torn Ukraine.

On that Friday at CPAC, the prospects of Ukraine withstanding a Russian insurgency seemed dim. CNN was reporting that according to "two sources familiar with the latest intelligence," Kyiv, Ukraine's capital, could fall "within days."[226] The intelligence assessment was essentially the exact opposite of the assessment when the US departed Afghanistan. In Afghanistan, President Biden told us that the chance of a Taliban takeover was "highly unlikely," and an April intelligence assessment suggested that any takeover would be "at least 18 months away."[227] In the end, both the Ukraine and Afghanistan intelligence—as reported—were wrong, and in fact, opposite.

As it turns out, Afghanistan fell within about forty-eight hours while Ukraine withstood the onslaught of the full force of the Russian military, thanks to the bravery of its citizens. And make no mistake, Vladimir Putin saw the disastrous US withdrawal from Afghanistan and took note of it. In fact, the *Washington Post* report on US intelligence specifically said that "[t]he Russian leader...believed that the Biden administration was chastened by the humiliating U.S. withdrawal from Afghanistan and wanted to avoid new wars."[228] The embarrassing Afghanistan withdrawal, in other words, had consequences across the world.

CPAC CONCLUDED THAT February weekend, and as I expected, the Russia-Ukraine war dominated our discussions on *Outnumbered* for the weeks to come. Along with the war came coverage of the refugee crisis—the largest refugee exodus since World War II.[229] The vulnerable crowded into trains in a rush to flee the country—"16, 17, 18 people in compartments that usually carry six, sleeping on the floor and on top of one another," *The Economist* reported.[230] "Women, children and the elderly have priority to board."[231]

Other refugees fled by foot. Battling freezing temperatures and falling snow, desperate Ukrainians traveled long distances to find a safe haven. *The Economist* described the plight of refugees near Medyka, Poland, where temperatures reached as low as negative twenty-eight degrees Fahrenheit.[232] "Tens of thousands of Ukrainians...queue on the Ukrainian side of the border in the cold, sometimes for more than a day. The traffic is such that many had no choice but to leave their cars behind and continue on foot. Holding a bag in one hand, her young daughter's hand in the other, and carrying her toddler in a sling, Anastasia describes having to walk 17km to the border. She was greeted by scenes of chaos, she says, including impenetrable crowds and vigorous shoving. A young couple remember seeing a village consumed by flames on the way. 'It was hell...'" *The Economist* described.[233]

Anastasia, a mother, traveled seventeen kilometers holding one child's hand, while *carrying* another—that is nearly ten and a half miles!

Imagine that.

I read this passage in my magazine shortly before carrying my daughter on what seemed like a trek—a very comfortable trek through the warmth of Newark airport while rolling a suitcase in one hand and holding my two-year-old on my hip. As I took that ten-minute walk, huffing and puffing along the way with the occasional stop to put Blake down and enjoy a brief reprieve, I could not help but think of Anastasia. She had not one child, but two, walking through the snowy abyss as she left her home and fled the horror behind her. There was no warm car waiting for Anastasia at the other end of her ten-and-a-half-mile journey.

Perspective.

As I write this in June of 2022, nearly seven million Ukrainians have fled their home for a neighboring territory.[234] Millions more have been displaced within the war-torn country. Each day, on *Outnumbered*, we reported on the refugee crisis and the dire images and emotional stories emerging from the war in Ukraine. With our program airing at noon eastern, the time in part of Ukraine was 7:00 p.m. During our lunchtime hour on the east coast of the United States, night was approaching in Ukraine. Oftentimes, crushing images of war came during our hour—like on Wednesday, March 9, 2022.

Russia had purportedly established a half-day stop to its relentless shelling and bombing to permit safe exit for civilians.[235] But that did not spare the bombing of a maternity hospital in Mariupol, Ukraine. Sitting on the *Outnumbered* couch, my co-hosts and I saw the devastation in real time. Plastic incubators for premature babies scattered among debris. Brightly colored pastel walls—green, yellow, and pink—destroyed. A white crib crunched between jumbled medical equipment. The bombed hospital, which welcomed new life routinely, was now decimated—the target of Russian bombs.

By the end of the noon hour, a disturbing picture emerged. Four men carried a pregnant woman from the wreckage on a gray stretcher lined with a vibrant red and green watermelon blanket. Her black pants were bloodstained with her left hand clutching her visibly pregnant belly. As we covered the image on *Outnumbered*, I grew emotional, trying my best to hold back my tears. I could not help but remember the day I had my daughter. Cloaked in hospital clothes and lying in a perfectly sanitized hospital room, I remember seeing Blake for the first time alongside my husband. As it should be for any mother, the moment was joyous—a far cry from the depiction of this Ukrainian mother fighting for her life and her baby's.

I found out days later that the mother was taken to another hospital, leaving the blown out maternity ward behind her. Doctors tried to save both her and her child. The mother's severe injuries meant that she had to have a cesarean section. Upon the baby's arrival, there were "no signs of life."[236] When the young woman learned that her newborn baby would not make it, she reportedly cried, "Kill me now."[237] The mother, unfortunately, succumbed to her wounds, and as a doctor shared with the Associated Press, medical professionals attempted "more than 30 minutes of resuscitation" that "didn't produce results. Both died."[238] Her husband

and father came to retrieve her remains. As the AP wrote, "Doctors said they were grateful that she didn't end up in the mass graves being dug for many of Mariupol's dead."[239]

Pictures and stories like these proliferated the news cycle. One evening, I walked into my living room to turn on *Cocomelon*, the popular, brightly colored cartoon, for my two-year-old. When I turned on the television, the news came on. Injured Ukrainian children appeared across the screen, and my daughter briefly saw the disturbing images.

"Mommy, baby hurt," she said in her innocent, soft voice.

The moment stuck with me. Here was my daughter—for a moment catching a glimpse of the unspeakable atrocities halfway across the globe. Meanwhile, in Ukraine, I had heard about one mother having to shield her child's eyes from bodies along the side of the road as they were walking together. I simply could not imagine.

These were the realities of war, and America watched from afar. After twenty years of war and the loss of 6,840 of America's best, there was understandably no appetite for war.[240] No one wanted to see American troops enter another endless war, especially with a nuclear power like Russia. Nevertheless, as with any international conflict, watching the war in Ukraine weighed heavy on the American conscience as wartime images of pain and suffering pierced our hearts. For anyone, these tragedies are incomprehensible and difficult to make sense of. But, for the Christian, we can look to an all-loving, all-knowing, all-powerful God for answers.

CHAPTER 4

AN ALL-POWERFUL GOD AND A SUFFERING WORLD

A father wailing at the sight of his now lifeless six-year-old little girl in a pink jacket. A new mother and her baby taken needlessly in the pastel hallways of a once joyous maternity hospital. Hundreds of churches razed to the ground, including a sixteenth-century monastery—among the "holiest Orthodox Christian sites."[241] These are the realities of war, and they are particularly difficult to square with the reality of an all-loving, all-powerful God.

The devastation abroad that we have witnessed most recently in Afghanistan and Ukraine raises all sorts of complicated questions. These questions are amplified by the pain we endure here at home—like the inexplicable, gut-wrenching loss of sweet little Eliahna "Ellie" Garcia and twenty other innocents at Robb Elementary School in Uvalde, Texas, on May 24, 2022. Nine-year-old Ellie Garcia was a remarkable young girl, whose faith in Christ was both beautiful and awe-inspiring.

Some time prior to her death, Ellie posted a video on social media, sharing her testimony with the world. "Jesus. He died for us. So, when we die, we'll be up there with Him," she said in her little voice, while pointing upward. "In my room, I have three pictures of him."[242] When Ellie posted that video, neither she nor her parents knew that the day she would meet her heavenly Father would come so soon.

Ellie's father wrote about his young daughter's devotion to prayer before her passing. "Caught my Ellie Gee in the middle of her talk with our almighty. I love you baby girl and I love the way you pray," he wrote alongside a picture of Ellie lying in her bed under the covers, eyes tightly closed as she held her hands in a praying position.[243] In the wake of Ellie's death, Ellie's father re-shared the image, alongside a message expounding upon her love for prayer and ending with these words: "These memories are all I have left...."[244]

Before her passing, the Primera Iglesia Bautista (First Baptist Church) had chosen Ellie to read Deuteronomy 6:18 on Sunday, May 29, 2022—the first Sunday after the Uvalde massacre.[245] "And you shall do what is right and good in the sight of the Lord, that it may go well with you, and that you may go in and take possession of the good land that the Lord swore to give to your fathers," the verse reads.[246] Ellie never got to read those words, for she was ruthlessly murdered five days earlier. "Instead," *Time* reported, "three of her friends from Sunday school recited the verse in her honor, with a picture of Ellie projected behind them."[247] Just days before her tenth birthday, Ellie was laid to rest in a pink and purple pastel-colored dress adorned with ornate flowers. The dress, provided by the Walt Disney Company, was modeled after the movie *Encanto*, one of Ellie's favorite movies.[248]

Why was Ellie taken from us so soon? Why were her parents—a good, faithful, loving mother and father—left to pick up the pieces? Their lives will never be the same. As a parent to a toddler girl and a newborn son, I have wondered this myself. Many nights I have lain awake trying to comprehend the horrifying, life-changing reality of these parents. My daughter, husband, and I have prayed for them often, turning to God and asking for Him to comfort the families of the fallen.

Whether facing war, our nation's worst tragedies, or personal plight, Americans seek answers. A poll conducted by George Barna posed this question: "If you could ask God only one question and you knew he would give you an answer, what would you ask?"[249] The question offered most by those polled was "[w]hy is there pain and suffering in the world?"[250]

In his book, *The Problem of Pain*, C. S. Lewis explores this very question.[251] He begins by recalling his life as an atheist and answers the question, "Why do you not believe in God?" Lewis offers a multi-page response from the purview of his atheistic days, citing all of the pain and suffering in the world, leading him to eventually state: "If you ask me to believe that this is the work of a benevolent and omnipotent spirit, I reply that all the evidence points in the opposite direction. Either there is no spirit behind the universe, or else a spirit indifferent to good and evil, or else an evil spirit."[252] For the layman, he articulates the problem simply in chapter two: "If God were good, He would wish to make His creatures perfectly happy, and if God were almighty, He would be able to do what He wished. But the creatures are not happy. Therefore, God lacks either goodness, or power, or both. This is the problem of pain, in its simplest form."[253]

And yet, the strange reality is that people, in the midst of unimaginable hurt or tragedy, often find themselves turning to God—sometimes expressing their anger and oftentimes finding faith amid tragedy. A pastor in Ukraine wrote, "'Bomb shelter ministry' is, I must admit, not a ministry profile I thought I'd ever have. And yet, we are already seeing how fruitful it's been. Our neighbors have heard more about Christ, heard more Scripture, and been led in more prayer in the last week than most of them probably have in their lives."[254]

In Uvalde, *Time* reported, "Much of Uvalde spent Sunday morning [following the tragedy] attending church services, together mourning the loss of 21 beloved community members. In this devout town—85% of people identity as some denomination of Christianity, according to a Public Religion Research Institute 2020 Census of American Religion—many have sought healing through faith."[255]

In his book, *The Language of God*, Dr. Francis Collins—a renowned scientist—writes about his bedside conversations with patients in North Carolina.[256] "I witnessed numerous cases of individuals whose faith provided them with a strong reassurance of ultimate peace, be it in this world or the next, despite terrible suffering that in most instances they had done nothing to bring on themselves," he writes.[257] "If faith was a psychological crutch, I concluded, it must be a very powerful one. If it was nothing more than a veneer of cultural tradition, why were these people not shaking their fists at God and demanding that their friends and family stop all this talk about a loving and benevolent supernatural power?"[258]

In Newtown, Connecticut, twenty-six innocents—many just six and seven years old—were shot by a deranged gunman at Sandy Hook Elementary School. Referencing the tragedy, Christian theologian Timothy Keller, in his book *Walking with God through Pain and Suffering*, highlights a column by Samuel G. Freedman in the *New York Times* called, "In a Crisis, Humanists Seem Absent."[259] Freedman notes that, following the Newtown tragedy, the community turned to faith, not humanism—"an umbrella term for those who call themselves atheists, agnostics, secularists and freethinkers."[260]

Drawing on examples from Freedman's piece, Tim Keller writes, "Connecticut is hardly the center of the U.S. Bible Belt, yet every single family in Newtown who lost a child chose to hold religious services, which took place in Catholic, Congregational,

Mormon, and Methodist churches, as well as in a Protestant mega-church and a Jewish cemetery.... President Obama delivered a eulogy that was essentially a sermon, speaking of God 'calling the children home.' He quoted extensively from 2 Corinthians 4 and 5 and used its hope for a world and life beyond this one to console and make bearable the losses we experience here and now."[261]

Nevertheless, "the problem of pain"—as C. S. Lewis calls it—indeed engenders many challenges to God's existence. It raises the most difficult question of "why." But the experience of hurt—and the deepest, most searing form of pain—simultaneously brings men and women to the very foot of God, dialoguing with the creator as they endure some of life's cruelest moments.

It is particularly in these moments of adversity, whether a small personal struggle or an enormous interpersonal one like the loss of a loved one, that we choose the prism through which to view our moment of crisis. I would argue that there is a decided difference in the way that the secular world and the community of faith handles the matter.

Several months into the COVID-19 pandemic, Pew conducted a survey comparing the religious and non-religious response to suffering in the world.[262] Christians tended to show more gratitude for gifts in their own life (by a twenty-point margin), more "sadness for those who are suffering" (by an eleven-point margin), and more of a "desire to help those who are suffering" (by an eight-point margin) than their non-religious counterparts.[263] Conversely, Christians expressed less of a "worry that something similar" would happen to them (by a four-point margin).[264]

These differences in views are reflected in action. In the wake of the Newtown shooting, as with almost any tragedy or natural disaster, the faith community flooded in to help, not just with charitable outpouring, but also bringing the hope of heaven during the darkest of times. Freedman, in his *New York Times* piece, contrasts the response of the humanist, prefacing his analysis with this—"[t] o raise these queries is not to play gotcha, or be judgmental.... In fact, some leaders within the humanist movement...are ruefully and self-critically saying the same things themselves."[265]

Freedman then depicted the response from the humanists: "The Ethical Culture Society chapter in Teaneck, N.J., helped organize a gun-control rally there. The Connecticut branch of the American Humanist Association contributed about $370 to Newtown families from a winter solstice fund-raiser. The organization American Atheists reports on its Web site that it has collected more than $11,000 in online donations toward funeral expenses in Newtown.... Still, when it comes to the pastoral version of 'boots on the ground'—a continuing presence in communities, a commitment to tactile rather than virtual engagement with people who are hurting—the example of Newtown shows how humanists continue to lag."[266]

The Christian community "boots on the ground," by contrast, seems to be ever-present in times of tragedy. Detailing the response to Hurricane Katrina, PBS reported, "Hundreds of faith-based volunteers rushed into the devastated areas to help with rescue operations, while others mobilized to provide desperately needed food, medicine, and shelter. Southern Baptists initially committed to providing 300,000 meals a day for the next 90 days, but a spokesman expected that number to rise to more than one million. Congregations from almost every denomination opened their facilities and became emergency shelters."[267]

The faith community's mobilization in response to suffering is nothing new. In fact, there is a long tradition of Christian activism during tragedy. Keller writes, "Early Christian speakers and writers not only argued vigorously that Christianity's teaching made more sense of suffering, they insisted that the actual lives of Christians proved it. Cyprian recounted how, during the terrible plagues,

Christians did not abandon sick loved ones nor flee the cities, as most of the pagan residents did. Instead they stayed to tend the sick and faced their deaths with calmness."[268]

Contrasting the pagan and the Christian response to the plague, Dionysius of Alexandria, a third-century bishop wrote, "At the first onset of the disease, they [nonbelievers] pushed the sufferers away and fled from their dearest, throwing them into the roads before they were dead and treated unburied corpses as dirt.... Most of our brother Christians showed unbounded love and loyalty, never sparing themselves and thinking only of one another. Heedless of danger, they took charge of the sick, attending to their every need and ministering to them in Christ, and with them departed this life serenely happy.... Many, in nursing and curing others, transferred their death to themselves and died in their stead."[269] In fact, it was Christians who were responsible for creating hospitals, now used to care for the sick in every corner of the globe.[270]

Not only does the response to suffering differ between the believer and nonbeliever, so, too, does the explanation. In the secular view of suffering, there simply is no explanation. The well-known atheist scholar Richard Dawkins, as quoted by Keller, wrote, "In a universe of blind physical forces and genetic replication, some people are going to get hurt, other people are going to get lucky, and you won't find any rhyme or reason in it, nor any justice. The universe that we observe has precisely the properties we should expect if there is, at bottom, no design, no purpose, no evil, no good, nothing but pitiless indifference."[271]

Nothingness. Total randomness.

That is the response of the atheist scholar.

In his argument, Dawkins asserts that "you won't find...any justice" in the universe. But how can Dawkins insert the concept of "justice" in a world where he asserts there is "no evil, no good"? For isn't the concept of "justice" totally dependent on using "good" and "evil" to discern what is "just"? Lewis makes a similar case, writing "[m]y argument against God was that the universe seemed so cruel and unjust. But how had I got this idea of *just* and *unjust*? A man does not call a line crooked unless he has some idea of a straight line. What was I comparing this universe with when I called it unjust?"[272] Dawkins finds himself in a moral conundrum, one that C. S. Lewis finally elucidates and rejects, concluding that "...in the very act of trying to prove that God did not exist—in other words, that the whole of reality was senseless—I found I was forced to assume that one part of reality—namely my idea of justice—was full of sense. Consequently atheism turns out to be too simple."[273]

Lewis has a point. In order to condemn the evils of this world, there must be some neutral barometer for determining what is good and what is evil. Keller draws out this concept through a pointed line of questioning: "What right have you to tell people they are obligated to stop certain behaviors if their feelings tell them those things are right, but you feel they are wrong? Why should your moral feelings take precedence over theirs? Where do you get a standard by which your moral feelings and sense are judged as true and others are false? On what basis do you say to someone, 'What you have done is evil,' if their feelings differ from yours?"[274]

Now, let us apply this logic with a specific example and extend Keller's line of questioning into criminal law. For instance, consider the proposition: "Stealing is wrong." It is a proposition that is widely accepted, but what if your neighbor decides that stealing is perfectly acceptable behavior? Sure, there is a law on the books for which he will be punished for the action of stealing, but who is to say that your neighbor is morally wrong in his viewpoint? Who is to say that the law is morally right? Besides, the law is a human creation that could change at any moment. What if a majority suddenly decided to do away with vast provisions of criminal law? Does that then change the concept of what is right and wrong? To what source of moral authority can you point—absent a God—for asserting that his point of view is incorrect and inferior to your own? Or is right and wrong something more enduring, more permanent, something etched in the human heart? In other words, is there some sort of moral law, and thus some moral lawgiver?

Lewis, as quoted by Keller, states the atheist's dilemma with artful precision: "The defiance of the good atheist hurled at an apparently ruthless and idiotic cosmos is really an unconscious homage to something in or behind that cosmos which he recognizes as infinitely valuable and authoritative: for if mercy and justice were really only private whims of his own with no objection and impersonal roots, and if he realized this, he could not go on being indignant. The face that he arraigns heaven itself for disregarding them means that at some level of his mind he knows they are enthroned in a higher heaven still."[275]

Without a doubt, appeal to a higher being who has created for us a higher moral code above our own predilections and whims is necessary for creating a good and just society that most of us—secular or of faith—would hope to find ourselves living in. After all, we have seen, painfully, how depraved human-created moral codes can become whether in the current Uyghur genocide occurring in China or the horrors of the Holocaust in Nazi Germany.[276]

By contrast to the illogic of the atheist, the faith community offers a far more wholesome, rich response to suffering—not just in deed—but also in rationale. While the believer finds comfort in scripture and ultimate solace in the restoration of the afterlife, the community of Christian scholars has offered some response to the question of why evil exists.

As a Christian, I believe that the Bible—the greatest book ever written—provides answers to life's biggest questions. How was the world created? What is the nature of God? How are we to view injustice? What is the purpose of life? What is my purpose?

All of these questions and more are answered. Supplementing my understanding of scripture is a body of work called Christian apologetics—a "verbal defence" or a "reasoned statement or argument" for the Christian faith.[277] Apologetics seeks to use human logic to rationalize and understand biblical truth. A big part of Christian apologetics is Christian philosophy, a field of deeply thought-provoking literature I discovered while taking a course at Georgetown University. Among the authors I read during my Christian philosophy course was Alvin Plantinga, an author and professor.

Plantinga first distinguishes the difference in providing a "theodicy" versus a "defense" to the question of "why does evil exist?" He describes the difference this way: "A theodicy would be an attempt to answer that question and say 'Well, here's why God permits it for the following reasons.' Whereas a defense could be offered by someone who says, 'I don't know what God's reasons are. Maybe his reasons are totally beyond us, but at least I can show you that there isn't any contradiction between the existence of evil on the one hand and God's being holy, good, and omniscient and omnipotent on the other hand."[278]

This idea of not knowing all of the answers comports with biblical truth. Isaiah 55:9 reads, "As the heavens are higher than the earth, so are my ways higher than your ways and my thoughts than your thoughts."[279] Similarly, Proverbs 3:5–6 cautions believers about relying on our own conception: "Trust in the Lord with all your heart and lean not on your own understanding; in all your ways submit to him, and he will make your paths straight."[280] Trust, after all, is a central component of faith.

To this end, Plantinga offers the so-called free will defense—"not to say what God's reason *is*, but at most what God's reason *might possibly be*."[281] While Plantinga provides a one hundred-plus page rationale in *God, Freedom, and Evil*, the free will defense, put simply, goes like this: "To create creatures capable of *moral good*, therefore, He must create creatures capable of moral evil; and He can't give these creatures the freedom to perform evil and at the same time prevent them from doing so.... The fact that free creatures sometimes go wrong, however, counts neither against God's omnipotence nor against His goodness; for He could have forestalled the occurrence of moral evil only by removing the possibility of moral good."[282] In other words, in a world where moral good is possible, so too is moral evil—both byproducts of a free world.

In his writings, Lewis directly addresses the question that arises: Why couldn't God have created beings that are free to commit good but unable to commit evil? Lewis writes, "If a thing is free to be good it is also free to be bad. And free will is what has made evil possible. Why, then, did God give them free will? Because free will, though it makes evil possible, is also the only thing that makes possible any love or goodness or joy worth having. A world of automata—of creatures that worked like machines—would hardly be worth creating."[283]

So where did creation go wrong? How did we descend from beings made in the image and likeness of God to creatures capable of the worst forms of human atrocity? As Lewis says, reflecting the Genesis story, "What Satan puts into the heads of our remote ancestors was the idea that they could 'be like gods'—could set upon their own as if they had created themselves—be their own masters—invent some sort of happiness for themselves outside of God, apart from God. And out of that hopeless attempt has come nearly all that we call human history—money, poverty, ambition, war, prostitution, classes, empire, slavery—the long terrible story of man trying to find something other than God which will make him happy."[284]

From this choice to commit evil comes suffering, but in God we find renewed hope. Keller notes this phenomenon when he references an essay by David Bentley Hart, written in the aftermath of the 2004 tsunamis that killed nearly a quarter of a million people. Hart writes, "Our faith is in a God who has come to rescue His creation from the absurdity of sin and the emptiness of death, and so we are permitted to hate these things with a perfect hatred.... As for comfort, when we seek it, I can imagine none greater than the happy knowledge that when I see the death of a child, I do not see the face of God, but the face of His enemy. It is...a faith that...has set us free from optimism, and taught us hope instead."[285]

In this passage, Hart illuminates a key truth: Suffering and death were *never* part of God's plan. They are an aberration, an abomination, a nuisance brought about by man's sin not God's divine and perfect will for our lives. In 2018, I published my first book, *The New American Revolution*.[286] I interviewed men and women who had lost loved ones, some of whom lost children. Among the Americans with stories of loss I profiled was Kim Copeland, a mom from Lakeway, Texas, who went on a dream vacation to Nice, France, with her two stepchildren; her eleven-year-old son, Brodie; and her husband, Sean.

Their European vacation turned into unimaginable horror when a terrorist rammed a nineteen-ton refrigerator truck through a crowd and into a candy stand, killing both Brodie and Sean. In mere moments, Kim's life changed—her son and her husband gone, their pictures now splashed across the news. You might remember that well-known image that crossed America's television screens—Brodie and Sean standing on a baseball mound, Brodie looking up with his glove hanging alongside him, looking into his dad's eyes. With only memories now, Kim was left to pick up the broken pieces of her life.[287]

In interviewing Kim for my book, I asked her if she ever became angry with God. "Oh, yeah," she said. Not only had Kim lost her son and husband, but she had also lost her mother at a young age and her beloved grandmother later in life. She told me that she used to ask God questions like, "What did I do, God? What did I do to deserve this?" But then one day her pastor offered this: "You're going to hear some crazy stuff, Kim. People are going to tell you this was God's plan. This was not God's plan. He did not plan this to happen. He allowed it, but he did not plan for your life to be this way."[288]

As I wrote at the time, "Kim had a realization. God did not plan for evil to extinguish innocence on that day in Nice or for cancer and Alzheimer's to steal the lives of her mom and [grandmother] Maw-Maw. Evil and subsequent hurt are a result of human sin, not part of God's outline for Kim's life. 'You have to figure out what you're going to do on this side of it,' Kim's pastor advised. After hearing those words, Kim had a choice: to let the anger consume her or fall into the arms of her loving heavenly father. She chose the latter."[289]

And God indeed comforted her, providing Kim with miraculous and unexplainable signs of His presence amid her pain and even the assurance that her loved ones were in heaven with Him.[290] I found that to be a common theme with all of the families I interviewed. A father who lost his police officer son, a mother who also lost her son, and a wife who lost her veteran husband—all saw miraculous outreach from God amid their hurt. As I interviewed these men and women who did not know one another and lived in all different parts of the country, a common theme could be best summed up by C. S. Lewis's renowned words: "God whispers to us in our pleasures, speaks in our conscience, but shouts in our pain: it is His megaphone to rouse a deaf world."[291]

Not only can we hear God more clearly during times of adversity, He can and often does use our adversity for good. We see this, for example, in the tragic story of Stephen, the first Christian martyr. The Bible tells us that Stephen was "full of grace and power," and he "was doing great wonders and signs among the people."[292] Those who challenged Stephen "could not withstand the wisdom and the Spirit with which he was speaking."[293] Much like Jesus, Stephen was falsely accused, seized, and taken before a council. Scripture tells us,

"And gazing at him, all who sat in the council saw that his face was like the face of an angel."[294]

In response to the council, Stephen gives a speech about the history of Israel and the truth of the Lord and Savior Jesus Christ.[295] But, according to scripture, "when they heard these things they were enraged, and they ground their teeth at him."[296] Stephen proceeds to tell the crowd that he sees "the heavens opened, and the Son of Man standing at the right hand of God," but the crowd "rushed together at him...and stoned him."[297] As they killed Stephen, Stephen ended his life in witness: "And as they were stoning Stephen, he called out, 'Lord Jesus, receive my spirit.' And falling to his knees he cried out with a loud voice, 'Lord, do not hold this sin against them.' And when he had said this, he fell asleep."[298]

I'm sure, to many at the time, Stephen's death was unfathomable. The Bible tells us that Stephen was doing "great wonders and signs among the people." So why did his life end? Wouldn't a long life for Stephen have brought about much good for God's kingdom? Not only that, Stephen's death marked the beginning of "a great persecution against the church in Jerusalem, and they were all scattered throughout the regions...."[299] How did any of this make sense?

The Jeremiah Study Bible explains that "Stephen's death jump-started the persecution that sent the church into the world with the gospel of Jesus.... If Stephen's sermon and death had not begun the wave of persecution that they did, the believers would never have left Jerusalem.... This was the beginning of the missionary movement. God used the persecution that people intended for evil to evangelize the world."[300]

Moreover, in the stoning of Stephen, we get the first mention of "Saul"—the infamous persecutor of Christians, who underwent a radical transformation in becoming Paul the Apostle. During the stoning of Stephen, we are told that "witnesses laid down their garments at the feet of a young man named Saul."[301] Stephen's martyrdom was instrumental in Saul's eventual conversion to becoming Paul. As the Jeremiah Study Bible notes, "We know this event created a lasting impression on Saul because he made reference to the event when responding to a vision he had of Christ after his conversion: 'Lord...when the blood of Stephen your witness was being shed, I myself was standing by and approving and watching over the garments of those who killed him.' (22:19, 20). Paul never forgot what he had done to contribute to Stephen's death. But we have to believe Stephen's prayer for forgiveness of those attacking him was granted (7:60). As Saint Augustine later, wrote, 'If Stephen had not prayed, the church would not have had Paul.'"[302] Paul, of course, went on to write much of the New Testament. In other words, Stephen's martyrdom and suffering made an eternal difference.

A biblical analysis of suffering would not be complete without a look at what are perhaps the two greatest stories of suffering in the Old and New Testament—the suffering of Job and the Passion of Jesus Christ. In Job, we find a man who is "blameless and upright, one who feared God and turned away from evil."[303] Described as the "greatest of all the people of the east," Job is a man with a very blessed life—a wife, seven sons, three daughters, ample cattle, and "very many servants."[304] But that all changes in moments. Job's children perish, his cattle and servants are lost as he suffers from debilitating illness and sores. Everything gone in the blink of an eye! Job's new reality is one of misery, from which he "arose and tore his robe and shaved his head and fell on the ground and worshiped."[305]

Amid inexplicable loss, Job worshiped, but he still questioned, asking, "'Why did I not die at birth, come out from the womb and expire?'"[306] "'Or why was I not as a hidden stillborn child, as infants who never see the light?'"[307] "'Why is light given to him who is in misery, and life to the bitter in soul, who long for death, but it comes not, and dig for it more than for hidden treasures, who rejoice exceedingly and are glad when they find the grave?'"[308]

To make matters worse, Job suffered the ill-conceived judgment of his friends. Job observes that, during prosperity, "'[m]en listened to me and waited and kept silent for my counsel.'"[309] "'But now they laugh at me, men who are younger than I...'" Job says.[310] "'I am a laughingstock to my friends...,'" he laments.[311] Job even describes men who "abhor" him and who "spit at the sight" of him.[312] His friends incorrectly suggest that Job must have brought this suffering upon himself. This incorrect logic is eventually rebuked by God, and the beginning of the book of Job tells us that, as Job's suffering began so treacherously, he "did not sin or charge God with wrong."[313]

In the end, God "restored the fortunes of Job" and "gave Job twice as much as he had before."[314] But this only comes after Job questions God, and in response, God confronts Job with what the Jeremiah Study Bible calls "divine cross-examination."[315] In explaining this portion of Job, Keller turns to sociologist Peter Berger, writing, "God confronts Job with his own finitude, his inability to understand God's counsels and purposes even if they were revealed, and his status as a sinner in no position to demand a comfortable life. Berger admits that this view of things has strong logic to it, but that all by itself such a vision would be 'hard to sustain for most people...only possible for certain religious 'virtuosi.' Fortunately for us, that is not the Bible's last word on suffering. Berger says that the 'unbearable tension of this problem brought about...by the Old Testament' is met with 'the essential Christian solution of the problem.' And that solution is that 'the incarnate God is a God who suffers.'"[316]

Indeed, the connection between the suffering of Job and the ultimate suffering of Christ is an undeniable corollary. One of Job's contentions during his suffering is that he has no arbiter between him and God, no one to plead his case. Speaking of God, Job says, "'For he is not a man, as I am, that I might answer him, that we should come to trial together. There is no arbiter between us, who might lay his hand on us both.'"[317] But this would change in the coming of Jesus Christ, which Job seems to foreshadow here. Indeed, in Job 19:25, Job states it definitively: "For I know that my Redeemer lives, and at the last he will stand upon the earth."[318]

How prescient are Job's words? Here is the book of Job—one of the oldest books in the Bible—already predicting the New Testament Gospel, as Job both laments the lack of a divine intercessory to God before declaring "My Redeemer lives!"[319] The Jeremiah Study Bible notes that "*Redeemer* means 'a go-between,' or 'one who will ransom.'"[320] The ransom is Jesus Christ who suffered not just physical pain and excruciating torture but the full weight of human sin—rape, murder, and all of its horrors—and the total absence of God as he was crucified. We see the heaviness of Christ's impending suffering on full display in the Garden of Gethsemane. "Sit here, while I go over there and pray," Jesus told his disciples as he went to pray in the Garden of Gethsemane just before Judas's betrayal.[321]

I had the humbling opportunity to visit the Garden of Gethsemane in Jerusalem, Israel, during my time as a producer with *Huckabee* on Fox News. Touring the garden with a tour guide and Governor Huckabee, who had been there several times, I was struck by the twisted olive trees lining the garden at the bottom of the Mount of Olives. Amazingly, these trees could very well have been the exact trees that Christ prayed beneath ahead of his crucifixion. "Jerusalem olive trees among oldest in world," reads one headline from Australian Broadcasting Corporation (ABC).[322]

Summarizing a study by the National Research Council of Italy Trees and Timber Institute, ABC writes, "Olive trees in the Jerusalem garden revered by Christians as the place where Jesus Christ prayed before he was crucified have been dated to at least 900 years old, a study released on Friday showed. The results of tests on trees in the Garden of Gethsemane have not settled the question of whether the gnarled trees are the very same which sheltered Jesus because olive trees can grow back from roots after being cut down, researchers said."[323]

It was amazing to consider. The trees I gazed at could be the very same ones Jesus Christ looked at, all twisted and "gnarled" as He considered the bodily gnarling He would face in crucifixion.

At the time Christ prayed in Gethsemane, Jesus is described as "sorrowful and troubled," with the Greek words indicating that He was experiencing "intense grief and extreme anguish."[324] Jesus told Peter, James, and John, "My soul is very sorrowful, even to death; remain here, and watch with me."[325] The Jeremiah Study Bible says that "[t]he phrase even to death is found often in the Septuagint [the Greek Old Testament] and refers to sorrow so overpowering that it almost kills. The intense anguish is further proof that Jesus was completely human as well as fully divine."[326]

In great anguish, Jesus "fell on his face and prayed, saying 'My Father if it be possible, let this cup pass from me; nevertheless, not as I will, but as you will.'"[327] The Gospel of Luke tells us that, as Christ prayed, "there appeared to him an angel from heaven, strengthening him."[328] Luke writes, "And being in agony he prayed more earnestly; and his sweat became like great drops of blood falling down to the ground."[329] In his book, *The Case for Christ*, Lee Strobel interviews Dr. Alexander Metherell, MD, PhD, who explains that drops of blood falling in this manner "is a known medical condition called hematidrosis. It's not very common, but it is associated with a high degree of psychological stress."[330] The National Institute of Health explains hematidrosis as "a condition in which capillary blood vessels that feed the sweat glands rupture, causing them to exude blood; it occurs under conditions of extreme physical or emotional stress."[331]

Luke's description of Jesus praying to the point of sweating "like great drops of blood falling down to the ground" speaks to the intense, inconceivable stress of Christ as He contemplated the pain He was about to endure to save humanity. Strobel investigated and studied the pain that Christ would have suffered on the cross. Summing it up, he writes, "The pain was absolutely unbearable. In fact, it was literally beyond words to describe; they had to invent a new word: *excruciating*. Literally, *excruciating* means 'out of the cross.'"[332]

When I was in middle school, I recall our music minister at my Southern Baptist church giving a sermon on Jesus's prayer in the Garden of Gethsemane. With a booming voice and all of the passion required to depict this scene, I remember him so eloquently describing the gravity of this moment. The savior of the universe— fully God and fully human—pleading with His Father for another way, painfully aware of the unfathomable fate He is about to suffer, and praying to the point of drops of blood falling into the soil on which He knelt. In all, Matthew writes that Jesus prayed to his Father three times, saying, "My Father, if this cannot pass unless I drink it, your will be done."[333] My music minister said that he believed when Christ looked into that cup of suffering, He saw you. He saw me. He saw our sins. He saw the pain he must endure to save us, and He deemed it a price worth paying.

In the Gospel of Mark, Mark uses slightly different wording in describing the prayer prayed by Jesus: "Abba, Father, all things are possible for you. Remove this cup from me. Yet not what I will, but what you will."[334] To my knowledge, this is the one and only time that Jesus uses the word "Abba," translated as "father" in appealing to God.[335] Ben Witherington III, PhD, who has taught at several academic institutions, including Duke University's Divinity School, told Lee Strobel that Abba is a "very personal" term.[336] Witherington continues, "It's the term of endearment in which a child would say to a parent, 'Father Dearest, what would you have me do?'…the significance of 'Abba' is that Jesus is the initiator of an intimate relationship that was previously unavailable. The question is, What kind of person can change the terms of relating to God? What kind of person can initiate a new covenantal relationship with God?... It implies that Jesus had a degree of intimacy with God that is unlike anything in the Judaism of his day."[337]

How significant to read of Jesus Christ talking to God in such intimate terms as a child appealing to his father, asking for a grave burden to be removed. You can just imagine the pain of the Almighty God, the pain of the Father knowing that to save all of humanity, He must permit the execution of His son. Note here also the contrast between the suffering of Job and the suffering of Christ. Where Job questions God's sovereignty at times before ultimately proclaiming it, Christ affirmatively declares in his prayer the total and complete sovereignty of God: "All things are possible for you."

Moreover, here we have—as described by Witherington—Christ "initiating a new covenantal relationship with God."[338] In other words, here is Christ as the "Redeemer" that Job proclaimed in the Old Testament, the "ransom" or the "go-between" between the Almighty God and His creation. Christ, in the cross, is repairing fallen man, providing a way to step beyond the evil we have created and return to a good, just, and right relationship with God in heaven.

In his book, Tim Keller crystallizes the necessity of the passion to save humanity. He writes, "Only through weakness and pain did God save us and show us, in the deepest way possible, the infinite depths of his grace and love for us. For indeed, here was infinite wisdom—in one stroke, the just requirement of the law was fulfilled *and* the forgiveness of lawbreakers secured. In one moment, God's love and justice were fully satisfied. This Messiah came to die in order to put an end to death itself. Only through weakness and suffering could sin be atoned—it was the only way to end evil without ending us."[339]

When I read these words from Keller, they struck me, for I had always seen the necessity of the passion and the suffering of Christ in the terms of "love" and "justice." Most theistic believers, who believe there is a God, accept the premise that, in order to be God, God must be perfect. To be perfect, God must be both perfectly just and perfectly loving. But how can you be both perfectly just and perfectly loving? The two attributes in their fullest appear to collide. Perfect justice would mean that humanity is castigated to eternal damnation. All of us are sinners. All of us are unworthy of heaven. We cannot be reconciled to a perfectly just God by our own merit. And yet subjecting humanity to the deserved fate of eternal damnation seems far from perfectly loving. So, what is God, a perfect being, to do?

"Take me," He would say. Take my son as ransom for the sins of humanity. Nail him to a cross along with the sins of the world. Resurrect Him to heaven on the third day, offering sinful men and women a path to justify their wrongdoing to an all-loving, perfect God and, in turn, join Him forever in eternity.

"Take me," is what our God said in an act of perfect love, perfect justice.

Berger quotes a passage from Albert Camus that sums it up beautifully: "Only the sacrifice of an innocent God could justify the endless and universal torture of innocence. Only the most abject suffering by God could assuage man's agony."[340]

Indeed, Christ's suffering paves the way for our own restoration. On a much smaller level, each of us, in our way and in our time will face our own Garden of Gethsemane. Maybe it is the betrayal of a spouse, the waywardness of a child, cancer, or terminal illness. Or perhaps it's the loss of a child, a pain that we must toil with for the rest of our lives, unable to understand why or how such a tragedy could have occurred. And unlike Christ, we are not fully God with divine understanding; instead, we are Job, searching for an answer through our pain, an answer from the Almighty.

Also, unlike Christ, we have access to the living God during our darkest moments. As you may recall, Christ said on the cross, "My God, my God, why have you forsaken me?"[341] Billy Graham's ministry describes Jesus's cry this way, "[I]n that moment He was banished from the presence of God, for sin cannot exist in God's presence. His cry speaks of this truth; He endured the separation from God that you and I deserve."[342] That is a depth of pain we will never know, and thanks to the sacrifice of Christ, we have access to a Father who can get us through the valleys of life.

While I don't believe that every answer will be given to us in this lifetime, I do believe that one answer can be found in the Garden of Gethsemane itself. When I visited the Garden of Gethsemane in Israel, I learned that it rested at the bottom of the Mount of Olives. Interestingly, from the garden, you are able to see the place where Christ is set to return to this earth. David Jeremiah said, "[T]he Bible does tell us the precise location of His return. Toward the end of the Old Testament, the prophet Zechariah predicted, 'In that day His feet will stand on the Mount of Olives, which faces Jerusalem on the east. And the Mount of Olives shall be split in two, from east to west, making a very large valley; half of the mountain shall move toward the north and half of it toward the south.'"[343]

How amazing is that juxtaposition? Standing in the Garden of Gethsemane, the very place where Christ struggled, imagining the spikes that would pierce His hands and His feet, you can see the very place where Jesus Christ will return in triumph. In this Second Coming, "Christ will return to defeat Satan…and commence His one-thousand-year reign on earth…. He will make right all the wrongs in our world," writes David Jeremiah.[344] It is fascinating to ponder that from this place of ultimate suffering, you can see the place of ultimate redemption. And therein lies the key point: without the suffering of Christ, you do not get the redemption of humanity.

LIFE

CHAPTER 5

THE HORRORS OF ABORTION

I grew up in a small town called Plant City, Florida—also known as the "Winter Strawberry Capital of the World." Raised by a father who built a successful business with few resources and a mother who was a teacher-turned-stay-at-home-mom, my home was filled with love, character, and traditional values. On Sundays, we graced the pews of our Southern Baptist church together, and on weekdays, I attended my all-girls Catholic school. Though my mother and father held conservative political views and occasionally discussed current events around the dinner table, my family was not involved in the political process beyond reliably casting their vote at each election. Despite not having a family firmly entrenched in politics, for some reason, politics and current events were of great interest to me from a young age. I suppose you would call it a natural love, a passion that God had impressed upon my heart.

There were of course an array of animating issues filling the national discourse throughout my young adulthood—the salacious scandals of the Clinton years, the highly charged 2000 election and its infamous hanging chads, and, of course, the wars in Iraq and Afghanistan. But no issue motivated me—the strawberry-blonde-haired, freckle-faced girl from Plant City, Florida—quite the same as the issue of life. The issue of abortion and its accompanying horrors resonated so deeply in my heart and, without a doubt, affirmed my view of the two major political parties and my place within them.

I remember, in particular, the debate surrounding partial-birth abortion that occurred during my sophomore year of high school. After an "eight-year-long congressional fight"—as described by NPR—the House and the Senate were on the verge of passing the "Partial-Birth Abortion Ban Act," which banned the controversial practice of partial-birth abortion defined as "[a]n abortion in which the person performing the abortion, deliberately and intentionally vaginally delivers a living fetus until, in the case of a head-first presentation, the entire fetal head is outside the body of the mother, or, in the case of breech presentation, any part of the fetal truck past the navel is outside the body of the mother, for the purpose of performing an overt act that the person knows will kill the partially delivered living fetus...."[345] President Bill Clinton had vetoed two bans on partial-birth abortion passed by the Republican Congress, and, in 2000, in a case called *Stenberg v. Carhart*, the Supreme Court had struck down a Nebraska law banning the practice; this new federal legislation—coming just three years later—was thus the subject of much discussion and debate.[346]

Amid the national dialogue, I recall being tasked with a school project that entailed researching and presenting a current event. While I don't recall the exact contours of the project, I do remember choosing to center my project on the issue of partial-birth abortion. I was rather young at the time—just fifteen years old, dressed in my school uniform (a plaid navy blue, green, yellow, and white skirt with a tucked-in white polo) when I decided to research partial-birth abortion on the internet. The pictures I discovered were nothing short of horrifying. Blood. Dismembered body parts. Nearly full-term children, cast aside as mere waste. The images haunted me, as did the description of the procedure.

"How could partial-birth abortion even be a subject of de bate?" I wondered. Is there anyone actually *for* this? Moreover, how could the Supreme Court of the United States essentially sanction this grotesque practice? Didn't the Declaration of Independence famously speak of "Life, Liberty, and the pursuit of Happiness" as unalienable rights? Presumably, children were recipients of this guarantee as well.

These were but a few of the questions I pondered as I completed my high school project. To me, there was something so intrinsic about the issue. While many issues in American political life are complicated, nuanced, and subject to debate, the dismemberment of children surely was not one of them. How does a young, fifteen-year-old girl—not even able to drive yet—recognize something so basic, so morally elementary that apparently a five-justice majority of the Supreme Court could not? It truly baffled me and still does to this day.

Today, by the grace of God, our country is in a much different place. In the summer of 2022, a 6–3 majority of the Supreme Court decided *Dobbs v. Jackson Women's Health Organization*, restoring the role of elected representatives in deciding abortion law. I will get into that tremendous victory in more detail in the following chapter, but, in the meantime, it is worth revisiting the tragic history of the abortion industry in this country.

The pro-choice movement chooses to ignore the heinous nature of the abortion industry, but it is vitally important to shed light on it—however hard it may be to read. The following pages may be difficult, but I believe they are necessary to understand the contours of the abortion debate in this country. Moreover, as important as is it to expose the monstrous practices of the now-convicted Kermit Gosnell, the abortion doctor who murdered children, it is likewise important to shed light on the state-endorsed, Supreme Court-sanctioned practice of partial-birth abortion, upheld in that 5–4 *Stenberg v. Carhart* Supreme Court opinion from 2000.

Speaking of the Gosnell case, Conor Friedersdorf wrote in *The Atlantic*, "The grand jury report in the case of Kermit Gosnell, 72, is among the most horrifying I've read. 'This case is about a doctor who killed babies and endangered women. What we mean is that he regularly and illegally delivered live, viable babies in the third trimester of pregnancy—and then murdered these newborns by severing their spinal cords with scissors,' it states."[347]

Writing separately of Dr. Leroy Carhart, the "celebrated" abortion doctor at the center of *Stenberg v. Carhart*, Shannen Coffin wrote this in the *National Review*: "There's very little difference between what Carhart does on a regular basis and what Kermit Gosnell stands on trial for."[348] The former received the endorsement of the Supreme Court; the latter received a conviction for murder.

You just read a portion of the Gosnell grand jury report. Now take a dive into the Supreme Court opinion from 2000 and decide for yourself how apt the comparison actually is.

At the center of *Stenberg* was a Nebraska statute that banned partial-birth abortion, described as "an abortion procedure in which the person performing the abortion partially delivers vaginally a living unborn child before killing the unborn child and completing delivery."[349] The law provided an exception where the "procedure is necessary to save the life of the mother whose life is endangered by a physical disorder, physical illness, or physical injury...."[350] Justice Stephen Breyer—writing for a five-justice majority of the court—wrote, "We hold that this statute violates the Constitution."[351]

The opinion begins by describing various abortion techniques in neutered but nevertheless excruciating detail. In fact, Breyer issues a rather telling warning to the reader before beginning his analysis: "Considering the fact that those procedures seek to terminate a potential human life, our discussion may seem clinically cold or callous to some, perhaps horrifying to others. There is no alternative way, however, to acquaint the reader with the technical distinctions among different abortion methods and related factual matters, upon which the outcome of this case depends."[352]

Should that not tell us something? If the discussion at hand is admittedly "clinically cold or callous to some, perhaps horrifying to others," then perhaps the actual procedure of partial-birth abortion is just that in practice.

Breyer goes on to explain that "[d]uring the first trimester, the predominant abortion method is 'vacuum aspiration,' which involves insertion of a vacuum tube...into the uterus to evacuate the contents."[353] The "contents"? Here the Supreme Court describes a growing human being as "contents." It is much more convenient, indeed, to depict the extermination of budding human life as merely an inanimate object.

In the second trimester, Breyer notes that the primary method of abortion is "dilation and evacuation" (D&E), which—according to an American Medical Association (AMA) report—is "'similar to vacuum aspiration except that the cervix must be dilated more widely because surgical instruments are used to remove larger pieces of tissue.'"[354] The AMA report cited by the court goes on to note that, during weeks thirteen and fifteen of pregnancy, "[b]ecause fetal tissue is friable and easily broken, the fetus may not be removed intact."[355]

So here you have the baby, initially described as "contents" by the Supreme Court, now evolving into "larger pieces of tissue." But, in actuality, the baby at fifteen weeks of pregnancy is far more than just "contents" or "larger pieces of tissue." Indeed, at fifteen weeks, "your baby is growing rapidly," according to Mayo Clinic.[356] The baby has a heartbeat, moving arms and legs, closed eyes that are able to sense light, and a scalp with a "forming...hair pattern."[357]

Pregnancy+—a pregnancy app developed by Philips Avent that gives me weekly updates on my phone regarding my pregnancy—described the baby at week fifteen this way: At nearly four inches long, "[y]our little one is able to taste the food you eat.... Your baby's hairline is forming and hair is starting to grow on your baby's head. Even the eyelashes and eyebrows are growing.... Even though your baby is hiccupping regularly, there is no sound produced as your baby's windpipe is full of fluid at this stage."[358]

Sure sounds like "contents" and "large tissue," right? Not quite.

After fifteen weeks, the Supreme Court—once again citing the AMA report—describes the abortion procedure of D&E like this: "'Because the fetus is larger at this stage of gestation (particularly the head), and because bones are more rigid, dismemberment or other destructive procedures are more likely to be required than at earlier gestational ages to remove fetal and placental tissue.'"[359] And, after twenty weeks, "'[s]ome physicians use intrafetal potassium chloride or digoxin to induce fetal demise prior to a late D&E...to facilitate evacuation.'"[360]

The court goes on to discuss "dismemberment of the fetus," described by Dr. Carhart this way: "'It takes something that restricts the motion of the fetus against what you're doing before you're going to get dismemberment.'"[361] Allow me to emphasize a portion of Dr. Carhart's testimony: "to restrict the motion of the fetus." In other words, the baby is indeed moving at this point of pregnancy and, gruesomely, must be restricted to be dismembered.

Furthermore, where the majority opinion describes D&E in sterile, clinical terms, the dissent authored by Justice Anthony Kennedy reveals some of Dr. Carhart's testimony that Breyer chose to avoid. For instance, as we just discussed, in performing D&E dismemberment, it is necessary for the abortionist to establish "traction...between the uterus and the vagina."[362] This entails "us[ing] instruments to grasp a portion (such as a foot or hand) of a developed and living fetus and drag[ging] the grasped portion out of the uterus and into the vagina."[363] Why? Here is the portion left out by Breyer: because "attempting to abort a fetus without using that traction is described by Dr. Carhart as 'pulling the cat's tail' or 'drag[ging] a string across the floor, you'll just keep dragging it. It's not until something grabs the other end that you are going to develop traction.'"[364]

So the child is no longer described as "contents" and "large tissue," but is now being analogized to a "cat" or a "string." Speaks for itself, doesn't it? Believe it or not, Kennedy's references to Carhart's testimony get even worse than the abortion doctor's comparisons of babies to animals and to inanimate objects like "string."

Kennedy correctly notes that "[t]he fetus, in many cases, dies just as a human adult or child would: It bleeds to death as it is torn from limb [to] limb. The fetus can be alive at the beginning of the dismemberment process and can survive for a time while its limbs are being torn off."[365] This is a proposition that the abortion doctor, Dr. Carhart, acknowledged. Dr. Carhart even went so far as to note that, at times with "extensive parts of the fetus removed," he has "observed fetal heartbeat via ultrasound," in Kennedy's words.[366] Perhaps most troubling of all was Dr. Carhart's admission that he "knows of a physician who removed the arm of a fetus only to have the fetus go on to be born 'as a living child with one arm.' At the conclusion of a D&E abortion no intact fetus remains. In Dr. Carhart's words, the abortionist is left with a 'tray full of pieces,'" Kennedy wrote.[367]

Stop and think about that. The Supreme Court of the United States heard testimony from an abortion doctor that a heartbeat was evident as a baby was being torn apart limb by limb. They also heard about a baby born "as a living child with one arm" because his or her arm had been torn off during a D&E abortion procedure. Apparently, totally unfazed by this, the Supreme Court nevertheless voted 5–4 in *Stenberg v. Carhart* to strike down a Nebraska law banning the procedure.

Amazing.

Returning to the majority opinion, Breyer goes on to explain a form of D&E called "intact D&E" used after sixteen weeks of pregnancy. It involves "removing the fetus from the uterus through the cervix 'intact,' in one pass, rather than in several passes" and is used at this point "as vacuum aspiration becomes ineffective and the fetal skull becomes too large to pass through the cervix."[368] Breyer notes that "[t]he intact D&E proceeds in one of two ways, depending on the presentation of the fetus. If the fetus presents head first (a vertex presentation), the doctor collapses the skull; and the doctor then extracts the entire fetus through the cervix. If the fetus presents feet first (a breech presentation), the doctor pulls the fetal body through the cervix, collapses the skull, and extracts the fetus through the cervix."[369] If part of this rather chilling description sounds familiar, it is because the language in the opinion closely mirrors the language used three years later in the Partial-Birth Abortion Ban Act of 2003.

Later in the opinion, just after declaring Nebraska's law in violation of the federal Constitution, Breyer points out that the second version of intact D&E—the "breech presentation" version also known as D&X—"reduces the incidence of a 'free floating' fetal head that can be difficult for a physician to grasp and remove...."[370]

Notice how cavalier the discussion of the baby is. Now resembling a fully formed human being—rolling and flipping, able to hear, heart pumping blood—the court expresses no concern for the child.[371] In fact, there is little discussion of the baby at all, outside of self-described "clinically cold," "callous," and "horrifying" terms detailing the process of abortion.

For example, where is the discussion of what the baby feels during these abortion procedures? We know that the baby is moving just before dismemberment. So where is the inquiry into what the baby feels? From my reading of the majority opinion in *Stenberg*, there is no detailed and protracted discussion of this question. In fact, a search for the term "pain" in the opinion yields precisely zero results. Meanwhile, a 2020 paper in the *Journal of Medical Ethics* notes, "Many papers discussing fetal pain have speculated a lower limit for fetal pain under 20 weeks' gestation."[372] One would think that this is a pertinent line of inquiry when discussing the dismemberment of babies at twenty weeks and beyond.

Kennedy's dissent goes on to describe the D&X procedure, once again including details left out by the Breyer majority. He begins in saying, "The fetus' arms and legs are delivered outside the uterus while the fetus is alive; witnesses to the procedure report seeing the body of the fetus moving outside the woman's body.... With only the head of the fetus remaining in utero, the abortionist tears open the skull. According to Dr. Martin Haskell, a leading proponent of the procedure, the appropriate instrument to be used at this stage of the abortion is a pair of scissors. Witnesses report observing the portion of the fetus outside the woman react to the skull penetration. The abortionist then inserts a suction tube and vacuums out the developing brain and other matter found within the skull.... Brain death does not occur until after the skull invasion, and, according to Dr. Carhart, the heart of the fetus may continue to beat for minutes after the contents of the skull are vacuumed out."[373]

As Kennedy correctly points out, D&X takes on a strong "resemblance to infanticide."[374]

In his dissent, Justice Clarence Thomas recounts the words of a nurse who was a witness to the D&X procedure. The nurse's words are chilling: "The baby's little fingers were clasping and unclasping, and his little feet were kicking. Then the doctor stuck the scissors in the back of his head, and the baby's arms jerked out, like a startle reaction, like a flinch, like a baby does when thinks he is going to fall. The doctor opened up the scissors, stuck a high-powered suction tube into the opening, and sucked the baby's brains out. Now the baby went completely limp."[375]

In reflecting on the *Stenberg* majority opinion, the late, great Justice Antonin Scalia opens his dissent with this: "I am optimistic enough to believe that, one day, *Stenberg v. Carhart* will be assigned its rightful place in the history of this Court's jurisprudence beside *Korematsu* and *Dred Scott*. The method of killing a human child—one cannot even accurately say an entirely unborn human child—proscribed by this statute is so horrible that the most clinical description of it evokes a shudder of revulsion."[376]

Wow.

That is quite a statement.

Korematsu and *Dred Scott* represent some of the darkest days of the Supreme Court. In *Korematsu*, the court upheld World War II-era internment camps for Japanese Americans; in *Dred Scott*, the court upheld the practice of slavery, refusing to acknowledge Dred Scott as a citizen of the country. Both grave injustices, at one point, upheld by the Supreme Court. Here was Scalia, putting the court-sanctioned partial-birth abortion among the grave sins of America's past.

"The notion that the Constitution of the United States, designed, among other things, 'to establish Justice, insure domestic Tranquility…and secure the Blessings of Liberty to ourselves and our Posterity,' prohibits the States from simply banning this visibly brutal means of eliminating our half-born posterity is quite simply absurd," Scalia wrote.[377]

Scalia was exactly right. After the two Clinton-era vetoes striking down legislation banning partial-birth abortion and the incomprehensible *Stenberg* decision of the Supreme Court, President Bush triumphantly signed into law the Partial-Birth Abortion Ban Act on November 5, 2003.[378] The vote in the Senate was 64–34, and as the *New York Times* noted, "Seventeen Democrats voted in favor, giving the legislation a bipartisan cast that has been rare in votes involving abortion."[379] In signing the 2003 legislation, President Bush stated, "For years, a terrible form of violence has been directed against children who are inches from birth, while the law looked the other way.... The best case against partial birth abortion is a simple description of what happens and to whom it happens.... Our nation owes its children a different and better welcome. The bill I am about to sign protecting innocent new life from this practice reflects the compassion and humanity of America."[380]

But Dr. Leroy Carhart was not finished yet. Shortly after the Partial-Birth Abortion Ban Act became the law of the land, Dr. Carhart challenged it in federal court, prevailing at the district court and in the Eighth Circuit. In 2007, *Gonzales v. Carhart* reached the Supreme Court.[381] This time, rather than voting 5–4 to strike down a partial-birth abortion ban—as the court did to Nebraska's law in *Stenberg*—the court voted 5–4 to uphold the federal ban on partial-birth abortion. The nomination and confirmation of Justice Samuel Alito in replacing the retired justice Sandra Day O'Connor made a key difference in the court's newfound respect for life and renewed interest in fidelity to the Constitution.[382] A triumph indeed.

I recognize the difficulty in reading about partial-birth abortion. It is equally tough to write on the matter, even now, nearly twenty years after I discovered its gruesome realities as a fifteen-year-old girl. But I believe it is necessary. It is vitally important to know about a practice that the pro-choice movement embraced with open arms just fifteen years ago. While we are a decade and a half out from the partial-birth abortion debate, the rhetoric of the pro-choice movement, the gruesome nature of the abortion industry, and the undeniable consequences it has globally are alive and well. The pro-choice rhetoric of today, and even the policy positions of the Democrat Party, do not depart dramatically from the days of the partial-birth abortion debate.

ON JANUARY 9, 2019, Democrat Virginia delegate Kathy Tran put forward House Bill No. 2491, permitting abortion until birth. Ironically, as the *Daily Caller* pointed out, this was the very same day that Tran introduced House Bill No. 2495, "protect[ing] the lives of 'fall cankerworms' during certain months" in the words of the *Daily Caller*.[383] Because, of course, long live the cankerworms and the "gypsy moths" but not the full-term babies. When asked by Virginia House majority leader Todd Gilbert, "Where it's obvious a woman is about to give birth…would that be a point at which she could still request an abortion?" Tran replied, "My bill would allow that, yes."

When Democrat governor of Virginia Ralph Northam was asked about the abortion bill the following day, he professed his support and then described what would happen if a mother was in labor and sought an abortion. "If a mother is in labor," Northam said, "I can tell you exactly what would happen. The infant would be delivered. The infant would be kept comfortable. The infant would be resuscitated if that's what the mother and the family desired, and then a discussion would ensue between the physicians and the mother."[384]

So the baby would be resuscitated *if* that is what the mother desired, and *if* resuscitation were to occur, "a discussion would ensue" in the aftermath. A discussion? We are now talking about a living, independent, viable child outside of the womb. What Northam described was nothing short of state-sanctioned infanticide.

By the end of January, Senator Ben Sasse introduced the "Born-Alive Abortion Survivors Protection Act," which would "prohibit a health care practitioner from failing to exercise the proper degree of care in the case of a child who survives an abortion or attempted abortion."[385] Sounds pretty reasonable, right? Not for the left. Senate Democrats blocked the bill with only three Democrat senators joining Republicans in support.[386] Republicans continued to request unanimous consent for the bill, but Democrats blocked its path at least seventy-five separate times.[387] In the new, Republican-controlled House, the Born-Alive Abortion Survivors Protection Act was among the first bills passed by the GOP majority. Notably, 210 Democrats—almost every Democrat member of the House—voted against it.[388]

Now, you may ask how necessary a bill like this actually is. Surely, contrary to Governor Northam's suggestion, babies born alive receive care, just as any other human being would in a time of need. Not so. Jill Stanek, a former registered nurse at Christ Hospital in Illinois, has testified before several legislative bodies about what she witnessed during abortions when the baby survives. Stanek, who testified as recently as 2020, noted, "My experience was 20 years ago, but as Governor Northam made clear, it could have happened—and probably did—yesterday."[389]

In her testimony, Stanek recounts that, during her time at Christ Hospital, babies born alive were taken to the "Soiled Utility Room to die," including a baby boy born with Down syndrome whom Stanek rocked until he passed away forty-five minutes later.[390] "He was too weak to move very much, expending all his energy attempting to breathe," Stanek said. "Toward the end he was so quiet I couldn't tell if he was still alive unless I held him up to the light to see if his heart was still beating through his chest wall."[391]

In another case, Stanek told the Senate Judiciary Committee, "A Support Associate told me about accidentally throwing a live aborted baby in the garbage who had been left on the counter of the Soiled Utility Room wrapped in a disposable towel. When she realized what she had done, she started going through the trash to find the baby, and the baby fell out of the towel and on to the floor."[392]

Stunning.

Stanek also remembered the case of a baby born with a 39 percent chance of survival. Typically, Stanek noted, a neonatologist, pediatric resident, neonatal nurse, and respiratory therapist would be at a delivery of this kind to administer treatment before moving the child to the Neonatal Intensive Care Unit, but because the mother chose to abort, the baby "was merely wrapped in a blanket and kept in the Labor & Delivery Department until she died 2-1/2 hours later."[393]

Stanek further testified that another nurse at Christ Hospital "described walking into the Soiled Utility Room on two separate occasions to find live aborted babies left naked on a scale and the metal counter."[394] She describes that one mother was shocked that her baby was born alive and demanded treatment for the child, but it was too late. "The mother was so traumatized that my friend had to give her a tranquilizer," Stanek noted.[395]

"Christ Hospital has never publicly refuted the incidents I describe in my testimony," Stanek said.[396]

The Senate Judiciary heard Stanek's testimony in February of 2020, so, too, did other legislative bodies on twelve occasions.[397] Do you know who else heard these eye-opening stories? Then-Illinois senator Barack Obama.[398] He heard Stanek's testimony, and according to *National Review*, "[i]n the Illinois senate, he opposed Born-Alive [legislation] tooth and nail."[399] Andy McCarthy writes, "The shocking extremism of that position—giving infanticide the nod over compassion and life—is profoundly embarrassing to him now. So he has lied about what he did. He has offered various conflicting explanations...."[400]

While the position might have been "profoundly embarrassing" for Obama—in the assessment of McCarthy—the "shocking extremism" of this abortion position is still alive and well today. Consider the so-called "Women's Health Protection Act of 2021," supported by President Joe Biden.[401] After the point of viability for a baby, this act would permit abortion "when, in the good-faith medical judgment of the treating health care provider, continuation of the pregnancy would pose a risk to the pregnant patient's life or health."[402] The "health" exception gives practitioners wide latitude to permit late-term abortion for a myriad of reasons. As Catholic News Agency points out, in *Doe v. Bolton*, the court "broadly defined what 'may relate to health,' including 'all factors—physical, emotional, psychological, familial, and the woman's age—relevant to the wellbeing of the patient.'"[403]

Taken together, the Daily Signal notes that, in advocating for the "Women's Health Protection Act," "Democrats seek to pass what could be the world's most permissive abortion bill."[404] "[T]he world's most permissive abortion bill" would have compounded the United States' already aberrational abortion regime, which, prior to the *Dobbs* decision, was among the world's most permissive. Pre-*Dobbs*, the United States was *one of only seven* countries to green-light elective abortion post-twenty weeks.[405] According to the Charlotte Lozier Institute, forty-seven of fifty European countries place limitations on elective abortion after fifteen weeks, and twenty-seven European countries do not permit abortion after the twelve-week mark.[406] "No European nation allows abortions up to the moment of birth, as do some liberal states such as California and New York," the Daily Signal observes.[407]

During the *Dobbs* oral arguments, where the Supreme Court considered Mississippi's fifteen-week abortion ban, Chief Justice John Roberts highlighted this reality. "I'd like to focus on the 15-week ban because that's not a dramatic departure from viability," Roberts said. "It is the standard that the vast majority of other countries have. When you get to the viability standard, we share that standard with the People's Republic of China and North Korea...."[408]

That's right, the United States' abortion laws post-*Roe* and pre-*Dobbs* shared the good company of North Korea and the People's Republic of China. As I have said previously, our country—the beacon of freedom and justice—was a pariah among nations when it came to our abortion laws. Nevertheless, President Biden insisted after the *Dobbs* decision that the Supreme Court has "made the United States an outlier among developed nations in the world."[409] As outlined above, the statement is an easily debunked lie.

But lies are not foreign to the abortion industry. There was the lie that abortion was intended to be "safe, legal, and rare." Meanwhile, sixty-three million babies have been killed in the United States due to abortion. There was the lie that the baby growing within a mother's belly was simply a blob of tissue. Ultrasound has proven otherwise. There is the lie that women suffer no emotional repercussions following an abortion. In fact, many women do. And then there is the lie that abortion is a celebrated act of female liberation. The treacherous history of Planned Parenthood's founding and the way in which abortion has been used and is still used to further eugenic ends tells a far different story.

MARGARET HIGGINS SANGER, the founder of Planned Parenthood, was an atheist, a socialist, and a eugenicist.[410] While some have tried desperately to deny these facts, her words speak for themselves. Kristan Hawkins, writing in *USA Today*, notes that she "advocated for a eugenics approach to breeding for 'the gradual suppression, elimination and eventual extinction, of defective stocks—those human weeds which threaten the blooming of the finest flowers of American civilizations.'"[411] In an openly racist letter, written in 1939 to Dr. C. J. Gamble, Hawkins notes that Sanger pushed for a "full time Negro physician" to be brought on staff since—in the words of Sanger—"colored Negroes…can get closer to their own members and more or less lay their cards on the table which means their ignorance, superstitions and doubt."[412] She sought to have the involvement of religious leaders in her endeavor. Sanger asserted, "We do not want word to go out that we want to exterminate the Negro population, and the minister is the man who can straighten out that idea if it ever occurs to any of their more rebellious members."[413]

Think about how toxic, how racist, how truly abominable those statements are. From these insidious views emerged the modern day Planned Parenthood, responsible for the killing of millions of children. Even Planned Parenthood acknowledges the horrid views of its founder. "Sanger…believed in eugenics—an inherently racist and ableist ideology that labeled certain people unfit to have children…." reads a Planned Parenthood document entitled "Opposition Claims About Margaret Sanger."[414]

"Margaret Sanger was so intent on her mission to advocate for birth control that she chose to align herself with ideologies and organizations that were explicitly ableist and white supremacist. In doing so, she undermined reproductive freedom and caused irreparable damage to the health and lives of generations of Black people, Latino people, Indigenous people, immigrants, people with disabilities, people with low incomes, and many others," the document continues before noting, "Planned Parenthood denounces Margaret Sanger's belief in eugenics."[415] Nevertheless, it is a sad reality that the vast majority of abortions in the United States have been black and Hispanic children.[416]

Margaret Sanger's perverted musings are not the only time that eugenics have been discussed in the context of abortion. Abortion has been used to perpetrate some of the globe's worst atrocities. Look no further than the People's Republic of China to see the devastating consequences that follow when life is devalued. China is in the process of waging a genocide against the Uyghurs, a minority, primarily Muslim population living in the Xinjiang province in Northwest China. The Trump-era State Department, at the time led by Secretary of State Mike Pompeo, labeled China's atrocities against the Uyghurs a "genocide" in January of 2021.[417] According to *Vox*, "[i]t is the largest mass internment of an ethnic-religious minority group since World War II."[418] Moreover, the Associated Press (AP) points out that birth rates among Uyghurs in two regions of the country have fallen an astonishing 60 percent between 2015 and 2018.[419]

How is China doing this? The AP headline tells the story: "China cuts Uighur births with IUDs, abortion, sterilization."[420] After conducting more than two dozen interviews with former detainees and even a former detention camp instructor, the AP concluded that "[t]he state regularly subjects minority women to pregnancy checks, and forces intrauterine devices, sterilization and even abortion on hundreds of thousands, the interviews and data show."[421]

China is waging a campaign of sheer terror against this minority population. Police go into residences and search for hidden children. If a parent is found with three or more children, they are sent to detention camps. In these camps, women are "force-fed birth control pills or injected with fluids, often with no explanation. Many felt dizzy, tired, or ill, and women stopped getting their periods. After being released and leaving China, some [former detainees] went to get medical check-ups and found they were sterile."[422]

One woman recounts authorities finding WhatsApp on her phone, an encrypted messaging application. She was sent to the hospital, where she gave a urine sample and found that she was two months pregnant. The baby would have been her third child, but Chinese officials forced her to have an abortion. "During the procedure, medics inserted an electric vacuum into her womb and sucked her fetus out of her body," according to the AP.[423] Sounds familiar, right? As one Uyghur woman told the AP, "God bequeaths children on you. To prevent people from having children is wrong."[424] She is exactly right.

In considering why and how this is happening, James Leibold, an expert on Chinese policy, said this: "It links back to China's long history of dabbling in eugenics…you don't want people who are poorly educated, marginal minorities breeding quickly. What you want is your educated…to increase their birth rate."[425]

I will pose the question once again: Does this sound familiar? It should. Going back to our discussion about Sanger, recall that Sanger sought "the gradual suppression, elimination and eventual extinction, of defective stocks—those human weeds which threaten the blooming of the finest flowers of American civilization."[426] Sanger's words are hauntingly familiar to Leibold's description of the Uyghur genocide in China.

A Uyghur genocide is what happens when life is devalued, unappreciated, and discarded. But the eugenic outcome of abortion happens in far more subtle ways too. Indeed, the most vulnerable among us suffer at the hands of the abortion industry. Abortion, in essence, has become a societally acceptable way to eliminate a type of person. A revealing article in *The Atlantic* called "The Last Children of Down Syndrome" details just how this has happened, how abortion has led to the eradication of Down syndrome children in some countries.[427]

Sarah Zhang in *The Atlantic* writes, "Few people speak publicly about wanting to 'eliminate' Down syndrome. Yet individual choices are adding up to something very close to that."[428] She notes examples from several countries. In the United States, about six thousand babies are born with Down syndrome annually. In Denmark, by comparison, "only 18 were born in the entire country" in the year 2019.[429] Headlines from across the media echo this sad reality.

"Why Down syndrome in Iceland has almost disappeared," reads CBS News.[430]

"Could this be the last generation of Down's syndrome children?" asks *The Telegraph*.[431] Answering their own question, the publication notes, "Globally, the Down's syndrome population is plummeting—leading to suggestions that we may be witnessing the elimination of the condition."[432]

But is it the elimination of a condition? Or is it, instead, the elimination of individual, unique children with something beautiful to add to society?

The answer lies in scripture: "For you created my inmost being; you knit me together in my mother's womb. I praise you because I am fearfully and wonderfully made; your works are wonderful, I know that full well."[433] Psalm 139:14 tells us that God personally knit us together in our mother's womb. How powerful, how purposeful was His plan for each and every child conceived, and how distorted is society's view of callously choosing which lives are worth living? But that is exactly what society now instructs new parents to do: select who is deserving of life.

The subheading of *The Atlantic* article reads "prenatal testing is changing who gets born and who doesn't. This is just the beginning." What a terrifying prospect that is! And "[t]his is just the beginning," Zhang notes.[434] Writing of the advent of Down syndrome testing in the 1980s, Zhang writes, "Suddenly, a new power was thrust into the hands of ordinary people—the power to decide what kind of life is worth bringing into the world."[435] She continues, "The forces of scientific progress are now marching toward ever more testing to detect ever more genetic conditions. Recent advances in genetics provoke anxieties about a future where parents choose what kind of child to have, or not have. But that hypothetical future is already here. It's been here for an entire generation."[436]

This issue is personal to me, for I was presented with just such a scenario when I began to have children. As I discussed in my previous book, *For Such a Time as This*, I carry a genetic mutation called BRCA2 that predisposes me to breast and ovarian cancer.[437] Over the course of my lifetime, I have an 84 percent chance of breast cancer and a 27 percent chance of ovarian cancer.[438] These odds are pretty clearly reflected in my family history. Eight extended relatives on my mom's side got breast cancer, and some at a very early age. My mother carried the gene and chose to get a preventative double mastectomy. Though she never had breast cancer, she chose to take this preventative measure, and in doing so, brought down her chances of breast cancer to virtually zero. I decided to follow in her footsteps, opting to have a preventative mastectomy at the age of thirty.

Despite having the surgery and reducing my own chances of breast cancer, I am still a carrier of the gene and can pass it to my children. On several occasions, well-intentioned doctors informed me that modern medicine meant that I have the choice to isolate non-BRCA2 eggs and ensure that I have a child without the BRCA genetic mutation. Upon first hearing about this option, my heart sunk. It immediately occurred to me that, had my own mom been given this choice and pursued it, I would not be here. If this option had been available down my family line, perhaps my mom would not be here, nor would my grandfather who passed her the gene. The thought was haunting, for I believe that God put me and my BRCA2 family members on this earth for a purpose, for a reason, by design. If my mother would have chosen to eliminate her BRCA2 eggs, I would not be here, and God's plan for my life never realized, never executed.

Moreover, had I selected that path, my beautiful daughter, Baby Blake, might not be here. I do not know if she has the BRCA2 gene or not. That is a test that she will choose to take at the right stage of her life, but I know this: my daughter's life—BRCA2 or not—is intentional. She is the most beautiful gift from God. I look at her every day and see a perfect, growing, fun-loving, and smart girl who will one day become a young woman. God has a bright plan for Baby Blake, and I know without a doubt that she was meant to be on this earth, knit together within my womb for a reason. I did not design her. The God of all the universe did, and she is perfect in my eyes.

To be clear, I do not fault or in any way think negatively of the doctors who suggested isolating my non-BRCA2 eggs. As I noted, they were well-intentioned and doing their due diligence in informing me of medical options at my disposal. Nor do I in any way cast judgment upon anyone choosing to select their healthy eggs. BRCA2 indeed comes with many challenges, which I recounted in my last book—mammograms, ultrasounds, MRIs, and all kinds of false alarms that added worry and anxiety to the decade of my twenties. Moreover, while BRCA2 has good prophylactic treatment options—mastectomies for preventing breast cancer and, when the time is right, a hysterectomy for preventing ovarian cancer—there are any number of genetic disorders that do not. And while—in my view—abortion is certainly never the answer to situations like this, genetic testing prior to a pregnancy and isolating certain eggs may be an answer for some. Without a doubt, every parent in the world wants their child to be healthy, having the absolute best chance at life. For me personally, when it came to BRCA2, I know that my life was intentional as was my mother's and my daughter's. God put us here for a reason.

The solution to human life devalued and the devastating repercussions of such a worldview is life reevaluated through the eyes of Christ. That is the single biggest antidote to so many of the problems that plague our society, and I am heartened to say that, on June 24, 2022, our country took a huge leap in that very direction.

CHAPTER 6

THE BEAUTY OF LIFE

In the summer of 2021, my husband, Sean, and I decided that we were ready to have a second child and make our daughter, Baby Blake, a big sister. My first pregnancy happened rather quickly, and we felt blessed that God had given us a beautiful daughter with relative ease. The second time around was different. Several months passed, and negative pregnancy tests were ample. As spring of 2022 approached, part of me began to worry. Why wasn't I getting pregnant? I attempted to overcome worry by leaning on faith.

A good friend of mine, Abigail Robertson, who is the White House correspondent for Christian Broadcasting Network (CBN), had recently given me a book called *Draw the Circle* by Mark Batterson.[439] The book issues a forty-day prayer challenge and provides uplifting and, at times, challenging messages to help your walk with Christ. Amid our hopes and efforts to bring a new life into the world, Sean and I decided to read the devotional that Abigail had given to me.

The opening pages of *Draw the Circle* talk about "liv[ing] in holy anticipation, knowing that God is orchestrating supernatural synchronicities."[440] The book goes on to say that we must trust God with both the big things and the little things. Batterson specifically cites "helping us to conceive" as an example of where we must trust God—a mention that personally resonated for both Sean and me.[441] Batterson correctly notes that "what God loves more than anything else is childlike faith.... It's simple childlike trust. It's the bedrock belief that God is bigger than our problem, bigger than our mistake, bigger than our dream."[442] He powerfully advises that "[t]here comes a moment when you must quit talking to God about the mountain in your life and start talking to the mountain about your God. You proclaim His power. You declare His sovereignty. You affirm His faithfulness. You stand on His Word. You cling to His promise."[443]

I realized that this is exactly what I needed to do—pray with expectation, knowing that God was going to act in my best interest and in accordance with His plan. But praying with expectation is sometimes easier said than done. We have a tendency to expect immediate results. That is a natural human inclination, one that I certainly fall into myself. As I tried to pray with expectation, Satan did his best to infiltrate with worry, doubt, and frustration.

I remember this frustration consuming me one Saturday in March. I was just about to give a speech in Tulsa, Oklahoma, when I was overcome with worry about my ability to have a second child. All of my friends seemed to be getting pregnant, but for some reason, it just wasn't happening for me. I pondered why as I got ready for the Christian conference I was about to speak at—the Extraordinary Women Conference 2022, appropriately titled "Pursuing an Unfailing God." I arrived at the conference and, for about an hour, had the pleasure of listening to testimony from Mandisa, prayers taking place just outside of my room, and inspiring Christian music ringing through the building. It took my mind off of personal struggle and put my focus where it needed to be—on the "way maker," my God, who has perfect timing.[444]

Two weeks later, I traveled to Collinsville, Illinois, to speak to another group called Mosaic Pregnancy and Health Centers (PHC), an organization that offers pregnancy resources to women in need and, as I learned that night, changes lives in doing so. At the event, which featured a dinner and a keynote speech from me, I met Kathy Sparks Lesnoff, president and CEO of Mosaic PHC. Kathy is a beautiful woman, filled with energy and drive and overflowing with the Holy Spirit. Right after my arrival, Kathy had her team gather together and pray over the events of the evening. Each member of her team spoke with passion about their faith, praying to God about their hopes for their biggest event of the year.

During the dinner, I sat with Kathy and her children, including Kathy's daughter-in-law who rocked her new baby—just a few weeks old. I opened up about my desire to have a second child with Kathy and her family, and without hesitation, Kathy asked if she could pray over me. I agreed, and right there at our dinner table, Kathy and I bowed our heads while she said a heartfelt prayer for God to bless me with a child.

"The last time I said a prayer like this, God blessed the young woman with twins!" she shared with me at the conclusion of our prayer. I smiled from ear to ear at the thought!

As dinner finished and the speaking portion of the night began, a young woman took the stage and shared her story. Pregnant, scared, and completely alone, she had gone from hopelessness to hope thanks to Mosaic. She shared how Mosaic's compassion and kindness had changed her life, leading her to keep her baby, who she now could not imagine living without. Near the end of her testimony, her little one joined her on stage, bringing many in the room to tears, including me—the beautiful gift of life on full display in front of us.

When I returned home from Illinois, Sean and I prayed together, asking God to bless us with a child. This time, though, we prayed with expectation. Unbeknownst to me at the time, my dad's Bible study that he attended every Friday morning was praying for me too, specifically praying for a future pregnancy. As Matthew 18:20 tells us, "For where two or three gather in my name, there am I with them."[445] And there Christ certainly was.

Three days after Sean and I said a prayer together, I decided to take a pregnancy test. I had already taken about five or six that month. All were negative. Nevertheless, for some reason, I felt the urge to take one that Tuesday morning, three days after our prayer. I suppose you could say I took the test that morning with expectation. A few minutes after taking the test, I saw a slight pink double line, indicating a pregnancy.

"Is this real?!" I wondered.

I took a second just in case, and sure enough, two solid pink lines!

Our prayers were answered!

That Tuesday morning, I went for a run. I was bursting with energy and filled with joy. I listened to the Christian song "Way Maker," which sings praise to the miracles, omnipotence, and unfathomable ways of God. I put my hand in the air and belted out the words, completely in awe that He had heard my prayers—the prayers of Kathy; the prayers of Sean and me; and, now I know, the prayers of my dad's Bible study, all given in the days prior to that positive pregnancy test.

After my workout, I put the positive pregnancy test in my pocket and walked downstairs to share the good news with Sean. I was wearing my "Play for Dad" shirt—a shirt featuring a blue baseball that Sean was given on Father's Day during his time playing in Major League Baseball. It was certainly appropriate! With a knowing smile on my face, I found Sean in the office, working on his iPad, and I scurried up to the table beside him. I set the two tests on the table, displaying two pink lines on each one. He wrapped me up in a big hug. Our journey with our second child was just beginning.

For Sean and me, our worries about getting pregnant lasted only a few months. Moreover, they came after we had been blessed with our first child. For millions of women, struggles with pregnancy occur for far longer than a few months, and for some, pregnancy is simply not possible, even though they pray with hopeful expectation and faith, as Sean and I did. My heart breaks for these women, and I imagine the struggle can be incomprehensible.

Why did God answer my prayers? I do not have an answer, for we will never know God's mysteries in full while here on earth. But I do know that Philippians 4:6–7 promises that God will bring peace to the faithful even when our prayers are not answered: "Do not be anxious about anything, but in every situation, by prayer and petition, with thanksgiving, present your requests to God. And the peace of God, which transcends all understanding, will guard your hearts and your minds in Christ Jesus."[446]

In the weeks that followed my positive pregnancy test, I told a few people about my second pregnancy. My mom was the first to prod the news out of me during a trip to the grocery store. I remember being in the freezer aisle on the phone with her when she said, "Have you taken a pregnancy test lately?" I had intended to find a way to surprise my family with the big news in the coming days but could not help myself in sharing the news on the spot!

Despite my eagerness, the circle that knew about my pregnancy remained small. That's why the voice message I received from my friend Abigail was such a surprise to me. Over the several years I had been friends with Abigail, I had witnessed what an incredibly close relationship with Christ she had. Both my sister and I had attended her Bible study, and Abigail had repeatedly sent me messages with a word on her heart that Christ had placed to share with me. Her texts always relayed an uncanny awareness of exactly what I needed to hear in a given moment—a word of encouragement, a verse speaking to my exact situation, or a prayer that spoke to my needs. There was no doubt in my mind that Abigail had a close relationship with God. Her message just a few weeks into my new pregnancy confirmed it once again!

I had not spoken to Abigail in months, which is what made her message all the more surprising. Out of nowhere I received this voice message: "This might sound really random...but I feel like the Lord was giving me a word of knowledge for you...I felt like the Holy Spirit was telling me that you might be pregnant or you want to be a pregnant and to be praying over that. And I just feel like the Lord was saying 'boy,' and then I also feel like God was saying that it's going to work out, invite the Lord into all of it, believe in miracles, Hosanna in the highest. So I don't know if any of that resonates, and I was kind of second guessing myself before I even reached out to tell you...I just know that I am praying for you and speaking life into you, and I'm praying over your growing family. I know that the Lord has you all in the palm of his hand, and He is going to carry you through whatever is going on...."

"How does she know I'm pregnant?!" I wondered. I was in complete disbelief at Abigail's message and immediately shared it with Sean and my mom. What an incredible word from the Lord that I had just received through Abigail, an emissary for Him and a true light in my life!

Even more incredible was Abigail's prediction of my baby's gender. Sean and I had been hoping for a boy, but like any parent, we only truly wanted to have a healthy child. When Abigail messaged me, I was just over six weeks pregnant, meaning there was no way of knowing the gender at that point. Even so, I was so confident in the revelation she had given me that I began to buy boy clothes. My mother and I went to Bloomingdale's and bought my new baby a blue blanket, a blue winter sweater, and his first onesie—a soft baby blue garment with an assortment of little puppies. I even picked out furniture for a boy's room, though I didn't purchase it yet just in case!

A month later, my doctor called me on a Friday evening with the results of my blood test. I was bathing Baby Blake when I got the surprise call. "You're having a healthy baby," I remember him saying. "Do you want to know the gender?"

"Of course!" I answered, having a feeling that I knew the gender before he even said it.

"You're having a boy!" he informed me.

I can't say I was even a bit surprised. Abigail was right!

Being pregnant with new life is one of God's greatest miracles that we as humans experience. Seeing your little one move around on an ultrasound, feeling him or her kick robustly inside your belly—there really is nothing like it.

Yes, life as a mom has its challenges. During the early days of my pregnancy, getting out of the house was a little bit of a scramble. For me, my morning routine begins with an early morning workout. Blake typically wakes up just before I step off the treadmill, and I look after her as I get ready for work. Oftentimes, that means watching her prance around in a pair of my colorful high heels that she has poached while I madly try to pick out a dress for *Outnumbered*. Then, I rush out the door to begin the workday.

In the first few weeks of my pregnancy, I experienced exhaustion and fatigue but fortunately no morning sickness! I no doubt had a little bit of what I affectionately call "pregnancy brain"—a proclivity to forget or do, at times, inexplicable things. One morning, for example, I was on my way to work when I received a call from my husband.

"Are you okay?" he inquired.

"Why wouldn't I be?" I responded.

"I opened the door to the refrigerator, and I found baby wipes on the shelf!" Sean said.

Or there was the time when I accidently brought my baby monitor to work with me. I discovered it just after sitting down on the *Outnumbered* couch, stowed away in a pocket of my purse and completely useless so far away from home.

Pregnancy brain!

"Was I losing it?!" I thought, laughing off my mistake. Even if I was, every single moment was worth it. Nothing I have done in life—being White House press secretary or co-hosting a television show—no worldly success will ever compare to the joy of being a mother. In fact, as I write this on a flight, Blake is sitting beside me, curled up under a little pink blanket and sleeping. I look at her with total amazement and adoration. God has never created a more perfect creature (though I am biased!). My love for my daughter is a reflection of His love for us—selfless, unconditional, and all-consuming.

I thought it appropriate to share a little of my personal journey in the spring and summer of 2022 because this was the reality I was living when the most consequential Supreme Court decision of my lifetime—*Dobbs v. Jackson Women's Health Organization*—became the law of the land. As I experienced my second pregnancy, the overturning of *Roe* took on an entirely new and more significant light.

I RAPIDLY DESCENDED my staircase and entered a small room-turned-makeshift television studio, prepared to join *Hannity* as I do on every Monday night. It was the first Monday in May of 2022, and it felt like any other Monday night—routine, ordinary, no surprises.

But I was wrong—very wrong.

During the show that I co-host every day at noon, *Outnumbered*, there is often breaking news. The collapse of the Surfside condominium in south Florida, a shooting at the Highland Park Fourth of July parade, and the attack on our troops at Kabul airport in Afghanistan are but a few examples of breaking news that unfolded in the noon hour. During *Hannity*, in the prime-time hours at 9:00 p.m., breaking news is far less frequent. That's what made the evening of May 2, 2022, all the more surprising.

As 9:00 p.m. approached, a producer's voice came through my earpiece, informing me that my topic would be changing because the Supreme Court opinion on *Roe v. Wade* had leaked. Stunned, my disposition changed from a relaxed posture to one of urgency as I opened my phone to discover the breaking news.

"Read Justice Alito's initial draft abortion opinion which would overturn Roe v. Wade," read the *Politico* headline.[447]

"*Roe v. Wade* overturned?! This cannot be true!" I thought in total disbelief.

Thanks to President Trump, the ideological makeup of the Supreme Court had changed, with conservative Justice Amy Coney Barrett replacing liberal Justice Ruth Bader Ginsburg. Even so, I never thought *Roe* would be overturned entirely. I had listened to oral arguments in *Dobbs v. Jackson Women's Health Organization*, the case at issue, and while I anticipated that the case would uphold Mississippi's ban on elective abortion after fifteen weeks, I never anticipated that the court would go so far as to overturn *Roe*, thereby returning the power to decide abortion law to the people. But here was a draft opinion doing just that.

"We hold that *Roe* and *Casey* must be overruled. It is time to heed the Constitution and return the issue of abortion to the people's elected representatives," read the draft majority opinion, written by Justice Samuel Alito—a truly consequential holding from the Supreme Court, perhaps the most significant in decades.[448]

As we approached my appearance on *Hannity*, I tried to contain my excitement. Millions and millions of lives would be saved in a post-*Roe* world. This was cause for celebration. The draft opinion was particularly special to me, as I was newly pregnant with my second child. Just eight weeks into my pregnancy, few were aware of this exciting, personal news outside of family and a few friends. But a new life was growing inside my womb, and it made the *Dobbs* draft opinion so real, so very significant.

Even so, I kept in mind that this was merely a leak and not a final opinion of the court—an unprecedented leak of a tightly guarded Supreme Court opinion. Moreover, it was a leak for a purpose, very likely intended to put immense pressure on the justices, who could certainly change their decision-making ahead of opinions being released throughout the summer months. Notably, the concurrences and dissent were not leaked—only the majority opinion, suggesting a leaker with a motive to pressure members of the majority. I speculated on *Hannity* that evening that the *Dobbs* leak likely generated from a young Supreme Court clerk, unhappy with the overturning of *Roe*. The number of people with access to these drafts was very small—justices, clerks, and a small group beyond that. It was hard to envision a sitting justice engaging in an extreme measure of this nature.

If creating a pressure campaign was the goal, the leaker succeeded. The media lit the forest fire of outrage as they so often do. Liberal co-host of *The View*, Joy Behar, said that her "worry" was that the court may "go after" *Brown v. Board of Education*, the landmark Supreme Court decision that ended racial segregation of schools.[449] It was a preposterous assertion with no basis in fact. The truly deranged and baseless comment was clearly designed to enrage.

Rage indeed followed the leaked draft. Protesters took to the streets, posting the addresses of conservative Supreme Court justices. They brought their protest activity to the front doors of justices' homes while the White House seemed to endorse this method of protest.

"Does the President feel that the demonstrations outside of, say Justice Alito's home—are those attempts to interfere or intimidate?" a White House correspondent asked Press Secretary Jen Psaki.[450]

"So I know that there's an outrage right now, I guess, about protests that have been peaceful to date—and we certainly continue to encourage that—outside of judges' homes. And that's the President's position," Psaki responded in part.[451]

Here was the White House press secretary condoning confronting justices at their homes—an action that was plainly illegal with 18 US Code Section 1507 reading, "Whoever...with the intent of influencing any judge...in the discharge of his duty, pickets or parades...in or near a building or residence occupied or used by such judge...shall be fined under this title or imprisoned not more than one year, or both."[452]

Just a few weeks later, a young man, clad with weaponry, was arrested outside of Justice Brett Kavanaugh's home.[453] The affidavit says that the man "decided that he would kill the Supreme Court Justice."[454] The Justice Department noted that the suitcase and backpack he was carrying contained "a black tactical chest rig and tactical knife, a pistol with two magazines and ammunition, pepper spray, zip ties, a hammer, screwdriver, nail punch, crow bar, pistol light, duct tape, hiking boots with padding on the outside of the soles, and other items."[455]

One would think that such a shocking and alarming action would garner a bold, forceful, and unequivocal condemnation from President Joe Biden's lips, particularly given that the White

House had encouraged protesting outside of justices' homes. But that never happened. While the president condemned the actions of the would-be assassin through spokespeople, he never used his megaphone to condemn the activity himself, though he had myriad opportunities.

Without a verbal condemnation from the president, abortion activist groups grew increasingly hostile and explicit in their threats. Pro-choice group Ruth Sent Us appeared to take aim at the children of Justice Amy Coney Barrett. "If you're in the DC metro area, join us. Our protests at Barrett's home moved the needle to this coverage. Falls Church is a People of Praise stronghold," they wrote, referencing a Christian group that Barrett had an affiliation with. "She sends her seven kids to a People of Praise school that she sat on the Board of Directors of. She attends church DAILY."[456] Protesters did show up outside of Barrett's home, dressed in faux bloody garb and holding baby dolls with signs that read, "Abortion on demand and without apology."[457]

A group called Jane's Revenge proclaimed, "We have demonstrated in the past month how easy and fun it is to attack.... We promised to take increasingly drastic measures...and those measures may not come in the form of something so easily cleaned up as fire and graffiti.... [I]t's open season.... Everyone with the urge to paint, to burn, to cut, to jam: now is the time. Go forth and manifest the things you wish to see."[458] In response to this threat, the White House issued a condemnation of "violence and destruction of property," but the violent activity continued.[459]

In keeping with the demonization of these pro-life centers, Senator Elizabeth Warren chose to marginalize them, alleging that they "are there to fool people looking for pregnancy termination.... We need to shut them down all around the country."[460] Nothing could be further from the truth.

Throughout the spring and summer of 2022 and leading up to the actual release of the *Dobbs* decision, I spoke to several pro-life groups and met many heads of pregnancy crisis centers. I know the pro-life community well. They are gentle. They are kind. And they are often a support system for pregnant women who feel alone, deserted by their male partner and sometimes without supportive family of their own. These centers can become families to these women, holding their hand throughout their pregnancies, providing resources, medical care, and love. But here they were, being attacked and marginalized, and I feared for their safety.

In the wake of these attacks, President Biden's Department of Justice (DOJ) did little to address the unlawful activity outside of justices' homes. They did not aggressively pursue those who attacked and defaced pregnancy crisis centers, and as of August 8, 2022, the *National Review* reported that "no arrests have been made as a result of the FBI's investigations."[461]

"Meanwhile," the *National Review* continues, "the criminal-justice process moved much more efficiently after a July 31 attack on a Kalamazoo, Michigan Planned Parenthood clinic...."[462] Also, of note, Biden's Department of Justice moved far more quickly when the National School Boards Association, a special interest group, demanded that parents at school board meetings be investigated. As you'll read in the pages that follow, Biden's DOJ expeditiously issued a memo to the FBI asking them "to address threats against school administrators, board members, teachers, and staff."[463]

All in all, in the wake of the *Dobbs* draft leak, at least forty pro-life pregnancy centers and churches were attacked with "incidents of violence, vandalism and intimidation."[464] The Biden DOJ, meanwhile, sat on its hands as America waited to see if the draft *Dobbs* opinion would become the official majority opinion of the Supreme Court of the United States.

ON THURSDAY, JUNE 23, 2022, I had just gotten home from taping *Outnumbered*. Blake was napping, and I intended to use every valuable second of silence to write part of this manuscript. I quickly ate lunch and ran upstairs to change into comfortable workout clothes. As I started to change, I felt a little something jerk in my stomach. I tilted my head down and saw what I thought was a slight shift in my stomach.

"Sean, come in here!" I shouted. "I think he's moving."

Our little baby boy was moving for the first time, perhaps doing a preliminary dance of joy for the great news on the horizon.

The next day, I went through my typical morning routine—a workout, some time with my daughter, and a brisk walk to the car. It felt like any other Friday afternoon. I knew that I had to travel to Washington, DC, after work for a Fourth of July interview that I was taping, so I had any number of things on my mind. Had I packed everything? Was I ready for the array of topics we would be discussing in the noon hour?

I knew that the Supreme Court was set to release opinions just after 10:00 a.m. (ET), but I was convinced that the *Dobbs* decision would be among the last batch released by the court. I didn't expect Friday, June 24, 2022, to be the day. Just before I arrived at the studio, news broke that the *Dobbs* opinion had come down from the court.

I began to stream Fox News on my phone, and I heard the news with my own ears—the Supreme Court had issued the *Dobbs* decision. *Roe v. Wade* had officially been overturned. Immediately, tears of joy began to roll down my cheeks. The magnitude of this moment was not lost upon me.

As I previously mentioned, sixty-three million children had lost their lives to the abortion industry since the passage of *Roe*. Sixty-three million. Stop and think about that. That is roughly one-fifth of the current population of the United States. Sixty-three million lives never lived, potential never realized. This was over a five-decade period.

As the Associated Press noted just before the *Dobbs* decision, "[t]he number and rate of U.S. abortions increased from 2017 to 2020 after a long decline.... The report from the Guttmacher Institute, a research group that supports abortion rights, counted more than 930,000 abortions in the U.S. in 2020. That's up from 862,000 abortions in 2017, when national abortion figures reached their lowest point since the 1973 U.S. Supreme Court ruling that legalized the procedure nationwide."[465]

So much for the left's mantra of "safe, legal, and rare!"

Worldwide, the numbers are far worse. According to Life International, "Abortion alone, in which the life of a preborn child is ended, claims the lives of more than 150,000 people every day—56 million every year around the world."[466] In other words, the domestic consequences of *Roe* essentially happen every single year internationally. A truly sad reality.

Contrary to the left's hyperbole in the aftermath of the *Dobbs* decision, the overturning of *Roe* did not mean the end of abortion nationwide. The *Dobbs* decision simply restored decisions surrounding abortion to the American people.

"*Roe* abruptly ended that political process. It imposed the same highly restrictive regime on the entire Nation...," Justice Samuel Alito's majority opinion observed, before later stating, "...and we thus return the power to weigh those arguments to the people and their elected representatives."[467]

Roe, without grounded legal reasoning based on the Constitution, history, and tradition, had usurped the power of the people to decide abortion law. It effectively silenced half of the country, robbing pro-life Americans of their ability to go to the ballot box and have their voices heard. Nine unelected justices in black robes had unilaterally decided to concoct a constitutional right that did not exist from thin air.

"For the first 185 years after the adoption of the Constitution, each state was permitted to address the issue [of abortion] in accordance with the views of its citizens," Alito wrote. "Then, in 1973, this Court decided *Roe v. Wade*. Even though the Constitution makes no mention of abortion, the Court held that it confers a broad right to obtain one."[468] The opinion was so ahistorical and nonsensical that even proponents of abortion and liberal legal scholars questioned it.

The late Justice Ruth Bader Ginsburg had previously criticized *Roe*, saying that "*Roe*...halted a political process that was moving in a reform direction and thereby, I believed, prolonged divisiveness and deferred stable settlement of this issue."[469]

Liberal law professor Laurence Tribe called *Roe* a "verbal smokescreen, the substantive judgment on which it rests is nowhere to be found."[470]

Professor Mark Tushnet deemed it a "totally unreasoned judicial opinion."[471]

President John F. Kennedy's solicitor general, Archibald Cox, asserted that *Roe* "read[s] like a set of hospital rules and regulations" that "[n]either historian, layman, nor lawyer will be persuaded... are part of...the Constitution."[472]

These were but a few of the many liberal *Roe* critics expressing an honest view of the weakness of *Roe*, finally made right in *Dobbs*.

On that Friday morning, I darted out of my car and toward the Fox News studio. I ran up to my office and pressed print on the 213-page *Dobbs* decision before collecting the opinion from the printer and rushing to the hair and makeup room. I endeavored to make good on every minute leading into the noon hour, hoping to be prepared with detailed analysis on the breaking news.

In preparation for this moment, I had spent the last few days reading Alito's leaked draft opinion. My hard copy of the draft was littered with highlights, underlines, and tabbed pages. As I got my hair and makeup done, I compared the draft decision with the newly released opinion, wanting to ensure that I made note of any discrepancies between the two.

One of the main takeaways I had from reading the draft was the oddity of *Roe* reading more like a statute enacted by the legislature than an opinion issued by the court. Factual findings were the purview of the legislature, whereas interpreting the law—not making it—was the purview of the court. *Roe* inverted those roles.

"The weaknesses in *Roe's* reasoning are well-known," wrote Alito. "Without any grounding in the constitutional text, history, or precedent, it imposed on the entire country a detailed set of rules much like those that one might expect to find in a statute or regulation."[473] The majority opinion similarly notes that "[o]ne prominent constitutional scholar wrote that he 'would vote for a statute very much like the one the Court end[ed] up drafting' if he were 'a legislator,' but his assessment of *Roe* was memorable and brutal: *Roe* was 'not constitutional law' at all and gave 'almost no sense of an obligation to try to be.'"[474]

In *Roe*, the court acted much like a legislative body in articulating a trimester-based framework with rules that varied by trimester. By contrast, the majority opinion in *Dobbs* did not engage in fact-finding or lines of scientific inquiry more appropriately left for legislatures; rather, *Dobbs* appropriately cited the factual findings of the Mississippi state legislature.

For instance, the court shows that the Mississippi legislature had laid out the progression of human life during pregnancy on a week-by-week basis.

At five to six weeks: "[an] unborn human being's heart begins beating."

At eight weeks: "[the] unborn human being begins to move about in the womb."

At nine weeks: "all basic physiological functions are present."

At ten weeks: "vital organs begin to function" and "[h]air, fingernails, and toenails…begin to form."

At eleven weeks: "an unborn human being's diaphragm is developing" and the baby "move[s] about freely in the womb."

At twelve weeks: "[the] unborn human being [has] taken on 'the human form' in all relevant respects."[475]

Moreover, Alito wrote that the legislature "found that most abortions after 15 weeks employ 'dilation and evacuation [D&E] procedures which involve the use of surgical instruments to crush and tear the unborn child,' and it concluded that the 'intentional commitment of such acts for nontherapeutic or elective reasons is a barbaric practice, dangerous for the maternal patient, and demeaning to the medical profession.'"[476] In other words, the gruesome "dilation and evacuation procedure" or D&E procedure I described in the previous chapter in horrifying detail used to be federally sanctioned by the court in the *Roe* era but still remains alive and well in some jurisdictions in the *Dobbs* era.

On the Friday that the *Dobbs* opinion was released, I endeavored to walk through several of these facts on *Outnumbered*. I wanted to approach the decision in a breaking news fashion, explaining the x's and o's of the Supreme Court decision and making good use of the great legal minds we would have on the show. I also wanted to speak to viewers as an almost-four-month-pregnant mother who had just felt her little baby kick one day before the *Dobbs* decision. I found that opportunity about midway into the show when I revealed the cherished family moment of feeling my son move for the very first time.

During the segment, I also pointed out that the *Dobbs* decision did not ban abortion nationwide; instead, the decision simply allowed pro-life voters to have a say in the political process.[477] And that is really the whole point of *Dobbs*—allowing the American people to decide the issue of abortion. For decades, the pro-life movement had peacefully made their viewpoint heard with little recourse. *Roe* made it such that elective abortion was the law of the land. Pro-life voters could elect pro-life legislators or presidents, but they did so knowing that their only real solution was the courts. Electing pro-life presidents would hopefully mean appointing law-abiding, Constitution-respecting justices to the court, who would undo the legally unsound *Roe* decision. It was always a long shot, though, a goal that seemed almost unattainable.

Nevertheless, the pro-life movement did what they could. Ever since the first anniversary of *Roe* on January 22, 1974, pro-life voters assembled in Washington, DC, for the March for Life, where at times hundreds of thousands of activists would march peacefully in support of life. The March for Life happened annually for decades, and the pro-life movement showed up dutifully. As a high school girl, I remember my brother high school, Jesuit High School in Tampa, Florida, taking a group of high school boys every year.

As a young professional in DC working at the Republican National Committee years later, I recall Jesuit students being at the March for Life along with thousands of other students and adults. In 2016, an impending blizzard could not even shut down the March for Life. "As DC shuts down for a blizzard, a small, faithful crowd still joins the March for Life," read the *Washington Post* headline.[478]

Little did they know, in 2016, that the election of President Donald J. Trump was on the horizon. President Trump would, of course, go on to nominate three justices faithful to the Constitution and the rule of law—Justice Neil Gorsuch, Justice Brett

Kavanaugh, and Justice Amy Coney Barrett. Their confirmation processes would vary in difficulty from the relatively easy confirmation of Gorsuch to the hard-fought, mudslinging confirmation of Kavanaugh. The circumstances of their confirmations, at times, would be hard to believe like the confirmation of Barrett just weeks before the 2020 presidential election. But the appointments of these three justices would, without a doubt, lead to the *Dobbs* victory just a year and a half after the Trump presidency—a God-ordained miracle in every sense of the word.

The scourge of *Roe* can never be fully undone or made right. Sixty-three million lives have been lost. They cannot be brought back on this earth, though I fully believe we will meet these beautiful, innocent little ones in heaven. While *Roe* cannot be wiped away or forgotten, at least in some states, our country is no longer a pariah among nations.

IN THE LEAD-UP to the 2016 election, I recall my pastor giving a sermon just weeks before election day. As I recounted in my first book, the topic centered on how people of faith should cast their ballots.[479] My pastor did not name candidates nor did he name political parties. The purpose was not to advocate for a campaign but to elucidate the principles of Christian voting. My pastor outlined several numbered bullet points that should animate the vote of a Christian, but one stood out above the rest: if there is one issue and just one issue that should determine Christian voting, it should be the issue of abortion. Voting for a pro-choice candidate is simply not an option for a Christian voter.

My pastor was exactly right.

Insanely, we have seen the left try to use their faith as a shield when it comes to their pro-abortion views. When the topic of

Biden's Catholic faith and his abortion position came up in a White House press briefing, Jen Psaki responded, "Joe Biden is a strong man of faith. The president's faith is personal. It's something that has helped guide him through some challenging moments in his life. And that's how many Americans see their faith as well, not through a political prism."[480] But abortion is not a political issue. No, it is a life and death issue, touching on the very epicenter of faith, which bridges this life with the next life.

President Biden, for his part, overtly misstated his own church's position on abortion. When Senator Lindsey Graham proposed federal legislation to ban elective abortion after fifteen weeks—a move that would put our abortion laws in line with those of the Western world—Biden actively misled about what the bill proposed and then distorted the Catholic Church's theology. "Think about what these guys are talking about," Biden said. "No exceptions—rape, incest—no exceptions, regardless of age. I happen to be a practicing Roman Catholic. My church doesn't even make that argument now."[481]

For starters, Graham's bill did include exceptions for rape, incest, or saving the life of the mother.[482] The larger point, however, is Biden's totally false statement about the Catholic Church's teachings. While I am a Southern Baptist girl, I did spend more than a decade in Catholic school, and it appears that I know Catholic catechism better than our Catholic president. Paragraph 2271 of the Catholic Church's catechism states in no uncertain terms, "Since the first century the Church has affirmed the moral evil of every procured abortion. This teaching has not changed and remains unchangeable. Direct abortion, that is to say, abortion willed either as an end or a means, is gravely contrary to the moral law."[483]

Democrat governor of California Gavin Newsom, likewise, distorted the Christian faith and biblical text in his abortion advocacy. Newsom posted billboards in several red states urging women to come to California to procure abortions. "Texas doesn't own your body. You do," one such sign read.[484] The most galling part of the ad campaign was Newsom's effort to use scripture to justify his position. One sign featured the words of Mark 12:31: "Love your neighbor as yourself. There is no greater commandment than these."[485]

"Seriously?" I thought in disbelief as I read these words.

As a pregnant woman writing this chapter, I can tell you that there is no closer neighbor than the little boy growing inside my womb!

House Speaker Nancy Pelosi's invocation of biblical principles when responding to a similar question on faith and abortion proved no better or more logical than Newsom's. "I believe that God has given us a free will to honor our responsibilities," she said.[486] Pelosi went even further in calling the pro-life position "sinful."[487] Georgia's Democratic nominee for governor, Stacey Abrams, took a similar tone in invoking her faith when addressing abortion, saying in part that "the value that should overhang everything is the right to make our own decisions, the free will that the God I believe in gave us."[488] Free will is certainly a biblical concept, but it is one that the House Speaker and the Democrat gubernatorial candidate distorted. Free will is not a means to justify the choice to sin; rather, it is an explanation for why sin, evil, pain, and suffering exist in the world. God has given us free will, and when we disobey his edicts, hurt and the maladies of this world ensue.

In addition to using faith incorrectly in defense of abortion, Abrams also made a rather peculiar scientific declaration. Sitting on stage at a campaign event, Abrams pronounced, "There is no such thing as a heartbeat at six weeks. It is a manufactured sound designed to convince people that men have the right to take control of a woman's body."[489] Manufactured? I heard my baby's heartbeat at my very first prenatal appointment, around six weeks of pregnancy. My husband and I both marveled at how fast our little one's tiny heart pounded on the monitor. And here was Abrams telling us that the sound was "manufactured"—as if there is some evil cabal among medical professionals to mislead parents? Right!

Beyond this first-hand evidence, the scientific community has been clear on this point. FoxNews.com gathered the words of various scientific entities to illustrate this. The National Library of Medicine observes that at five weeks, "the baby's brain, spinal cord, and heart begins to develop," and at six weeks the "heart continues to grow and now beats at a regular rhythm. This can be seen by vaginal ultrasound."[490] March of Dimes states that at five weeks the "baby's heart and lungs are developing, and baby's heart starts to beat."[491] And Mayo Clinic writes, "A baby's cardiovascular system begins developing five weeks into pregnancy, or three weeks after conception. The heart starts to beat shortly afterward."[492] Presumably, Stacey Abrams respects "the science."

But as we have seen so often throughout COVID-19, "the science" often evolves to match liberal talking points. Around the same time as Abrams's absurd remark, Planned Parenthood engaged in what FoxNews.com described as "stealth-edit[ing]" of its website.[493] Timothy Nerozzi wrote, "As recently as July 25 of this year, Planned Parenthood stated that in the fifth and sixth weeks of gestation 'a very basic beating heart and circulatory system develop' within the fetus.... Now, Planned Parenthood instead claims that at five to six weeks 'a part of the embryo starts to show cardiac activity.'"[494]

The liberal media, meanwhile, decided to run cover for Abrams. The *Huffington Post* griped, "Stacey Abrams Enrages Republicans By Citing Science On 'Fetal Heartbeats."[495] Glenn Kessler, the *Washington Post* "fact checker," described "fetal heartbeat" as a "misnomer."[496] "The ultrasound picks up electrical activity generated by an embryo. The so-called 'heartbeat' sound you hear is created by the ultrasound. Not until 10 weeks can the opening and closing of cardiac valves be detected by a Doppler machine...."[497] Notably, Glenn—the great "fact" checker—provides no "facts" to explain away the beating heart that you can see with your own eyes on ultrasound at six weeks.[498]

In lockstep with the liberal media, social media, too, deceived the public in vouching for Abrams. In the Twitter trend section, Twitter typically provides an agnostic description for why a subject matter is trending—unless it is a conservative, in which case, the description always seems to skew negatively. For Abrams, though, they chose to engage in advocacy in describing the reason her name was being mentioned so often on the platform. "Georgia gubernatorial candidate Stacey Abrams said there is 'no such thing' as a fetal heartbeat at six weeks of pregnancy, and doctors agree one doesn't exist during this early stage of pregnancy, reports from NBC News and NPR confirm."[499] In other words, gone with the science!

Isn't it interesting how that happens? A Democrat gubernatorial candidate says something blatantly false, in total disregard of nearly every reputable scientific source currently available, and special interest groups, the liberal media, and social media all snap into unison running cover for the Democrat Party and changing the science. The Abrams controversy reminded me of when the CDC suddenly dropped "pregnant women" for "pregnant and recently pregnant people"—just as the Squad and other radical liberals chose to embrace the latter terminology.[500] Once again, gone with the science!

But regardless of the nonsense that media and social media chose to propagandize, Abrams' scientific justification was just as incorrect as her faith rationale. Now, I am certainly not here to cast aspersions on anyone's faith. Biden and Pelosi, for example, both claim to be devout Catholics, and I am in no place to assess their faith walk or level of devotion. That is between them and God, but I feel confident in saying they are wrong to assert Christian faith and scripture as a justification for abortion.

The Bible, while written centuries ago, has remarkable, enduring principles applicable to modern-day issues. When it comes to life, the Bible is unmistakable in clearly stating the value of life. Here is just a cursory glance of scripture centered around the concept of life. In addition to these, several additional verses supporting the protection of life were compiled by Focus on the Family.[501]

Jeremiah 1:5 says, "Before I formed you in the womb I knew you, before you were born I set you apart; I appointed you as a prophet to the nations."[502] How awe-inspiring is that? The Bible says that *before* God formed you in the womb, He knew you—*before*. In other words, before our parents even conceived of our existence, Christ did. Isaiah 49:1 echoes this concept, saying in part, "Before I was born the Lord called me; from my mother's womb he has spoken my name."[503]

Psalm 139:13-16 further elaborates in saying, "For you formed my inward parts; you knitted me together in my mother's womb. I praise you, for I am fearfully and wonderfully made. Wonderful are your works; my soul knows it very well. My frame was not hidden from you, when I was being made in secret, intricately woven in the depths of the earth. Your eyes saw my unformed substance; in your book were written, every one of them, the days that were formed for me, when as yet there was none of them."[504] Here we move from the pre-conception concept of life to the growth of the baby during a mother's pregnancy. Scripture tells us that God Himself "knitted me together in my mother's womb." How powerful!

Speaking to the value of human life, Luke 12:7 quotes Jesus Christ as saying, "Indeed, the very hairs of your head are all numbered. Don't be afraid; you are worth more than many sparrows."[505] How significant you are in Christ's eyes! For He does not just know your name, your desires, your wants, your needs, your proclivities. No, He knows the very number of hairs on your head—so intimate a detail revealing how special you are to Him.

Genesis 1:27 tells us that we were indeed made in God's image: "So God created mankind in his own image, in the image of God he created them; male and female he created them."[506] Indeed, God Himself created you. He designed you for a purpose. Any number of Bible verses reflect this very idea.

"Did not He who made me in the womb make them? Did not the same one form us both within our mothers?"—Job 31:15[507]

"From birth I was cast on you; from my mother's womb you have been my God."—Psalm 22:10[508]

"The Spirit of God has made me, and the breath of the Almighty gives me life."—Job 33:4[509]

"Your hands made me and formed me."—Psalm 119:73a[510]

"When Elizabeth heard Mary's greeting, the baby leaped in her womb, and Elizabeth was filled with the Holy Spirit."—Luke 1:41[511]

"Children are a heritage from the Lord, offspring a reward from him."—Psalm 127:3[512]

Are you sensing a trend? You should. For the Bible is imminently clear.

We are *created* by God.

We are *made* in His image.

And we are to *respect* His creation.

Perhaps Deuteronomy 30:19 says it best: "I call heaven and earth to witness against you today, that I have set before you life and death, blessing and curse. Therefore choose life, that you and your offspring may live."[513]

As Christians, we must follow this biblical instruction and "choose life," and as Proverbs 31:8 says, "Speak up for those who can't speak for themselves. Speak up for the rights of all those who are poor."[514]

Though *Dobbs* has re-empowered people of faith and the pro-life movement, our work is not done. State by state, legislature by legislature, we must make our voices heard, speaking for those "who can't speak for themselves." As I say often, it is really quite simple: it is not a woman's right to choose, but a baby's right to live.

EDUCATION

CHAPTER 7

THE FORSAKEN GENERATION

In the fall of 2018, an eleven-year-old girl began her sixth-grade year at Buena Vista Middle School. For the purposes of her privacy, I will refer to her as A.G. Shortly after the school year commenced, A.G.'s friend invited her to an "Equality Club" meeting, a club managed by two teachers where LGBT+ and gender issues were discussed. A.G. decided that the club was not for her but decided to rejoin the club after one of the founding teachers assured her that she "fit in perfectly."[515]

According to the complaint filed by A.G.'s mother against the school district, "[a]t these meetings and in other discussions...[two teachers] planted the seed in A.G.'s mind that she was bisexual. That idea did not originate with A.G. In fact, she did not fully understand what that term meant."[516] A.G.'s feeling that she was bisexual soon evolved into a belief that she was transgender. Again, this was a term that she did not fully comprehend. "At the time, A.G. was pre-pubescent."[517]

By the spring semester, A.G. was experiencing "depression and stress." The Equality Club teachers urged A.G. to take a boy name, so A.G. soon began dressing in boy clothes and going by "S.G." Under what the complaint alleges was a "Parental Secrecy Policy," the two teachers "instructed A.G. not to tell her mother about her new identity or new name, saying that her mother might not be supportive of her and that she couldn't trust her mother."[518] At the end of the year, one of the Equality Club teacher's signed A.G.'s yearbook: "S.G., Stay you! Looking forward to working with you next year."[519]

Imagine that.

Two teachers knowing intimate details of this young sixth grader's life.

Her mother left totally and completely in the dark.

During the summer, A.G. contacted her teachers asking them which name she should put on her school materials. "[W]rite whatever your mother will approve and we'll fix it when you get to school," one of the teachers allegedly replied.[520] During the year, at one point, A.G. received transgender literature, which A.G. was forced to read at the insistence of her teacher. Perhaps in line with the Parental Secrecy Policy, A.G.'s teacher told her how to conceal the material from her mother. Harmeet Dhillon, A.G.'s family's attorney, said that educators even instructed A.G. about "binding her breasts to make sure that they don't grow as part of the transition process."[521] When A.G. specifically inquired about informing her mother of the decision during the fall of her seventh-grade year, the teacher told her not to do so.

By December of 2019—almost a year and a half since A.G. had first started attending Equality Club meetings—the principal summoned A.G.'s mother to the school, where she was finally told about her daughter's new identity. According to the complaint, A.G.'s mother "was taken aback by this news, and she reasonably believed that if she did not process what was going on quickly enough, [the school] would take efforts to attempt to have her daughter taken from her."[522]

During the spring of 2020 when COVID-19 hit, like many schools, Buena Vista transitioned to remote learning. While school closures were a detriment to students across the nation, it did have a "silver lining" for A.G. and for many families—it exposed the toxic, anti-parent, radical left indoctrination taking place at far too many of our nation's schools. "Freed from [her teachers'] influence, A.G. began to return to her old self," the complaint reads.[523]

In an article about a related matter, the *San Francisco Chronicle* noted that "[t]he district and the two teachers declined to comment on the lawsuit. But California law does not require teachers to inform parents about students' gender identities.... The California Department of Education says that school staff should not disclose information about students' gender identity without student permission under AB1266, which protects transgender students' rights and went into law in 2014."[524] The lawsuit between A.G.'s mother and Spreckels Union School District is ongoing as I write this in September of 2022.

The story is a remarkable one, and unfortunately, does not appear to be isolated to a town in California. Harmeet Dhillon, CEO of the Center for American Liberty and the attorney for A.G.'s family, told *Fox & Friends* that she has heard from parents that clubs like the Equality Club and the coaching that accompanies are happening all over the country.[525]

Indeed, Buena Vista does not appear to be the exception to the rule.

In Clay County, Florida, parents filed a similar lawsuit, alleging that their twelve-year-old daughter (called A.P. for privacy purposes) underwent school therapy sessions for months as she dealt with gender identity issues. Like A.G., A.P. assumed a new name and pronoun, her parents left totally uninformed. When were A.P.'s parents notified about this extraordinary life decision? Only when A.P. attempted to commit suicide twice in the school bathroom.[526] The school district insists that the allegations are "completely false," but the parents stand by their account and litigation is ongoing.[527]

In New Jersey, meanwhile, the Department of Education has what is, in essence, a statewide parental secrecy policy. The state's "Transgender Student Guidance" says, "A school district shall accept a student's asserted gender identity; parental consent is not required."[528] Not only that, the school district will instruct students on gender ideology as young as first and second grade, when students are just six and seven years old.[529] Developed in 2020 and slated to go into effect in September of 2022, the "New Jersey Student Learning Performance Expectations" state that, "by the end of grade 2," students should be able to "[d]iscuss the range of ways people express their gender and how gender-role stereotypes may limit behavior."[530] In second grade!

Pursuant to this directive, the Westfield Board of Education provided parents with sample lesson plans. The *first-grade* lesson plan, entitled "Purple, Pink, and Blue," included this language: "You might feel like you're a boy even if you have body parts that some people might tell you are 'girl' parts. You might feel like you're a girl even if you have body parts that some people might tell you are 'boy' parts. And you might not feel like you're a boy or a girl, but you're a little bit of both."[531] A lesson sure to leave six-year-old children completely confused!

The *second-grade* lesson plan, called "Understanding Our Bodies," is even worse. "[T]here are some body parts that mostly just girls have and some parts that mostly just boys have. Being a boy or a girl doesn't have to mean you have those parts, but for most people this is how their bodies are," the sample plan reads. "Most people have a vulva and a vagina or a penis and testicles, but some people's bodies can be different."[532] Keep in mind, this is a lesson plan for seven-year-old children. Simply amazing. In response to an inquiry, Westfield Public Schools told Fox News that the plans are "not state-mandated" and are just part of a "sample list of resources."[533]

In neighboring New York City, the perverse education for elementary school-age children continues.[534] At the famous Dalton School, where tuition is $55,000 per year, first graders received quite an education from "health and wellness" teacher Justine Ang Fonte.[535] In one case, the six-year-old kids were shown a cartoon video where a young boy asks an adult who appears to be his teacher, "Hey, how come sometimes my penis gets big sometimes and points in the air?"[536]

"That's called an erection," the teacher replies.[537]

"Sometimes I touch my penis because it feels good," the boy responds, followed by the little girl immediately chiming in, "Sometimes when I'm in my bath or when Mom puts me to bed, I like to touch my vulva too."[538]

In reply, the teacher expounds upon the young children's anatomy and says, "[I]t's okay to touch yourself and see how different body parts feel, but it's best to only do it in private."[539]

As I viewed this cartoon in real time, I simply could not believe the utter filth that I was watching, being pushed into the young minds of children.

In response to the New York Post's request for comment, a representative for the Dalton School defended the video as "evidence-based and age-appropriate...for students 4 years and older."[540] "These videos align with nationally recognized methodologies and standards," the statement continues.[541]

The report on the Dalton School came on the heels of another New York Post report about this same educator, Justine Ang Fonte, teaching a "porn literacy" workshop at the $47,000-a-year Columbia Grammar & Preparatory School, another New York City school.[542] The eleventh-grade students were taught "how porn takes care of 'three big male vulnerabilities.'"[543] One slide featured a portion of a woman's naked body tied in ropes with the question "Art or Porn?"[544] Another discussed the so-called "orgasm gap in heterosexuals," noting that straight women are less likely to have orgasms than gay or bisexual men or women.[545]

Additionally, the presentation seems to list out what it calls "mainstream" pornography as "consensual or 'vanilla,'" "incest-themed," "barely 'legal,'" "anime," "kind and BDSM (waterboard electro)."[546] It also elaborates on the "most searched" terms for pornography, which include "creampie," "anal," "gangbang," and "stepmom" among other peculiar terms.[547] I would venture to guess, like me, you probably have never heard of these terms. Just picture your high schooler coming home from their private school one day and teaching you about various erotic pornographic terms and facts that they had learned—all for $47,000 a year!

To make matters worse, the porn presentation went on to reference an online application called OnlyFans, described by the *New York Post* as "the hot new app used mostly for sex work."[548] The slide, as the *Post* notes, features a picture of a girl seeming to promote the app while the presentation apparently did not even caution against sexting and its hazards.[549]

Like with A.G.'s transgender coaching, this porn literacy presentation was given during the pandemic, meaning that most kids participated on Zoom.[550] Once again, remote learning exposed the cultural rot being taught to our nation's students, in this case, at one of the country's most elite schools. This time, however, instead of defending the clearly inappropriate presentation as the Dalton School's spokesperson did, the head of the school told parents that the "content and tone of the presentation did not represent our philosophy...."[551]

Gender inappropriate material has not only been limited to deep blue states like California, New Jersey, and New York, though;

even states like Texas and Virginia have seen grotesque literature in their school libraries. Two books—*Lawn Boy* and *Gender Queer*—depict inappropriate sexual scenes and were featured in high school libraries. As described by the *Washington Post, Gender Queer* "shows the adult author engaging in fellatio with a romantic partner who is also an adult, while the author wears a dildo. The other image shows a sexual fantasy of the author's—in which an apparently teenage youth is about to engage in fellatio with an older, bearded man...."[552] Meanwhile, *The Post* also describes *Lawn Boy*, relating a scene that "involves an adult man recalling a sexual encounter he had with another fourth-grader when he was in fourth grade."[553]

In Virginia, parents protested the pair of books at a school board meeting. "St. Michael the Archangel, defend us in battle," the parents said in unison.[554] "Be our defense against the wickedness and snares of the Devil," they continued, praying the Prayer to St. Michael the Archangel. Their prayers were heard, at least temporarily, as Fairfax County Public Schools removed the two books pending review.[555] Unfortunately, the book removal was very temporary with both *Lawn Boy* and *Gender Queer* being placed back on library shelves less than two months later.[556] In response to Texas's uproar, one school district removed *Gender Queer* pending review but opted to remove several other books alongside it—including the Bible.[557]

A rational mind would clearly acknowledge that the material depicted from New York and New Jersey to Texas and Virginia is inappropriate, to say the least. Likewise, a rational mind would see the need for Florida House Bill 1557 (HB 1557)—the "Parental Rights in Education" bill signed into law by Governor Ron DeSantis. The bill states, rather plainly, that "[c]lassroom instruction by school personnel or third parties on sexual orientation or gender identity may not occur *in kindergarten through grade 3* or in a manner that is not age-appropriate or developmentally appropriate for students in accordance with state standards."[558] Nevertheless, controversy ensued.

Critics erroneously misnamed the bill the "Don't Say Gay" bill, leaving out that the bill only applied to K-through-3rd-grade education. Disney said that HB 1557 "should never have passed" and stated that its "goal as a company is for this law to be repealed...."[559] The Biden White House came out in full-fledged opposition to the law with then-press secretary Jen Psaki almost coming to tears during a podcast interview.

"I'm going to get emotional about this issue because it's horrible," she said, audibly fighting back tears. "It's little kids who are bullied and then all these leaders are taking steps to hurt them and hurt their families.... It's completely outrageous."[560] In response to Psaki, I suggested that, rather than crying about a ban on teaching sexuality to young children in our schools, she should instead shed tears for the millions of children lost to abortion who would not be able to attend elementary school.[561]

Meanwhile, polling reflected the common sense that most Americans display on the issue of education. While many polls distorted the language of the DeSantis bill, those that acknowledged the caveat that this applied to K-through-3rd-grade education saw majority support. A Politico/Morning Consult poll found that 51 percent of those polled supported "banning the teaching of sexual orientation and gender identity from kindergarten through third grade."[562] A Daily Wire/Lucid poll from March 2021, which directly cited language from HB 1557, revealed that 64 percent supported the Florida legislation, "including 62% of Democrats and 57% of registered Independents."[563] And a month later, in April of 2021, after the total and complete demonization of the DeSantis bill by the media, a Golden/TIPP poll found that "57% of Americans agreed with the legislation, while only 31% said they disagreed."[564]

In the end, it really is just common sense. While children as young as five years old should of course be taught that they are loved, they are special, and that they have something of value to add to the world, the idea that they should learn about sex and sexuality is jarring.

UNFORTUNATELY, FOR PARENTS today, radical gender ideology is not the only curriculum concern, so, too, is critical race theory (CRT). As Jonathan Butcher put it in a piece for the Heritage Foundation, "Critical gender theory is a close relative of critical race theory. Both theories put personal feelings over facts."[565] At its core, CRT asserts that every human is inescapably an "oppressed" or an "oppressor" by virtue of the color of their skin. It is a divisive and insidious ideology in every way, and the left denies its very existence in erroneous unison: "Critical race theory is not being taught in schools," they say. Along with the rest of the Democrat Party, for example, American Federation of Teachers (AFT) president Randi Weingarten declared, "Let's be clear: critical race theory is not taught in elementary schools or high schools."[566] One problem for Randi, though, is the evidence, and there is a lot of it.

No one has done more to expose CRT in America's schools than activist Christopher Rufo.[567] The accounts below are drawn from his extensive research on the topic.[568] In July of 2021, Rufo published a list of twenty-five schools and school districts pushing a book called *Not My Idea* by Anastasia Higginbotham.[569] One page of the book states, "[w]hiteness is a bad deal," while another page seems to show a demonic figure with flames protruding from its head, holding a "contract binding you to whiteness," stating that "whiteness gets to mess endlessly with the lives of your friends, neighbors, loved ones, and all fellow humans of color."[570] Schools from Seattle, Washington, to Cumberland, Maine—many of them elementary schools—either taught the book explicitly or listed it as recommended reading.

Meanwhile, in Arizona, schools decided to explore the racist tendencies of two-year-olds! The Arizona Department of Education created a document explaining the issue of race among babies from birth to six years old. At two years old, they determined that children "use race to reason about people's behavior" and by ages four or five "[e]xpressions of racial prejudice often peak...."[571] Also, at five years old, "[w]hite children at this age remain strongly biased in favor of whiteness."[572]

In Atlanta, Georgia, Kila Posey filed a federal discrimination complaint against Mary Lin Elementary School for allegedly segregating students into separate classrooms based on race. According to Kila, an administrator attempted to explain the policy in saying, "I just wish we had more Black kids, and then some of them are in a class because of the services that they need."[573] Kila said she found out about the situation when she made a routine call to the principal requesting a specific teacher for her daughter. "She said that's not one of the black classes," Kila recalled, to which Kila replied, "What does that mean?"[574]

Reflecting on the conversation, Kila told WSB-TV, "I was confused. I asked for more clarification. I was like, 'We have those in the school?' And she proceeded to say, 'Yes. I have decided that I'm going to place all of the black students in two classes.'"[575] In a statement, Atlanta Public Schools responded in saying that they do "not condone the assigning of students to classrooms based on race. The district conducted a review of the allegations. Appropriate actions were taken to address the issue and the matter was closed."[576] In other words, a non-denial of this clearly illegal act of segregation in a public school. Kila said, "It was just disbelief that I was having this conversation in 2020 with a person that looks just like me—a black woman."[577]

While the allegation is shocking, are we really that surprised? After all, segregated graduations have been going on for quite some time with Campus Reform reporting more than three dozen such incidences.[578] Yesterday, it was segregated graduations; today, it is segregated classrooms that allegedly occurred in at least one Atlanta, Georgia, school. There is indeed a great irony here. After all, *Brown v. Board of Education* held, "We conclude that in the field of public education the doctrine of 'separate but equal' has no place. Separate educational facilities are inherently unequal."[579]

Radical ideology on race, meanwhile, has found its way into the statewide "Ethnic Studies Model Curriculum" (ESMC) in the state of California.[580] The first attempt at developing the radical curriculum incurred broad criticism in August 2019 for "contain[ing] significant anti-Semitic sentiment, such as a poem insinuating that Jews control the media" among other anti-Semitic assertions as reported by the *Wall Street Journal*.[581] While these racist and baseless sentiments were removed, the ESMC approved by the State Board of Education on March 18, 2021, still has many flaws, to say the least.[582]

For starters, according to Rufo, the curriculum is based—at least in part—on the teachings of "Marxist theoretician" Paulo Freire.[583] Rufo also notes that R. Tolteka Cuauhtin, "the original co-chair" of the ESMC formed the basis for part of the curriculum. Rufo writes that Cuauhtin claimed that "white Christians committed 'theocide' against indigenous tribes, killing their gods and replacing them with Christianity.... The ultimate goal is to 'decolonize' American society and establish a new regime of 'countergenocide' and 'counterhegemony,' which will displace white Christian culture and lead to the 'regeneration of indigenous epistemic and cultural futurity.'"[584] As part of the curriculum, California children were to chant two Aztec chants—yes, Aztec chants.[585] After parents threatened a lawsuit against the California

Department of Education, the department, fortunately, agreed to remove this recommendation from the curriculum.[586]

But, nevertheless, the derision of Christianity in the guise of radical racial ideology has proven pervasive. In Cupertino, California, a teacher taught her elementary school children that "white, middle class, cisgender, educated, able-bodied, Christian, English speaker[s]" were "dominant."[587] The students then created "identity maps," wherein they ranked themselves by "power and privilege."[588] The lesson reflected what one teacher told the Loudoun County School Board was happening in Virginia: "Within the last year, I was told in one of my so-called equity trainings that White, Christian, able-bodied females currently have the power in our school and that 'this has to change.' Clearly, you've made your point. You no longer value me or many other teachers you've employed in this county," the teacher said before quitting her job.[589]

In Springfield, Missouri, at a diversity training, educators were asked to place themselves on an "oppression matrix."[590] The matrix, according to Rufo, asserted that "white heterosexual Protestant males" are "inherently oppressors."[591] Moreover, one teacher asserted that, at one point, "MAGA" was listed as a type of "covert white supremacy."[592] In Fairfax County, Virginia, students were instructed to play "privilege bingo." Among the "privileged" boxes they could check were being "white, Christian, male and able-bodied."[593] "There was also a box for being a military kid," NBC Washington reported.[594] Fairfax County Public Schools later apologized "for any offense it may have unintentionally caused...."[595]

Have you noticed a consistent theme in the examples above? If you haven't, you should. Embedded in the radical doctrines being taught at our schools is a distinct, undeniable anti-Christian emanating theme. "Christian" is often labeled outright alongside "white" as being chief among the characteristics of an oppressor. It was not enough to remove God from our schools; outright demonization of Judeo-Christian faith has always been the aim.

ON SEPTEMBER 17, 2020, when I was serving as White House press secretary, I accompanied President Trump to the National Archives Museum.[596] He was set to give a speech on the importance of patriotism in education, fittingly, on Constitution Day, which commemorates the signing of the Constitution on September 17, 1787. Surrounded by American flags in the National Archives rotunda and flanked by two enormous murals commemorating the creation of the Declaration of Independence and the Constitution, President Trump succinctly described the challenge we faced as a country: "We embrace the vision of Martin Luther King, where children are not judged by the color of their skin but by the content of their character. The left is attempting to destroy that beautiful vision and divide Americans by race in the service of political power. By viewing every issue through the lens of race, they want to impose a new segregation, and we must not allow that to happen."[597]

He explained exactly how the left was trying to achieve this and the consequences of such divisiveness. "Critical race theory, the 1619 Project, and the crusade against American history is toxic propaganda, ideological poison that, if not removed, will dissolve the civic bonds that tie us together," he continued. "It will destroy our country."[598] President Trump's speech so clearly portrayed the radical left-wing agenda at play in education, and he ended by announcing deliverables. In addition to banning critical race theory in federal government training, he announced a new executive order to create a "1776 Commission," devoted to furthering patriotic education.

Despite the speech's clear-eyed look at the state of American education and its inspiring vision for the future, the media chose to mock and demonize the speech.

"Trump unleashed a cascade of grievances from the National Archives Museum…," declared *Politico*.[599]

"President Trump's attack on the Critical Race Theory is sad," read an opinion piece in the *Sacramento Bee*.[600]

"Trump's dark National Archives speech was white resentment run amok," *Vox* mused.[601]

But Trump's speech—filled with references to God, unity, and patriotism—spoke for itself. Just a few months later, a very different president began his first term of office with a very different outlook on critical race theory and the role of parents in education.

A number of incomprehensible and radical Biden administration decisions have exposed where the current administration stands on education. All of them seem to fall beneath a guiding philosophy that Biden announced to a room full of teachers and union members in April of 2022. "You've heard me say it many times about our children, but it's true: They're all our children," Biden said. "They're not somebody else's children; they're like yours when they're in the classroom."[602] The remark got very little attention, though it was deserving of far more.

Your children? Absolutely not. I sit here six months pregnant with my second child as I write this chapter. While teachers play an important role in society, they do not carry the child in my belly. They do not raise my children. No, Sean and I will raise our son alongside our daughter, teaching them right and wrong, morality, and faith. In no way, shape, or form are our children "like yours [the teacher's] when they're in the classroom."[603] But this is the way Biden views our children, and this view has animated the reprehensible actions his administration has taken in radicalizing our schools.

A few months into President Biden's first term, the Department of Education (DOE) released its COVID-19 handbook: a "Roadmap to Reopening Safely and Meeting All Students' Needs."[604] Among the various instructions and recommendations was a link to the Abolitionist Teaching Network's "Guide for Racial Justice & Abolitionist Social and Emotional Learning," which claims that social and emotional learning "can be a covert form of policing used to punish, criminalize, and control Black, Brown, and Indigenous children and communities to adhere to White norms."[605] Amid criticism, the Department of Education claimed that the reference to the group pushing critical race theory was in "error," asserting that the DOE "does not endorse the recommendations of this group...."[606]

Psaki, for her part, insisted, "[W]e don't dictate or recommend specific curriculum decisions from the federal government."[607] The statement was indeed curious as it came less than two weeks after Psaki was asked about her view of the National Education Association supporting a variety of curricula, including critical race theory.[608] Rather than distancing the White House from CRT or suggesting that education curriculum should be left to localities, Psaki said, in part, that "kids should learn about our history."[609]

Far from leaving education to localities, and more specifically to parents, the Biden White House has involved itself in education on a variety of fronts, specifically taking its marching orders from powerful unions. We saw this very clearly when the Centers for Disease Control (CDC) adopted changes to guidelines on school reopening suggested by the American Federation of Teachers (AFT) almost verbatim.[610] Rather than committing to fully opening schools, which would have been in the interest of the child, more tempered language was issued, as suggested by the AFT.[611]

Despite slow-walking the opening of schools post-COVID, Press Secretary Karine Jean-Pierre falsely blamed the Trump administration when it was revealed that student test scores had dropped for the first time since the 1970s.[612] "[W]e must repair the damage that was done by the last administration, the mismanagement that was done…," Jean-Pierre said in response to a question on test scores.[613] The statement was laughable considering that I had stood at that very podium as White House press secretary in 2020 repeatedly calling for the reopening of our nation's schools—a position the Trump administration was often derided for on the left.[614]

Given the precedent of powerful unions dictating Biden administration CDC guidelines, perhaps it should have come as no surprise when the Department of Justice released a letter seeming to target parents at school board meetings for potential criminal prosecution, this time at the urging of the National School Boards Association (NSBA). On September 29, 2021, the NSBA sent a letter to President Biden, reading in part, "America's public schools and its education leaders are under an immediate threat…. [The NSBA] respectfully asks for federal law enforcement and other assistance to deal with the growing number of threats of violence and acts of intimidation occurring across the nation."[615] The letter "specifically solicits the expertise and resources of the U.S. Department of Justice, Federal Bureau of Investigation (FBI)" among other government entities while claiming that "threats against public school officials…could be the equivalent of a form of domestic terrorism and hate crimes."[616] The NSBA document even suggests that the government utilize the PATRIOT Act, a law passed in the wake of September 11, 2001, to prosecute terrorists.[617]

On October 4, 2021—five days after the NSBA sent this letter to President Biden—the DOJ, seemingly in lockstep with the NSBA, issued a memorandum for the director of the FBI "to address threats against school administrators, board members, teachers, and staff."[618] The memo noted the rising threats of violence and declared that "[i]n the coming days, the Department will announce a series of measures designed to address the rise in criminal conduct directed toward school personnel."[619]

"I am directing the Federal Bureau of Investigation, working with each United States Attorney, to convene meetings with federal, state, local, Tribal, and territorial leaders in each federal judicial district within 30 days of the issuance of this memorandum," the letter from the Attorney General instructed, featuring Merrick Garland's signature off to the right.[620] The very next day, on October 5, President Biden called Dr. Viola Garcia, the president of the NSBA Board of the Directors at the time, to thank her for the letter and invite her to visit the Oval Office.[621]

Meanwhile, the letter from the DOJ was met with widespread outrage. It seemed as though the DOJ was being weaponized against concerned parents and at the direction of the NSBA, an influential interest group. After a firestorm of criticism, the NSBA apologized for their letter, saying that there was "no justification for some of the language included in the letter."[622] Attorney General Merrick Garland, however, did not back down from the DOJ memorandum, instead saying that "[t]he letter that was subsequently sent does not change the association's concern of violence or threats of violence. It alters some of the language in the letter…that we did not rely on and is not contained in my own memorandum."[623]

The topic of reliance, though, is an interesting one. A months-long internal investigation of the NSBA incident by outside attorneys found significant coordination between the NSBA, the White House, and even the DOJ. For starters, the White House and the NSBA coordinated in advance of the initial letter being sent to the White House. For example, the then-interim CEO and executive director of the NSBA Board of Directors gave "advance[d] knowledge of the planned Letter and its specific contents" to a White House senior advisor, going so far as to also provide "an advance summary of the Letter's contents and its list of requests for federal intervention, along with the previously requested list of 'egregious examples,' so White House officials could 'include' the planned contents of the Letter in discussions with Department of Justice officials...."[624]

Not only that, the NSBA-initiated independent investigation conclusively stated that "evidence indicates that White House officials discussed the existence of the Letter, its requests, and the contents of the Letter with Department of Justice officials more than a week before the Letter was finalized and sent to President Biden."[625] In other words, here was another example of parents taking a backseat to special interest groups that seemed to be dictating the decision-making of the federal government.

The message that the Biden administration was sending to parents stood in stark contrast to the message embraced by the administration that I worked for. In his speech at the National Archives, President Trump stated his view in no uncertain terms: "There is no more powerful force than a parent's love for their children. And patriotic moms and dads are going to demand that their children are no longer fed hateful lies about this country. American parents are not going to accept indoctrination in our schools, cancel culture at our work, or the repression of traditional faith, culture, and values in the public square. Not anymore," he said.[626]

President Trump was exactly right, and Tuesday, November 2, 2021, would prove it.

IN THE FALL of 2021, America waited to learn the highly anticipated outcomes of the gubernatorial races in Virginia and

New Jersey. These races, which take place in an off-election year, are often looked to as a political bellwether for a first-year president. In Virginia, former Democrat governor Terry McAuliffe faced political novice and relatively unknown businessman Glenn Youngkin. In a year of economic turmoil and COVID-19, few expected education to take center stage, but it did as Loudoun County, Virginia, school board meetings commenced, with very vocal parents voicing their concern about radical gender curriculums and critical race theory.

McAuliffe, for his part, adopted the same erroneous line of the Democrat Party, claiming that critical race theory "has never been taught in Virginia."[627] His lie was quickly debunked, with Christopher Rufo noting a memo from the State Superintendent calling CRT "an important analytic tool...."[628] A 2015 presentation also emerged from the Virginia Department of Education's website that suggested teachers "embrace Critical Race Theory."[629] McAuliffe should have been well aware of this. After all, he was governor of the state of Virginia at the time.

Additionally, parents themselves were vocalizing that they were hearing CRT directly from their children with one parent at a Loudoun County school board meeting saying, "My six year old somberly came to me and asked if she was born evil because she was a white person, something she learned in a history lesson at school."[630] But CRT was just a figment of our imagination—so we were told.

McAuliffe also made the rather interesting and ill-advised choice of running an anti-parent campaign. On the debate stage, Youngkin said pointedly to McAuliffe, "You believe school systems should tell children what to do. I believe parents should be in charge of their kids."[631] McAuliffe replied with the infamous line that defined the campaign: "I'm not going to let parents come into schools and actually take books out and make their own decisions. I don't think parents should be telling schools what they should teach"—a curious line that he doubled down on in a later interview.[632]

The remarkable assertion that parents have no role in their child's education was prominently featured and displayed in Youngkin campaign ads across the state. Further demonization of parents continued with McAuliffe also stating that "I met a school board member, who said our school boards were fine. As soon as Glenn Youngkin got nominated, these people started showing up creating such a ruckus."[633] "These people" were of course concerned parents. McAuliffe even invited none other than AFT President Randi Weingarten to campaign with him.[634] Brilliant!

Education quickly became the top issue in Virginia with 21 percent of Virginians citing education as the most important issue followed by jobs at 15 percent and COVID-19 at 14 percent, two key areas now taking a backseat.[635] A similar Monmouth poll, also taken in October, reflected the rising importance of education in voters' minds with "education and schools" being the second issue to "jobs and the economy."[636] Education surged ten percentage points in importance from September to October.[637] Even more notably, in the same poll, Youngkin actually beat McAuliffe by one point when voters were asked which candidate was more trusted to handle education and schools. This was a notable shift from the late summer and early fall when Youngkin trailed McAuliffe by about four to five points.[638]

Just days before the election, a *Washington Post*-Schar School poll noted a similar remarkable swing on the issue of education. In September, voters with education as their top issue favored McAuliffe by thirty-three points; by late October, Youngkin had a nine-point advantage on the issue—a stunning forty-two-point shift![639]

While Republicans historically trail on the issue of education, that was not the case in Virginia in the fall of 2021, and vote totals reflected the polling. "Parents who wanted more voice in schools broke for Youngkin by a large margin in exit polls," NPR observed.[640] Similarly, Fox News's voter analysis found that a quarter of Virginia voters cited CRT as their top issue with 72 percent saying it was important.[641] Among education-motivated voters, 71 percent voted for Youngkin.[642]

Education, without a doubt, made a difference in Virginia and is making a difference in elections nationwide. In New Jersey, where Democrat governor Tim Murphy was supposed to win by eight or nine points, the actual result was much closer with Murphy beating Republican nominee Jack Ciattarelli by less than one point when the race was called.[643]

"What happened?" asked *New York Magazine*. "[I]n the absence of hard evidence, a consensus is already starting to emerge: It was the schools."[644] Just over three months later, in the liberal bastion of San Francisco, three far-left school board members were voted out in a recall election, after—along with other radical decisions—they sought to rename several institutions, Abraham Lincoln High School among them.[645] And in Florida's primary elections, Governor Ron DeSantis took the unprecedented step of making endorsements in local school board races.[646] Of the thirty candidates DeSantis endorsed, twenty-five either prevailed or moved on to a runoff election.[647] And, in two counties—Sarasota and Duval county—the ideological balance of the school boards flipped to conservative.

While education has taken a prominent place in American political life, it did not happen in a vacuum. COVID-19 and virtual learning uncovered a radical indoctrination of our nation's youth that has been going on for quite some time. This radical takeover began long before COVID-19 came to the shores of the United States; it all began when God was stripped from our nation's schools.

CHAPTER 8

FORGOTTEN GOD

Madalyn Murray O'Hair, born in Beechview, Pennsylvania, in 1919, had an enemy.[648] Of that, there is no doubt. Her life made it abundantly clear. Peculiarly, though, Madalyn had an enemy that she did not believe actually existed—God.

While serving abroad in the Army Corps during World War II, Madalyn became pregnant with her first child, William J. Murray III.[649] Though she was married at the time, Madalyn conceived William, not with her husband, but with a married pilot who she met overseas during the war.[650] The pilot refused to marry Madalyn, and while Madalyn's husband offered to remain with her and father the child as his own, Madalyn insisted on divorce.[651] Alone, Madalyn moved into her parents' home—a small shanty with no flooring or running water.[652]

In a rather ironic twist, William, Madalyn's first son, rejected his mother's atheist views in adulthood and actually became a Southern Baptist minister. William wrote books about his faith, and in one of them, he recalls a story that his grandparents shared with him.[653] One night, while Madalyn was pregnant with William, a fierce thunderstorm erupted, and lightning struck close to Madalyn's parents' home. Madalyn walked outside, and as William recalls learning, "challenged God to strike her and her unborn child dead."[654] Madalyn lived to tell the story, her atheism even more entrenched.

Madalyn's steadfast anti-religious views were matched with equally fervent political perspectives. As a member of the Socialist Labor Party, William recalls Madalyn hosting socialist meetings in their family basement.[655] Madalyn enjoyed reading communist publications and even applied to become a citizen of the Soviet Union in 1959.[656] Set on this plan, Madalyn took William and her second son to the Soviet embassy in Paris, France, to try and make her dream a reality.[657] But the Soviets were apparently unimpressed with Madalyn Murray O'Hair, as an official at the embassy told her, "I do not believe you have a true comprehension of Marxist principles in our motherland. It is against the law to be unemployed. The punishment for not being employed is hard labor at half pay. In looking at your work record, it seems you would be working for half pay most of the time."[658] Dismayed, Madalyn returned to the United States, where a new crusade that would leave an unmistakable mark on American society awaited her.

In his book, *Let Us Pray*, William recalls that fateful day that changed everything in 1960 at Woodbourne Junior High School.[659] Walking through the school's hallways one morning just before school commenced, Madalyn stopped at an open door where students were saying the Pledge of Allegiance.[660] William remembers his mother quipping, "They do this every day?"

"As we approached another classroom she stopped dead. The students were standing, heads bowed, reciting the Lord's Prayer," he writes. "With a burst of obscenities, she shouted, 'Why didn't you tell me about this?' 'We were going to the Soviet Union to become great commissars,' I said with bad timing and complete truthfulness."[661] The encounter prompted Madalyn to go straight to the counselor's office, where she curtly and crudely asked, "Why are those f--ing children praying? It's un-American and unconstitutional."[662] After leaving the school, William remembers his mother instructing him to take notes on all of the happenings at school, and when he inquired why, she responded—according to William—with this anti-Semitic remark: "The United States is nothing but a fascist slave-labor camp run by a handful of Jew bankers in New York City. The only way true freedom can be achieved is through the new Socialist man. Only when all men know the truth of their animal sameness will we have true freedom."[663]

Wow.

It was there that Madalyn Murray O'Hair's quest to eliminate God from America's schools began. That same year, Madalyn filed a lawsuit against the Baltimore City Public School System. Her son, William, was the plaintiff in the lawsuit called *Murray v. Curlett* that would make it all the way to the Supreme Court of the United States. The policy at issue was "Section 6—Opening Exercises" issued by the Board of School Commissioners of Baltimore City. It read, in part, "Each school, either collectively or in classes, shall be opened by the reading, without comment, of a chapter in the Holy Bible and/or the use of the Lord's Prayer.... Any child shall be excused from participating in the opening exercises or from attending the opening exercises upon written request of his parent or guardian."[664] But this accommodation did not satisfy Madalyn.

In 1963, *Murray v. Curlett* was combined with a similar case called *Abington School District v. Schempp* and appealed up to the Supreme Court. The Supreme Court heard the pair of cases just one year after deciding a landmark case called *Engel v. Vitale*. At issue in *Engel* was a short prayer recited in a school district in New York. The prayer was voluntary and referenced no religion in particular. It merely read, "Almighty God, we acknowledge our dependence upon Thee, and we beg Thy blessings upon us, our parents, our teachers and our Country."[665] Citing the First Amendment—the amendment that reads, in part, "Congress shall make no law respecting an establishment of religion, or prohibiting the free exercise thereof; or abridging the freedom of speech..."—the court ruled that the New York school district's prayer was not permissible.[666]

Specifically, the court relied on the "Establishment Clause" in making their decision, the portion of the First Amendment reading that "Congress shall make no law respecting an establishment of religion."[667] As a sidenote, the accompanying corollary to this part of the First Amendment is the "Free Exercise Clause" barring Congress from "prohibiting the free exercise" of religion. Writing alone in dissent, Justice Potter Stewart argued, "With all respect, I think the Court has misapplied a great constitutional principle. I cannot see how an 'official religion' is established by letting those who want to say a prayer say it.... For we deal here not with the establishment of a state church, which would, of course, be constitutionally impermissible, but with whether school children who want to begin their day by joining in prayer must be prohibited from doing so."[668]

The majority opinion in *Engel* went on to reference a phrase that you have no doubt heard often, as it is almost a part of American vernacular—"the constitutional wall of separation between Church and State."[669] The great irony, though, is this: nowhere in the United States Constitution is the term "separation between Church and State" ever utilized. As the Stewart dissent appropriately noted, "...I think that the Court's task...is not responsibly aided by the uncritical invocation of metaphors like the 'wall of separation,' a phrase nowhere to be found in the Constitution."[670]

Furthermore, Stewart went on to lay out in vivid detail how history and tradition showcase the extent to which religion and the state were intertwined. When engaging in constitutional interpretation, judges chiefly look to the plain text of the Constitution, history, tradition, and precedent. In this case, history and tradition are clear. As Stewart noted, since the 1800s, the Supreme Court itself began each day with the words "God save the United States and this Honorable Court."[671] Similarly, the Senate and the House of Representatives began with prayer.[672] As for the remaining branch of government, the executive, "[e]ach of our Presidents, from George Washington to John F. Kennedy, has upon assuming his Office asked the protection and help of God."[673]

Beyond God being in the halls of government, He has a place in our pledge and on our money. Stewart wrote, "In 1954, Congress added a phrase to the Pledge of Allegiance to the Flag so that it now contains the words 'one Nation *under* God, indivisible, with liberty and justice for all.' In 1952, Congress enacted legislation calling upon the President each year to proclaim a National Day of Prayer. Since 1865, the words 'IN GOD WE TRUST' have been impressed on our coins."[674] And even before that, at the very founding of our country, on July 4, 1776, America's founders acknowledged in the closing line of the Declaration of Independence that they wrote this document "with a firm reliance on the protection of divine Providence...."[675]

One year after the *Engel* decision, the court sided with Madalyn Murray O'Hair and against school prayer again. In *Abington School District v. Schempp*, the majority wrote that "the First Amendment, in its final form, did not simply bar a congressional enactment *establishing a church*; it forbade all laws *respecting an establishment of religion*. Thus, this Court has given the Amendment a 'broad interpretation....'"

But, notably, the majority sided with Murray O'Hair while also acknowledging the importance of religion in our history. The majority recognized that in a previous 1952 case "we gave specific recognition to the proposition that '[w]e are a religious people whose institutions presuppose a Supreme Being.' The fact that the Founding Fathers believed devotedly that there was a god and that the unalienable rights of man were rooted in Him is clearly evidenced in their writings, from the Mayflower Compact to the

Constitution itself."[676] Despite striking down voluntary prayer in schools, the majority contended that "[t]he place of religion in our society is an exalted one, achieved through a long tradition of reliance on the home, the church and the inviolable citadel of the individual heart and mind.... In the relationship between man and religion, the State is firmly committed to a position of neutrality."[677]

One of the student plaintiffs in this case, Madalyn's son, William Murray, now has different thoughts on school prayer in adulthood. William Murray rejects the notion that the State has taken a "position of neutrality," instead arguing that "[t]he Court thought that banning school prayer was tantamount to taking a neutral stance toward religion. I disagree. I think the Court privileged a secular value system and its stance was overwhelmingly hostile to religion."[678] Indeed, that has been proven true over time as I will illustrate.

This embrace of a secular value system is perfectly embodied by the woman who prompted the *Murray/Schempp* decision on behalf of her son: Madalyn Murray O'Hair. As the Supreme Court was considering the case, Murray wrote this response to an article in *Life* magazine, which advocated for school prayer: "We find the Bible to be nauseating, historically inaccurate, replete with the ravings of madmen. We find God to be sadistic, brutal, and a representation of hatred, vengeance. We find the Lord's Prayer to be that muttered by worms groveling for meager existence in a traumatic, paranoid world."[679]

Hardly a position of neutrality!

Following Madalyn's victory and America's loss, Madalyn began a group called "American Atheists." Her advocacy included pursuing various other legal challenges, including an effort to remove "In God We Trust" from our money and tax-exempt status from churches.[680] While America celebrated Apollo 8, the first spacecraft carrying humans to orbit the moon, O'Hair was busy suing NASA.[681] Why? On Christmas Eve of 1968, the Apollo 8 crew sent a broadcast message back to earth, reading from Genesis: "In the beginning, God created the heavens and the earth," they read before continuing with the following verses. "And from the crew of Apollo 8, we close with good night, good luck, a Merry Christmas and God bless all of you—all of you on the good Earth," they concluded.[682] But that was too much for Murray O'Hair, who took action in filing a lawsuit.

Time Magazine infamously stuck Madalyn Murray O'Hair with a label that would follow her for the rest of her life, calling her "the most hated woman in America."[683] According to the Texas State Historical Association, it was "a title she apparently enjoyed."[684]

As I mentioned at the start of this chapter, William Murray underwent quite a transformation. The *Baltimore Sun* observed, "The student who stood up at the back of this class in Woodbourne Junior High School to rebuff a teacher's Bible reading as 'ridiculous' is now the Rev. Bill Murray, a Southern Baptist and a fundamentalist evangelist based in Coppell, Texas."[685]

After succumbing to a miserable life of alcoholism and even drugs, Bill Murray found God through an Alcoholics Anonymous program. *The Oklahoman* noted, "Although the 12-step program did not give a specific name to this god, Bill said not long after that he felt directed by the 'Holy Spirit' to read the Bible, where he learned about Jesus Christ."[686] Murray said, "This was the one place I had never looked for the nature of God, for it was this very book that my mother had removed from our nation's schools by her lawsuit in 1963."[687]

In his book about Madalyn Murray O'Hair, *Ungodly*, journalist Ted Dracos writes, "[T]here couldn't be, and wouldn't be in the future, any doubt as to the authenticity of Bill's rebirth. His alcoholism and drug abuse ended. He became a marathon runner. His physical abuse stopped. His life went from chaos to an ordered and dedicated spreading of faith…. The naysayers could mock him, but Bill was, in reality, a new man."[688]

As for Madalyn Murray O'Hair's reaction? It was nothing short of a cruel and unfathomable rejection of her son, as alleged in Dracos' book. According to Dracos and other sources, she retorted: "One could call this a postnatal abortion on the part of a mother, I guess; I repudiate him entirely and completely for now and all times…. He is beyond human forgiveness."[689]

IN THE NEARLY six decades since prayer was exiled from our nation's schools, America has seen not "neutrality" toward religion but rather overt "hostility." Just a glimpse at case law pertaining to religion in our nation's schools tells the story.

In 1985, for example, the court struck down an Alabama law allowing a sixty-second moment of silence "for meditation or voluntary prayer" in school.[690] Student-led prayer before a football game at Santa Fe High School—even if "nonsectarian [and] nonproselytizing"—was barred.[691] Likewise, a rabbi could not offer a prayer at a public middle school graduation ceremony.[692] Nor could the Virginia Military Institute recite a daily prayer before dinner with its cadets.[693] The hostility toward faith from the court made its way into school curricula with the court striking down a Louisiana law called "The Balanced Treatment for Creation-Science and Evolution-Science Act," which mandated that where evolution is taught in school, creationism must be taught as well.[694] Pew surveys the aforementioned cases in more detail and points out that "[a]s a result [of the evolution decision], school boards have lost virtually every fight over curriculum changes designed to challenge evolution, including disclaimers in biology textbooks."[695]

In New York, a federal court upheld the New York City Department of Education's policy that allowed "[t]he display of secular holiday symbol decorations…includ[ing but not limited to], Christmas trees, menorahs, and the [Islamic] star and crescent" even though, according to Pew, "It explicitly forbids the display of a Christmas nativity scene in public schools."[696]

Meanwhile, in Denver, a teacher was stopped from silently reading his Bible during a fifteen minute "silent reading period" in his fifth-grade classroom, where students were free to read any book of their choice.[697] The school additionally forced the teacher, Mr. Roberts, to remove the Bible from his desk while permitting him "to teach actively about Navajo Indian religion" and "read silently a book dealing with the life of Buddha and keep it on his desk for some period."[698] The court admitted that the teacher, Mr. Roberts, "never read from the Bible aloud nor overtly proselytized about his faith to his students," but because he had a poster referencing "the hand of God" in his classroom as he silently read his Bible, the court found that Mr. Roberts had inappropriately "created the appearance that Mr. Roberts was seeking to advance his religious views."[699]

As you can see, for decades, courts across the country slowly whittled away at the free exercise of faith in our schools. Ironically, even in *Schempp*—Murray O'Hair's case that ended prayer in schools—the court admonished against expelling religion altogether in a way that would establish a so-called "religion of secularism." Citing the 1952 case, *Zorach v. Clauson*, the majority in *Schempp* went on to issue a very important admonition: "We agree, of course, that the State may not establish a 'religion of secularism' in the sense of affirmatively opposing or showing hostility to religion, thus preferring those who believe in no religion over those who do believe."[700] Regrettably, the court's warning against a "religion of secularism" was unheeded, for that is exactly what has developed in America's schools and society more broadly.

Yet, just a cursory look at history and tradition shows that the Founding Fathers intended the exact opposite. In the case *Elk Grove Unified School District v. Newdow*, a parent argued that children in the classroom hearing—even if not reciting—"under God" in the Pledge of Allegiance violated the First Amendment's Establishment Clause.[701] Amazingly, the notoriously liberal Ninth Circuit agreed that the words "under God" violated the Constitution, though the court later backtracked on this decision.[702] When the initial ruling of the Ninth Circuit reached the Supreme Court, the parent who brought the suit lost on a technicality, meaning that justices did not have to answer the substantive question at hand. Four justices, however, penned concurrences arguing that reciting the pledge in school did not violate the Constitution.[703]

In his concurrence, Justice William Rehnquist wrote, "The phrase 'under God' in the pledge seems, as a historical matter, to sum up the attitude of the Nation's leaders, and to manifest itself in many of our public observances."[704] Rehnquist then proceeds to outline the place of God in America's history. On April 30, 1789, at the first inauguration of President George Washington, Washington placed his hand on the Bible and turned to Psalm 121:1, which reads, "I raise my eyes toward the hills. Whence shall my help come."[705] Washington then recited the Presidential Oath of Office, ending with the words, "So help me God"—words still used to the this day at the presidential inauguration.[706] During the first Thanksgiving Proclamation, Washington referenced the "favors of Almighty God," "obey[ing] His will," and being "grateful for his benefits, and humbly to implore his protection and favor…."[707] As Rehnquist remarked, "Almost all succeeding Presidents have issued similar Thanksgiving proclamations."[708]

During what is perhaps the most famous presidential address ever given, the Gettysburg Address of 1863, President Abraham Lincoln vowed, "[W]e here highly resolve that these dead shall not have died in vain—that this nation, under God, shall have a new birth of freedom...."[709] Lincoln, likewise, invoked God during his second inaugural address on March 4, 1865, saying, "[w]ith malice toward none, with charity for all, with firmness in the right as God gives us to see the right...."[710] Rehnquist goes on to note that when President Woodrow Wilson declared war against Germany in 1917, he mentioned "God helping" America; when President Franklin Delano Roosevelt took office during the Great Depression, he "humbly ask[ed for] the blessing of God"; and, on D-Day, General Dwight D. Eisenhower told the Allied Forces, "Good Luck! And let us all beseech the blessings of Almighty God upon this great and noble undertaking."[711] Moreover, during the treacherous Civil War, "In God We Trust" was added to the US currency.[712] In 1956, Congress officially made "In God We Trust" our country's motto.[713] And our National Anthem, "The Star-Spangled Banner," has "In God is our trust" in the final verse.[714]

Taken together, Rehnquist writes this in response to the challenge of "under God" in our pledge, "The Constitution only requires that schoolchildren be entitled to abstain from the ceremony if they chose to do so. To give the parents of such a child a sort of 'heckler's veto' over a patriotic ceremony willingly participated in by other students, simply because the Pledge of Allegiance contains the descriptive phrase 'under God,' is an unwarranted extension of the Establishment Clause, an extension which would have the unfortunate effect of prohibiting commendable patriotic observance."[715]

I venture to say that our Founding Fathers would have agreed. In his book, William Murray explores the views of various thought leaders surrounding the founding of our country. John Locke—perhaps the greatest influence on our Founding Fathers and the Declaration of Independence—argued for the separation of church and state while also saying this of education in a letter to a friend:

"With the reading of history I think the study of morality should be joined. I mean not the ethics of the Schools fitted to dispute, but...Aristotle, and above all the New Testament [which] teaches wherein a man may learn how to live...."[716]

The term "separation of church and state"—while found nowhere in our founding documents—was used by Thomas Jefferson in this manner: the "legislature should 'make no law respecting the establishment of religion, or prohibiting the free exercise thereof,' thus building a wall of separation between church and state."[717] Murray makes an important and often ignored note— that Jefferson made his famous "separation of church and state" reference, ascribing it specifically to the legislature, not public schools.[718] Setting this statement aside, Jefferson made ample references to morality and virtue, writing this in a letter: "The defect of these virtues can never be made up by all the other acquirements of body and mind."[719] In other words, Jefferson understood and had high regard for morality. As Murray writes, "Jefferson's aim was not separation of church and state but the fullest possible freedom of belief and opinion."[720]

While the prohibition of a national religion is quite clear in the "Establishment Clause," our forefathers never sought to exile religion from school entirely. But that is exactly what has happened, and grave consequences have followed. William Murray noted, "July 17, 1963 was the first day Baltimore's children could not pray in schools. Before that date, there had never been a murder in a Baltimore school. The nurses gave out aspirins and teachers taught English, math, history and the sciences. Thirty years later, there is a Baltimore schools police force to deal with violence and drugs in schools. The nurses give out condoms and implant birth-control devices that allow teen-age girls to have unprotected sex."[721]

Those were Murray's words in 1993, thirty years after prayer was taken out of our schools. Now, almost sixty years later, where are we? Teachers are convincing middle school students, without parental notice, that they may be a different gender. Kindergarteners are learning about sexuality and body parts. Toxic social media, suicide, and fentanyl overdoses plague our nation's young people. Alongside the removal of God from education has come a series of ills that have tormented a generation. Nevertheless, the tide very well may be turning.

ON A FALL Friday evening in Bremerton, Washington, you could find Coach Joseph Kennedy kneeling in silent prayer on the 50-yard line of Bremerton High School's football field. The jovial, gray-haired former Marine-turned-football coach would briefly kneel alone for about thirty seconds and give "thanks through prayer" for "what the players had accomplished and for the opportunity to be a part of their lives through the game of football."[722] Over time, players from Bremerton and, eventually players from the opposing team, took notice of Coach Kennedy and voluntarily joined him in prayer at the 50-yard line.

As the majority opinion in *Kennedy v. Bremerton* points out, no one complained about Kennedy's kneeling for seven years, and the school only became aware of the coach's prayer "after an employee from another school commented positively on the school's practices to Bremerton's principal."[723] Soon after, Bremerton School District began their quest to stop Coach Kennedy from praying. In an effort to comply with the district, Coach Kennedy made several accommodations, for example, agreeing to pray once the players had departed the field. But the district insisted that Coach Kennedy display no "overt action...appea[ring] to a reasonable observer to endorse...prayer...."[724] Nevertheless, Coach Kennedy kept his vow to God, knelt silently at the 50-yard line, and lost his job because of it. As the Supreme Court would eventually note, "The District disciplined him *only* for his decision to persist in praying quietly without his players after three games in October 2015."[725]

For six years, Coach Kennedy waged a legal effort to protect his First Amendment right to pray silently. In fact, I wrote about Coach Kennedy's legal battle in 2017 when I published my first book.[726] First Liberty, the foremost legal organization representing men and women of faith in religious liberty cases, fought alongside Coach Kennedy, incurring several defeats along the way, but on Monday, June 27, 2022, everything changed when the Supreme Court of the United States ruled against Bremerton School District and for Coach Joseph Kennedy.[727]

Citing a 1969 opinion of the court, Justice Neil Gorsuch wrote, "[T]he First Amendment's protections extend to 'teachers and students,' neither of whom 'shed their constitutional rights to freedom of speech or expression at the schoolhouse gate.'"[728] As Gorsuch observed, "The Establishment Clause does not include anything like a 'modified heckler's veto, in which religious activity can be proscribed' based on 'perceptions' or 'discomfort.'"[729]

In the end, such a broad reading of the Establishment Clause would mean that "the only acceptable government role models for students are those who eschew any visible religious expression."[730] Based on Bremerton School District's understanding of the First Amendment, Gorsuch observed that "a school could fire a Muslim teacher for wearing a headscarf in the classroom or prohibit a Christian aide from praying quietly over her lunch in the cafeteria."[731] Both untenable outcomes totally antithetical to the free exercise of religion.

"Such a rule would be a sure sign that our Establishment Clause jurisprudence had gone off the rails," Gorsuch wrote. "In the name of protecting religious liberty, the District would have us suppress it. Rather than respect the First Amendment's double protection for religious expression [in the Free Exercise Clause and

Free Speech Clause], it would have us prefer secular activity.... We are aware of no historically sound understanding of the Establishment Clause that begins to 'mak[e] it necessary for government to be hostile to religion' in this way."[732]

And yet, for nearly sixty years—since the banishment of prayer from schools—isn't that exactly what the court has done? Teacher-led prayer was eliminated from schools. Bibles banished from desks. A sixty-second moment of silence struck down. Equal time for creationism in the curriculum barred. For more than half a century, the court had indeed succeeded in creating the very "religion of secularism" it spoke against.

Society and media echoed it. Previewing Kennedy's impending victory, *Sports Illustrated* dubbed the win "[a] win for Kennedy and an erosion of a bedrock of American democracy.... The expected result is a win for the coach—and the further erosion of the separation between church and state."[733] Here, protection of religious freedom is stunningly described as "an erosion of a bedrock of American democracy...." Wow!

Even during this fall into secularism, God made his presence known in the form of religious groups flourishing on campuses. The *Christian Science Monitor* notes that "[s]tudent ministries that started before the school prayer ban, or just after, have expanded to reach tens of thousands of public school students."[734] The Fellowship of Christian Athletes is on eight thousand campuses, and Campus Crusade for Christ (or Cru) has launched two hundred Christian clubs.[735] The Reverend Billy Graham's Youth for Christ is on 1,200 campuses; the Good News Club hosts classes at more than three thousand schools; and the prayer day "See You at the Pole" at our schools' flagpoles has anywhere from one million to two million participants.[736]

Moreover, there is good news on the legal terrain, too, as the court is slowly but surely eating away at the "religion of secularism" it created. In 1981, the court found that a public university could not exclude a Christian student group from using its facility based on the fact that it was a religious group.[737] Three years later, Congress passed the Equal Access Act, withholding federal funding from public schools that infringed on the rights of such groups to meet.[738] In the 1990s and 2000s, the court continually upheld the rights of religious student groups and publications to operate on equal footing with other secular groups.[739]

And in addition to *Kennedy v. Bremerton*, the court also decided *Carson v. Makin*, where the court found that Maine's tuition aid program could not bar parents from using the state's assistance to attend a religious school when a Maine public school was not available in the area.[740] This school choice victory is perhaps the greatest religious freedom victory of them all.

As the mom of a three-year-old daughter, I have been genuinely fearful for my daughter's education prospects. If schools—both private and public—are teaching children about body parts, sexuality, and gender ideology now, what will they be teaching when my daughter enters elementary school, middle school, and then high school? It's why I say often that the answer is not the public school or the private school, but rather the parochial—or religiously affiliated—school.

I feel incredibly blessed to have attended an all-girls Catholic middle school and high school. I learned the values of Christianity, the importance of morality, and how to be a good, prospering member of society. Although, in today's world, I have heard from far too many parents that even the parochial schools must be kept in check.

For my family, I will be carrying on the practice that my father started when I was a young girl. Every night, we would sit around the table, say a prayer, and begin our family dinner. I distinctly remember my dad asking each night what I learned at school. I would recount for him the various lessons from history or religion class that I had been taught. It was a way not only of instilling the importance of education, but also checking in on my school's curriculum—a wise move for any twenty-first century parent!

In the end, our children are our nest egg, the future of our country, and the guardrails for her protection. As President Ronald Reagan reminded us, "Freedom is never more than one generation away from extinction. We didn't pass it to our children in the bloodstream. It must be fought for, protected, and handed on for them to do the same, or one day we will spend our sunset years telling our children and our children's children what it was once like in the United States where men were free."[741] Embedded in freedom is the sacrosanct principle of religious freedom, and as President George Washington wisely admonished, "...reason and experience both forbid us to expect that national morality can prevail in exclusion of religious principle."[742] Indeed, with the eradication of God from schools came the exponential increase in the maladies that plague our nation's children.

But I believe that there is a great awakening happening in this country. Men and women of faith are showing up in great numbers—at school board meetings, at the ballot box—and our voices are propelling consequential victories. We saw it in Virginia in the election of Glenn Youngkin. We saw it in Florida in a tidal wave of conservative school board members. And now we are seeing it at the court, where Constitution-abiding justices have finally taken the bench and issued opinions in keeping with the undeniable faith tradition that underpins this country. While there is a spiritual battle going on within our nation's schools, rest assured that God is at work.

LIBERTY

CHAPTER 9

RELIGIOUS LIBERTY RESTORED

I sat behind the dark brown wooden desk and beneath the glimmering gold chandelier, flipping through the pages of my perfectly tabbed binder in preparation for the press briefing. On that Friday in May, an afternoon flight back to Florida awaited me, but before that, I would conduct a White House press briefing in the James S. Brady Press Briefing Room. As was typically the case, my day began early. Preparation—in my view—was the key to success, and this meant reviewing every conceivable news story, topic, or item that could possibly come up during my freewheeling question-and-answer sessions with the press.

After a full day of preparation, I felt ready for the variety of questions, mainly pertaining to the COVID-19 pandemic, that would come my way in the afternoon briefing—that is, until I received a call to come to the Oval Office. Surrounded by staff as the briefing time approached, I looked at my team and said something to the effect of, "Alright, I will be right back." I exited the back door of my office, took a right turn, and—after just a few steps—arrived in "Outer Oval," the area just outside the Oval Office where President Trump's personal staff sat.

Molly, the president's executive assistant, motioned for me to head into the Oval. I walked past the tall mahogany grandfather clock and onto the sunbeam-patterned rug from the Reagan era. I entered the world's most powerful office to find President Trump sitting at the Resolute Desk surrounded by a group of advisers. I assumed that the president had summoned me to ask my advice on a matter or to inquire about a story he had seen in the media, but instead, I learned that the administration would be announcing a new policy in labeling houses of worship as "essential." I was certainly heartened by the news. With an "essential" designation, this meant that theoretically churches, mosques, and synagogues would be able to open their doors after being shuttered amid nationwide lockdowns.

At the same time, I began to process what this meant from a functional standpoint as press secretary. My team and I had engaged in rigorous preparation for the afternoon briefing, which was now moments away. A policy change meant that I needed to be prepared for an entirely new line of questions. In an ideal world, this would mean studying the policy in great detail and dialoguing with various agencies—in this case, the Centers for Disease Control (CDC) and Health and Human Services (HHS). I would want to put in calls to CDC director Robert Redfield and HHS secretary Alex Azar among others.

Additionally, I would want to explore the ramifications of such a policy. For example, under what federal power was the president acting, and how might it interact or converge with the power of states? This would certainly be a question in the briefing room along with many others that I would need to anticipate and prepare for. This was quite a Friday afternoon surprise, but I was confident I could handle it. I just needed a little time, and without a doubt, a delay to the scheduled briefing time.

I walked back into my office and found my team still scattered around the room, ready to head out to the briefing. "The entire briefing just changed," I said to them, my voice taking on a tone of urgency. "We're announcing a new policy, right here in my hand. I haven't even read it yet!" My staff stared at me blankly, in disbelief of the sudden change, as I began to parse through the policy document, making highlights and markings along the way.

Before long, I was on my way to the briefing room, ready—as much as one could be—for the White House briefing and the unexpected topic change.

"Here we go," I thought.

President Trump walked out to the sound of clicking cameras, Dr. Birx and I filing into the room behind him. Dr. Birx took her seat off to the side, wearing a purple dress and one of her signature scarves. I sat beside her, still reviewing the guidelines in my lap—my prepared binder now virtually useless.

"At my direction, the Centers for Disease Control and Prevention is issuing guidance for communities of faith," President Trump announced. "Today, I'm identifying houses of worship—churches, synagogue [*sic*], and mosques—as essential places that provide essential services. Some governors have deemed liquor stores and abortion clinics as essential but have left out churches and other houses of worship. It's not right. So I'm correcting this injustice.... I call upon governors to allow our churches and places of worship to open right now. If there's any question, they're going to have to call me, but they're not going to be successful in that call."[743]

President Trump went on to urge governors to open places of worship immediately. "If they don't do it, I will override the governors," he vowed, raising that federal-state power issue that I had anticipated. "In America, we need more prayer, not less. Thank you very much. Thank you."[744]

With that, President Trump exited the room, and I introduced Dr. Birx to present some slides providing an update on COVID-19. After her presentation, Dr. Birx fielded a few questions with me finally intervening, "One more for Dr. Birx."

"Can I do a follow-up for Dr. Birx?" a reporter asked following her answer.

"You can do a follow-up with me," I stated, taking the podium in a light-yellow linen jacket, holding a rather thick binder prepared with everything but the very topic we were discussing. After my opening remarks, the White House correspondents asked nearly a dozen questions about churches potentially defying governors who were unwilling to following the president's new guidance. Would President Trump encourage that defiance?

"You're posing a hypothetical…." I said in response to one of the dozens of questions. "You're assuming that governors are going to keep churches shut down, and keep mosques shut down, and keep synagogues shut down. That is a hypothetical question, and we will leave it to those faith communities to reopen."[745]

Rather than hearing my answer, reporters chose to re-ask the same question in a variety of different ways. What a difference from the Biden days when reporters just accepted Psaki labeling Hunter Biden's laptop as "Russian disinformation" (it was not).[746] Or when they accepted her successor Karine Jean-Pierre's re-direction. "I refer you to his son's [Hunter's] representatives," Jean-Pierre said, answering a question about a voicemail left—not by Hunter—but by President Joe Biden prior to taking office.[747]

In the case of house of worship reopenings, reporters continued to ask the same question over and over. In response to one of the many iterations of the same question, I replied, "I am thankful that we have a president that celebrates the First Amendment. The same amendment that gives you all the ability to ask me questions is there to have the freedom of worship so imams and pastors can go to their churches, can go to their places of worship, and can celebrate what is a First Amendment right in this country, which is to pray to your God and to practice your faith."[748]

As it turns out, in the wake of President Trump's announcement that houses of worship were "essential," at least one blue state governor did reverse course. Just days before this briefing, on Wednesday, Minnesota churches had sent a letter to Minnesota governor Tim Walz saying that they would reopen their doors in defiance of the governor. On Friday, President Trump declared churches as "essential." And, as the *Wall Street Journal* editorial board notes, "By Saturday all parties agreed to an accommodation allowing churches to hold in-person services starting this Wednesday, provided they follow health guidelines such as limiting services to 25% capacity."[749]

"What changed Mr. Walz's mind? No doubt he recognized the bad politics of trying to enforce an arbitrary law against people going to church," the editorial board continued. "Mr. Walz probably recognized that a court would rule that he too was violating the First Amendment's religious-liberty protections."[750]

But, while Mr. Walz may have "seen the light," as the editorial board described it, many governors did not.[751] Indeed, the once-in-a-generation COVID-19 pandemic exposed the despotic, anti-freedom predilections of blue state governors across the nation. It also exposed a level of hostility toward religion completely at odds with the Constitution of the United States.

IN NOVEMBER OF 2020, Supreme Court justice Samuel Alito gave the keynote speech to the Federalist Society, the nation's preeminent conservative legal organization. It was nearly a year into the COVID-19 pandemic, and the world had changed in remarkable ways. Masks, social distancing, and lockdowns were now part of everyday life, and so, too, was religious suppression. "The pandemic has resulted in previously unimaginable restrictions on individual liberty," Alito told the Federalist Society. "[I]t is an indisputable statement of fact, we have never before seen restrictions as severe, extensive and prolonged as those experienced for most of 2020.... The COVID crisis has served as a sort of constitutional stress test. And in doing so, it has highlighted disturbing trends that were already present before the virus struck."[752]

Indeed, Justice Alito is correct to point out that COVID-19 highlighted and, in many ways, exacerbated an already existing pattern of religious liberty coming under attack. Kelly Shackelford, the president and CEO of First Liberty, has worked on religious freedom cases for decades and noted the trend: "We have had *14* cases at the Supreme Court of the United States in only *nine* years defending our 'first freedom.' Put in the context of legal history, the numbers are truly shocking. For the first 110 years of the American republic, the U.S. Supreme Court decided only *three* questions concerning religious liberty."[753]

COVID-19 threw accelerant on this fire; fortunately, though, the nomination and confirmation of Justice Amy Coney Barrett reversed the overtly hostile assault on the First Amendment freedom of religion. But prior to the victories came two major blows to religious freedom.

Just one week after President Trump deemed places of worship "essential," the Supreme Court issued a 5–4 ruling upholding California governor Gavin Newsom's restrictions on places of worship. His decree limited places of worship to 25 percent capacity or one hundred attendees, whichever was smaller. As Justice Brett Kavanaugh wrote in dissent, "The basic constitutional problem is that comparable secular businesses are not subject to a 25% occupancy cap, including factories, offices, supermarkets, restaurants, retail stores, pharmacies, shopping malls, pet grooming shops, bookstores, florists, hair salons, and cannabis dispensaries."[754]

Limit the churches. Open the cannabis dispensaries. Surely what our Founding Fathers intended!

Then, less than a month later, came the Nevada decision, which was perhaps even more shocking. In Nevada, while churches were limited to fifty people, casinos and other secular businesses were allowed to operate at 50 percent capacity, meaning that for some casinos, thousands were permitted to congregate. Calvary Chapel Dayton Valley challenged Nevada's regulation, hoping to host ninety people for church services, representing 50 percent of its capacity. Calvary took varying health measures "equal to or more extensive than those recommended by the CDC," in the words of experts.[755] But the court, nevertheless, allowed the disparate treatment to stand.

Alito's dissent puts the point quite bluntly: "The Constitution guarantees the free exercise of religion. It says nothing about the freedom to play craps or blackjack, to feed tokens into a slot machine, or to engage in any other game of chance. But the Governor of Nevada apparently has different priorities."[756] Gorsuch, also writing in dissent, noted the state of Nevada's distortion of the Constitution: "In Nevada, it seems, it is better to be in entertainment than religion. Maybe that is nothing new. But the First Amendment prohibits such obvious discrimination against the exercise of religion. The world we inhabit today, with a pandemic upon us, poses unusual challenges. But there is no world in which the Constitution permits Nevada to favor Caesars Palace over Calvary Chapel."[757]

Alito went on to highlight an additional disparity. When Black Lives Matter protests erupted across the nation, including in the state of Nevada, Nevada's governor, Steve Sisolak, "not only declined to enforce the directive but publicly supported and participated in a protest."[758] Explaining his support for the protest, Governor Sisolak said, "I think these are peaceful folks who are just speaking their mind.... This is important to them. It's encouraging to see the young generation participating so I'm thrilled to come and say hi to them."[759] When the attorney general of Nevada was asked about treating protests and churches differently, he replied, "You can't spit…in the face of law and expect law not to respond."[760]

That is, unless you're a Black Lives Matter protester.

From the outset of COVID-19, in states across the nation, churches were treated with irrationality and disdain. New York City mayor Bill de Blasio, for example, stated his hostility outright in March of 2020: "The NYPD, fire department, buildings department—everyone has been instructed that if they see worship services going on, they will go to the officials of that congregation, they'll inform them they need to stop the services and disperse. If that does not happen, they will take additional action up to the point of fines and potentially closing the building permanently," he said.[761] A "permanent" ban the mayor threatened, as if this would ever be permitted under the Free Exercise Clause of the Constitution.

Leading into Easter of 2020, churches sought to find innovative ways to allow parishioners to gather during what was a very dark and scary time for our country. Some Democrat governors and mayors, of course, would not have it.

Three days before Easter 2020, Louisville mayor Greg Fischer instructed Christian congregations not to hold church services on Easter Sunday, barring even drive-in worship services, where attendees would sit alone in their cars.[762] Fischer even went so far as to inform Louisville that the Metro Police Department would be attending services and collecting license plate numbers to be transmitted to the health department.[763] In contrast to the mayor, Kentucky attorney general Daniel Cameron said that "[a]s long as Kentuckians are permitted to drive through liquor stores, restaurants, and other businesses during the COVID-19 pandemic, the law requires that they must also be allowed to participate in drive-in church services, consistent with existing policies to stop the spread of COVID-19."[764]

A church called On Fire Christian Center sought to hold a drive-in service and filed a lawsuit just days before Easter Sunday. Fortunately, a federal district court sided with On Fire, issuing a temporary restraining order against the mayor's order just one day before Easter. Judge Justin Walker wrote, "On Holy Thursday, an American mayor criminalized the communal celebration of Easter. That sentence is one that this Court never expected to see outside the pages of a dystopian novel, or perhaps the pages of *The Onion*.... The Mayor's decision is stunning. And it is, 'beyond all reason,' unconstitutional."[765]

In Greenville, Mississippi, the mayor tried to take the same sad, shocking approach. Despite the fact that the governor of Mississippi, Tate Reeves, labeled houses of worship as "essential," thus meaning that they could operate in accordance with CDC guidelines, the mayor of Greenville, Errick Simmons, issued an "Executive Order Regarding Church Services."[766] This order barred church services, including drive-in services.

When a local church, Temple Baptist Church, held a drive-in service on April 8, 2020, broadcasting its service over low-power FM radio, eight police officers were sent to the service.[767] The officers, as detailed in a lawsuit filed by Temple Baptist Church, "began knocking on car windows, demanding driver's licenses, and writing citations with $500 fines."[768] Just over a week later, after receiving "clarification" from the governor, Mayor Simmons backed down from his plainly unconstitutional order.

As spring turned to fall, and America began to adjust to life with COVID-19, churches continued to experience unjust discrimination. Alito had noted in his *Calvary Chapel Dayton Valley* dissent in July of 2020, "The problem is no longer one of exigency, but one of considered yet discriminatory treatment of places of worship."[769] Fortunately, along with the continued discrimination, came a series of victories for places of worship.

In Washington, DC, Mayor Muriel Bowser put in place Mayor's Order 2020-053 in March of 2020, ceasing all "large gatherings" of ten or more whether indoor or in a closed-in outdoor area.[770] When DC began its phased reopening plan, though the large gathering ban remained in effect, certain places of business were allowed to operate freely under phase one—barbershops, hair salons, outdoor eateries, farmers' markets among them.[771] But houses of worship remained subject to the ban on ten or more congregants or faced "civil and administrative penalties authorized by law...."[772]

Discrimination against places of worship continued as the phased reopening proceeded with secular establishments given more liberalized treatment. In phase two, for example, the mayor "prohibit[ed] gatherings of over 100 people for purposes of worship, even if held outdoors and even if worshippers wear masks and practice appropriate social distancing."[773] Meanwhile, there were no limits on outdoor dining. The mayor's guidance even explicitly singled out religious venues, saying that "[p]laces of worship are encouraged to continue providing virtual services as everyone is safer at home."[774]

Mass protests for Black Lives Matter once again evaded large gathering restrictions. In fact, according to a complaint filed against the mayor, "on June 6, 2020, Mayor Bowser appeared personally at an outdoor gathering of tens of thousands of people at the corner of 16th and H Streets, NW and delivered a speech describing the large gathering as 'wonderful to see.'

"Similarly, on four occasions between June and August 2020, the District's Metropolitan Police Department closed city streets to accommodate protests and marches of thousands to tens of thousands of people."[775] And as the district court opinion in the case against the mayor stated, Mayor Bowser went on to praise these citywide protests. "Indeed, Mayor Bowser christened 'Black Lives Matter Plaza' when 'she directed the D.C. Department of Public Works to create a mural on 16 Street N.W., near the White House, to 'honor the peaceful protesters from June 1, 2020 and send a message that District streets are a safe space for peaceful protestors.'"[776]

Four days after Mayor Bowser's appearance at a rally addressing a "record crowd," Capitol Hill Baptist Church (CHBC) officially requested a waiver from the outdoor gathering prohibition.[777] CHBC has a long history of worship gatherings, dating all the way back to 1878, meeting every single Sunday except for a short three-week-long break when the Spanish flu was raging in 1918.[778] After submitting the request in June, the church resubmitted the waiver request in September before receiving notification from the mayor's office that the application had been rejected.[779]

Capitol Hill Baptist Church filed a lawsuit against the mayor with the complaint stating, in part: "The First Amendment protects both mass protests and religious worship. But Mayor Bowser, by her own admission, has preferred the former over the latter. When asked why she celebrates mass protests while houses of worship remain closed, she responded that 'First Amendment protests and large gatherings are not the same' because 'in the United States of America, people can protest.' In the United States of America, people can gather for worship under the First Amendment as well."[780] Acknowledging the clear disparity between the treatment of houses of worship and mass protest, the United States District Court for the District of Columbia enjoined Mayor Bowser's restrictions on outdoor worship, finding that "the District's actions impose[d] a substantial burden on its [CHBC's] exercise of religion."[781]

Later in the fall, in November of 2020, the Supreme Court, which had initially allowed onerous and discriminatory bans on religious worship to stand in Nevada and California, ruled against the state of New York and then-Governor Andrew Cuomo in his restrictions on places of worship. In *Roman Catholic Diocese of Brooklyn, New York v. Andrew M. Cuomo, Governor of New York*, the Supreme Court joined together two emergency applications for relief from the governor's restrictions—one from the Roman Catholic Diocese of Brooklyn and another from Agudath Israel of America.

For several months, both entities "complied with all public health guidance" and "operated at 25% or 33% capacity…without a single outbreak."[782] Nevertheless, the governor's rules "single[d] out houses of worship for especially harsh treatment."[783] For example, the governor color-coded areas of the state based on the level of COVID-19 in the area. In a red zone, while churches or synagogues were subject to a ten-person limit, "essential" businesses—like "acupuncture facilities, camp grounds, garages," among others—had no capacity limits whatsoever.[784]

In addition to discrimination against worship generally vis-à-vis other entities, Agudath Israel of America argued that Governor Cuomo had engaged in targeted discrimination against the Jewish community. A per curiam opinion issued by the Supreme Court (an opinion written in the name of the court rather than in the name of a specific justice) referenced this discrimination: "Citing a variety of remarks made by the Governor, Agudath Israel argues that the Governor specifically targeted the Orthodox Jewish community and gerrymandered the boundaries of red and orange zones to ensure that heavily Orthodox areas were included."[785]

Unlike the Supreme Court's opinions in Nevada and California, this time, the Supreme Court sided with places of worship and issued an injunction against Governor Cuomo's orders. "[E]ven in a pandemic, the Constitution cannot be put away and forgotten," the court noted. "The restrictions at issue here, by effectively barring many from attending religious services, strike at the very heart of the First Amendment's guarantee of religious liberty."[786] In his concurrence, Justice Gorsuch called New York's restrictions "just the latest example" of "treating religious exercises worse than comparable secular activities."[787]

Justice Gorsuch went on to make this powerful statement: "[I]t turns out the businesses the Governor considers essential include hardware stores, acupuncturists, and liquor stores. Bicycle repair shops, certain signage companies, accountants, lawyers, and insurance agents are all essential too. So, at least according to the Governor, it may be unsafe to go to church, but it is always fine to pick up another bottle of wine, shop for a new bike, or spend the afternoon exploring your distal points and meridians. Who knew public health would so perfectly align with secular convenience?"[788]

Think about how powerful that question really is: "Who knew public health would so perfectly align with secular convenience?"[789] Is that not the story of COVID-19? While health restrictions were obviously necessary, why were they used so differently when applied to places of worship—even drive-in services—than when applied to restaurants, liquor stores, and casinos? The answer certainly does not lie in science.

Indeed, the prevalence of these disparities is notable. "Nor is the problem an isolated one," Gorsuch wrote. "In recent months, certain other Governors have issued similar edicts. At the flick of a pen, they have asserted the right to privilege restaurants, marijuana dispensaries, and casinos over churches, mosques, and temples."[790]

This opinion striking down Governor Cuomo's disparate treatment was issued in November of 2020—nearly a year after the pandemic began. Making note of this, Gorsuch wrote, "Now, as we round out 2020 and face the prospect of entering a second calendar year living in the pandemic's shadow, the rationale has expired according to its own terms. Even if the Constitution has taken a holiday during this pandemic, it cannot become a sabbatical."[791]

In California, however, it appeared that the Constitution had indeed taken a "sabbatical" rather than a "holiday" lasting into the year 2021. As you'll recall, in May of 2020, the Supreme Court, in a 5–4 decision, upheld California's restrictions on in-person worship.[792] By November of 2020, Becket Law noted that "California stood alone in its absolute prohibition on indoor religious worship. Every other state permitted some form of indoor worship, with most states imposing no restrictions at all."[793]

Following the Cuomo decision in New York, South Bay United Pentecostal Church and Harvest Rock—two California churches—applied for injunctive relief against the state of California's regulations. This time, the challenge against California's restrictions turned out differently, with the court striking down the ban on indoor worship in a 6–3 vote, while upholding other restrictions like the ban on singing indoors.[794]

In a statement written by Justice Gorsuch and joined by Justices Thomas and Alito, Gorsuch wrote, "Since the arrival of COVID–19, California has openly imposed more stringent regulations on religious institutions than on many businesses. The State's spreadsheet summarizing its pandemic rules even assigns places of worship their own row."[795] With regard to the singing ban, Gorsuch acknowledged the potential efficacy and reasonableness of such a regulation but notes that, when examined closely, it appears that "California's powerful entertainment industry has won an exemption."[796]

Gorsuch went on to point out the moving goal posts for rules on places of worship. "No doubt, California will argue on remand, as it has before, that its prohibitions are merely temporary because vaccinations are underway," Gorsuch wrote. "But the State's 'temporary' ban on indoor worship has been in place since August 2020, and applied routinely since March. California no longer asks its movie studios, malls, and manicurists to wait. And one could be forgiven for doubting its asserted timeline."[797]

The Supreme Court again struck down California's onerous bans on worship in April of 2021, this time pertaining to private worship within the home. At the time, COVID-19 regulations in the state of California meant that indoor prayer gatherings in private homes must be limited to three households.[798] Stop and think about that—the government mandating the number of people who can gather in a private home for silent prayer. What extraordinary government overreach! In *Tandon v. Newsom*, the court struck down these regulations, which allowed "hair salons, retail stores, personal care services, movie theaters, private suites at sporting events and concerts, and indoor restaurants to bring together more than three households at a time."[799]

In fact, California governor Gavin Newsom himself enjoyed a dining experience with several friends. As was widely reported, Governor Newsom was photographed violating his own COVID restrictions during a dinner outing at the lavish restaurant, French Laundry, in November of 2020—masks and social distancing nowhere to be found.[800] But indoor prayer gatherings be limited!

The Supreme Court, however, righted the wrong and even issued an admonishment of sorts to the state of California. "This is the fifth time the Court has summarily rejected the Ninth Circuit's analysis of California's COVID restrictions on religious exercise," the court wrote in per curiam. "It is unsurprising that such litigants are entitled to relief."[801]

Unsurprising indeed.

IN HIS ADDRESS to the Federalist Society in the fall of 2020, Justice Alito noted that the pandemic-related restrictions tended to rely on one source of authority when challenged in court— *Jacobson v. Massachusetts*.[802] *Jacobson*, a Supreme Court decision dating back to 1905, upheld a smallpox vaccine requirement in Cambridge, Massachusetts. "Now, I'm all in favor of preventing dangerous things from issuing out of Cambridge and infecting the rest of the country and the world," Alito said. "It would be good if what originated in Cambridge stayed in Cambridge."[803]

I chuckled when I first heard Alito's line. His "Cambridge" reference referred to Cambridge, Massachusetts—the home of Harvard Law School. Cambridge, sometimes referred to as "The People's Republic of Cambridge," is notorious for its high population of liberal Democrats. As a graduate of Harvard Law School, I can attest that the name is well suited, and I endorse the notion of what originates in Cambridge remaining there. That would include *Jacobson v. Massachusetts*, which was twisted and contorted to substantiate and justify all sorts of COVID mandates. As Alito noted, a Cambridge restriction intended to solve a "problem of limited scope" was not meant to uphold "sweeping" and radical nationwide change "for extended periods" giving executives "unlimited…discretion."[804]

Thankfully, the Supreme Court managed to slam the brake on the COVID-related attacks on religious freedom. The court evolved from upholding these restrictions in California and Nevada in the summer of 2020 to rejecting them in New York and then California in the fall of 2020 and spring of 2021. The change in the court's jurisprudence came with the prolonging of the COVID-19 pandemic but also with a change in the makeup of the court in the addition of Justice Amy Coney Barrett.

On September 26, 2020, I sat in the Rose Garden, four rows back from President Trump as he announced the consequential, history-changing nomination of Amy Coney Barrett to the Supreme Court. She would be replacing liberal jurist Justice Ruth Bader Ginsburg, and in doing so, shifting the ideological balance of the court. Surrounded by her husband and seven children, Barrett accepted the nomination, sailed through the confirmation process, and took her place on the court, restoring religious freedom to millions across the nation.

As you can imagine, the liberal media was not happy.

Taking aim at religious freedom in the COVID-era, Reuters seemed to lament the restoration of religious freedom, writing that "though the temporary local, state and federal policies put in place to fight the COVID-19 pandemic may be expiring, they have left an indelible mark on the legal landscape, particularly in the area of religious liberty, legal experts say.... Litigation over COVID, however, has proved to be an accelerant, thanks to the court's so-called shadow docket, giving it multiple occasions to decide religious freedom issues on emergency motions and provide little reasoning."[805]

Headlines across the media reflected the sentiment.

"How the Supreme Court is dismantling the separation of church and state," read a CNN headline, authored by a "legal analyst and Supreme Court biographer."[806]

"The Supreme Court is leading a Christian conservative revolution," *Vox* pronounced.[807]

"'No Victory for Religious Liberty': In Ruling For Praying Football coach, the Supreme Court smashes what's left of separation between church and state," read *Vanity Fair* in the wake of Coach Kennedy's victory.[808]

Summing up the 2022 Supreme Court decisions, the Washington bureau chief of *The Guardian*, David Smith, wrote an article entitled, "Alarm as US supreme court takes a hatchet to church-state separation."[809] In the article, the bureau chief endeavored to place blame for the court's rulings because, of course, the rule of law prevailing could not be the answer.

"White Christians represented 54% of the population when Barack Obama first ran for president in 2008 but now make up only 45%," Smith wrote. "Former president Donald Trump's appointment of three rightwing justices, however, helped put the court on a very different track. And the nature of its rulings have been unusually radical and sweeping. Robert P Jones, founder and chief executive of the Public Religion Research Institute think tank in Washington, said: 'What we're seeing is a desperate power grab as the sun is setting on white Christian America. In the courts, instead of moving slowly and systematically, it's a lurch.'"[810]

That's right, it wasn't the Constitution at work, namely the First Amendment. It must have been—had to be—"white Christians."

Robert P. Jones—whom David Smith cited—went on to say rather apocalyptically that "we're going to be left with essentially an apartheid situation in the US where we're going to have minority rule by this shrinking group that's been able to seize the levers of power, even as their cultural democratic representation in the country shrinks."[811]

In a *New York Times* piece called "A Pro-Religion Court," which would be more aptly named "A Pro-First Amendment Court," the *Times* goes on to document the increasingly pro-First Amendment disposition of the court over time. "The Supreme Court has become the most pro-religion it's been since at least the 1950s, and it appears to include the six most pro-religion justices since at least World War II," the piece reads.[812]

The *Times* points out that "[s]ince John Roberts became chief justice in 2005, the court has ruled in favor of religious organizations in orally argued cases 83 percent of the time. That is far more than any court in the past seven decades—all of which were led by chief justices who, like Roberts, were appointed by Republican presidents."[813] And the 83 percent win rate for the First Amendment's Free Exercise Clause came before several of the recent 2022 religious freedom victories that would push that win ratio even higher.

It appears that we end where we began, with the media protesting the resurgence of religious freedom, and the Constitution restored—at least for now. Indeed, what the media laments, people of faith across the country celebrate—the freedom to worship, a value that our founders certainly held dear and a bedrock principle of America.

SOCIETY

CHAPTER 10

AN UNRECOGNIZABLE WORLD

"You are living in a world far different than the one that I grew up in." My mom says this repeatedly and often in reaction to news stories that shock the conscience, running far askew of our moral compass as Christians. Each time she made this point to me growing up, I would react with a contrarian view. Perhaps being naïvely optimistic, I would counter with the assessment that society has always been morally adrift and that we are just seeing a continuation of that. Though initially dismissive of the sentiment in young adulthood, now—as a wife, and especially as a mother—I realize that my mom was exactly right.

No matter where you look in society—television news, newspapers, social media—there is more violence and anger, less compassion and understanding. The rage is personal, cutting, direct, and shocking while bridge-building, civil conversation, and pleasant disagreement seem to be a thing of the past. To put it simply, there is more sadness and less joy. The word that often comes to mind as I peruse the news is "lost." Whether it is a video of a young child punching and cursing at a police officer, an Olympic alternate professing her desire to win a medal just so that she can burn the American flag on the podium, or the new trend of children attending drag shows, there is a general sense that we as a society are lost with no conception of right and wrong.[814]

At the heart of so many of our societal ills is the ever-present, all-consuming existence of social media. From teenage depression and increased drug use to toxic, hateful political division and cancel culture, social media platforms continue to exacerbate the problem. Selflessness and worship of the creator have been replaced with selfies and worship of created content that has no basis in truth or reality. We live in a lost society, increasingly so, and social media—among other societal ills—has amplified our world's broken compass.

SOCIAL MEDIA

MY CHILDHOOD WAS, for the most part, totally free of social media. Throughout middle school and most of high school, social media platforms simply did not exist. There was no Twitter, no Facebook, no Instagram, no TikTok. As a millennial, my childhood—unlike that of younger millennials or Generation Z—was free from the pressures of social media. I was not consumed with selfies, comparing myself to my friends' online profiles, or experimenting on photo editing software. Instead, I was focused on Friday night football games, Saturday morning debate tournaments, and in-person interaction.

Midway through high school, Myspace arrived on the scene, offering young people a chance to create a profile, post a picture, and share a little bit about their interests and hobbies. Soon after, came Facebook. My friends and I used the platform during our late high school and early college years, mostly as a means to check out who our classmates would be at our new college or to keep up with friends attending colleges in a different state.

Those days are gone. Now, a whole faux, unrealistic world has been created that young people, and especially young girls, feel they must live up to. Drug sales, crude pictures, and all kinds of maladies pervade the once-innocent platforms I used in my college years. As a mother, few topics concern me more than social media, its effect on society, and how it will shape the lives of my young children.

Though social media's toxicity is obvious to anyone taking a clear-eyed look, social media executives have continually down-played their platforms' negative effects. When questioned by Congress in March of 2021 on the effects of social media on children, Facebook CEO Mark Zuckerberg answered, in part, "Overall, the research that we have seen is that using social apps to connect with other people can have positive mental health benefits and well-being benefits by helping people feel more connected and less lonely."[815]

During a congressional hearing, Congresswoman Cathy Mc-Morris Rodgers pointed to the data: "Between 2011 and 2018, rates of depression, self-harm, suicides, and suicide attempts exploded among American teens. During that time, rates of teen depression increased by more than sixty percent, with the larger increase among young girls. Between 2009 and 2015, emergency room admissions for self-harm among 10 to 14-year-old girls tripled and suicides substantially increased. One study found that during that time, teens who used their devices for 5 or more hours a day were 66 percent more likely to have at least one suicide-related outcome compared to those who used their devices for just one."[816]

But when McMorris Rodgers questioned Zuckerberg on the connection, he insisted, "I don't think that the research is conclusive on that."[817] A few months later, Adam Mosseri, CEO of Insta-gram (which is owned by Facebook) parroted the claim, asserting the effect of Instagram on mental health was "quite small."[818]

But then came the *Wall Street Journal*'s September 2021 exposé: "Facebook Knows Instagram Is Toxic for Teen Girls,

Company Documents Show," the headline read followed by the sub-heading, "[i]ts own in-depth research shows a significant teen mental-health issue that Facebook plays down in public."[819] The *Journal* then outlines this research as depicted in a set of internal company slides.

For example, in March of 2020—one year before Zuckerberg's congressional testimony referenced above—a slide presentation created by Instagram researchers was published on Facebook's internal message board.[820] "Thirty-two percent of teen girls said that when they felt bad about their bodies, Instagram made them feel worse," one slide read.[821] "We make body image issues worse for one in three teen girls," a 2019 slide further noted.[822]

Another Instagram slide, posted by the *Journal*, details that Instagram initiated the following feelings in young people: 39 percent of US teens feel they "have to create the perfect image"; 41 percent said they were "not attractive"; 42 percent say they "don't have enough money"; 32 percent assert they "don't have enough friends"; and 24 percent feel they are "not good enough."[823] In some cases, Instagram research found that these feelings led to "clinical-level depression" and self-harm, according to Dr. Jean Twenge.[824] The *Journal* reported that "[a]mong teens who reported suicidal thoughts, 13% of British users and 6% of American users traced the desire to kill themselves to Instagram, one presentation shows."[825]

To make matters worse, Instagram algorithms appeared to curate content that exacerbated body image issues and eating disorders.[826] As detailed by the *New York Post*, Instagram researchers developed a "test user that followed dieting- and thinness-obsessed Instagram accounts."[827] Describing internal research from Instagram, the *Post* reported, "Instagram's algorithm then recommended more eating disorder-related content—including images of distressingly thin female bodies and accounts with names like 'skinandbones,' 'applecoreanorexic' and 'skinny._.binge.'"[828] Underscoring these findings, Senator Richard Blumenthal's office developed a fake thirteen-year-old female Instagram account, and according to the *Post*, "the account had been served content promoting eating disorders within one day."[829]

Confronting a Facebook executive, Blumenthal concluded, "Instagram's recommendations will still latch on to a person's insecurities—a young woman's vulnerabilities—about their bodies and drag them into dark places that glorify eating disorders and self-harm. That's what Instagram does."[830] As the *Journal* noted in its explosive report, an anonymous former company executive essentially admitted the truth about Instagram: "People use Instagram because it's a competition. That's the fun part."[831] It also happens to be the dangerous part, fueling self-image issues, self-doubt, and insecurities while prompting mental anxiety and even—at times—self-harm.

Instagram's alarming internal research should have led the company to take an honest, inward look about its role in society. Instead, though, Instagram and Facebook pursued plans to create platforms for children under the age of thirteen, who are currently barred from their platforms due to age restrictions. Despite being technically banned, however, children under thirteen often lie about their age and join Instagram and Facebook anyway.[832] According to the *Journal*, "Social media usage is common for kids under 13, research finds. In that demographic, roughly 30% use TikTok, while 22% use Snap Inc.'s Snapchat and 11% use Instagram, according to a survey last summer by investment research firm Piper Sandler."[833] The *Journal* continued in highlighting that the National Parents and Teachers Association found "social media was already nearly ubiquitous among pre-teens, with 81% of parents reporting their child began using social media between the ages of 8 and 13."[834]

Eight-year-old children using social media? That is striking to consider.

The old debate used to center around how much television to show young children; now, the new consideration appears to be whether your eight-year-old child is actively using a dangerous, toxic social media platform. And to think Instagram sought to officially sanction the practice of young use of their platform by creating an Instagram for kids!

Rare bipartisan outrage ensued surrounding the idea of Instagram for children. Attorneys general (AGs) from forty-four states and territories bound together in opposition, sending a letter to Zuckerberg expressing their opposition to his plan.[835] The press release for the National Association of Attorneys General cited a report that "found an increase of 200% in recorded instances in the use of Instagram to target and abuse children over a six-month period in 2018. In 2020 alone, Facebook and Instagram reported 20 million child sexual abuse images."[836]

The AGs went on to cite the "major concern" of cyberbullying: "A 2017 survey found that 42% of young Instagram users had experienced cyberbullying on the platform, the highest percentage of any platform measured. As children spend more time online during the COVID-19 pandemic, these issues have likely been exacerbated."[837] Amid fierce backlash, Instagram temporarily paused their plans to create an Instagram for kids with Adam Mosseri, Instagram head, saying "[w]hile we stand by the need to develop this experience, we've decided to pause this project."[838]

But the problems for teens on social media nevertheless persist, and the AGs were correct in suggesting COVID-19 exacerbated many problems for adolescents. One *Texas Tribune* headline reads: "Hospital admissions for teenage girls who may have attempted suicide have increased 50% nationwide."[839] JAMA Pediatrics published research finding that "[s]uicide-risk screenings have yielded higher positive results" during the COVID-19 pandemic, as reported by CNN.[840] CDC data further amplifies the connection between the pandemic and self-harm, finding that emergency room visits for suicide increased by more than 50 percent for young girls and 3.7 percent for boys between February and March of 2021 compared to that time in 2019.[841]

In 2021, the American Academy of Pediatrics (AAP) issued a "Declaration of a National Emergency in Child and Adolescent Mental Health."[842] While the AAP points out that COVID-19 "intensified" the crisis, the increase in adolescent suicides preceded the pandemic. "Rates of childhood mental health concerns and suicide rose steadily between 2010 and 2020 and by 2018 suicide was the second leading cause of death for youth ages 10-24," the AAP declaration noted.[843] Though the report does not cite social media as connected to the mental crisis, we do know—as observed above—that Instagram's own researchers found a link between using its platform and mental struggle.

With COVID-19 and the increase in self-harm came another alarming trend—an increase in drug overdoses, also tied to social media. CDC data published in November of 2021 showed the highest number of deaths from drug overdose ever recorded in a one-year period.[844] For the first time, the number of overdose deaths exceeded one hundred thousand.[845] This startling finding came after drug deaths fell in 2018—the first time this had occurred in three decades.[846] As Fox News reported, "Opioid-related deaths, mainly fueled by the potent drug fentanyl, accounted for about three quarters of the deaths through April, according to the CDC...."[847] Jim Crotty, a former deputy chief of staff at the Drug Enforcement Administration (DEA), described fentanyl to the *Wall Street Journal* as "the most pernicious, the most devastating drug that we have ever seen."[848]

Young people were not immune from the fatal trend with the *New York Times* pointing out that "[o]verdoses are now the leading cause of preventable death among people ages 18 to 45, ahead of suicide, traffic accidents and gun violence, according to federal data."[849] And there is a pattern to how these deaths transpire: "Law enforcement authorities say an alarming portion of them unfolded the same way…from counterfeit pills tainted with fentanyl that teenagers and young adults bought over social media."[850]

One example cited by the *Times* is the death of Zachariah Plunk, who was just seventeen years old. The "star high school football player" from Mesa, Arizona, purchased what he thought was a Percocet through Snapchat. The pill was delivered to his family home, and within the span of two hours, he was found dead. As it turns out, the pill was no ordinary Percocet, but a fentanyl-laced, deadly tablet.[851] "Zach went outside, swallowed a pill and fell to the curb," the *Times* reported.[852] When the *Times* published their exposé in May of 2022—"Fentanyl Tainted Pills Bought on Social Media Cause Youth Drug Deaths to Soar"—the Snapchat dealer who sold Zach the deadly pill was still operating on social media.[853]

Zach's death is not an aberrational one-off but an unfortunate trend. District Attorney Morgan Gire told the *Times*, "Social media is almost exclusively the way they [adolescents] get the pills. About 90 percent of the pills that you're buying from a dealer on social media now are fentanyl."[854]

Ninety percent. That is extraordinary!

The DEA has noticed the trend, publishing a chilling graphic called "Emoji Drug Code—Decoded."[855] The document has several drug names—Percocet and oxycodone, Xanax, and Adderall among them—alongside commonly used emoji combinations that young people use to purchase these drugs online. It also lists "dealer signals" like "high potency," denoted by an emoji rocket ship, bomb, and flash bang.[856] Illicit drugs like meth, heroin, cocaine, mushrooms, and marijuana are also listed. "These emojis reflect common examples found in DEA investigations," reads the disclaimer at the bottom of the document.[857] The DEA expounds, "This reference is intended to give parents, caregivers, educators, and other influencers a better sense of how emojis are being used in conjunction with illegal drugs. Fake prescription pills, commonly laced with deadly fentanyl and methamphetamine, are often sold on social media and e-commerce platforms—making them available to anyone with a smartphone."[858]

In the case of Kade Webb—a twenty-year-old who died from a fentanyl-laced Percocet in a supermarket bathroom—"the police opened his phone and went straight to his social media apps. There, they found exactly what they feared," the *Times* reported.[859] He had purchased the deadly pill on Snapchat like far too many other young people. Flowing from China, and oftentimes straight through America's lawless, open southern border, these lethal substances make their way into our children's smartphones and social media apps, offering an easy-to-purchase, deadly substance right at their fingertips.[860]

In August, the *Wall Street Journal* published a report called "How Two Mexican Drug Cartels Came to Dominate America's Fentanyl Supply."[861] The details are chilling: "At a half-built house in a barrio, a longtime Sinaloa cartel employee used a shovel to mix chemicals in a simmering oil barrel. His concoction was an illegal form of fentanyl.... [The cook] dons a hazmat suit, dark glasses and a black cloth mask. If he gets queasy, he said, he drinks milk. Jugs line the roughly 10-by-10 foot lab, including one containing a clear liquid marked 'Pure Acetone.' Others are marked 'Fentanyl XXX,' and 'Chinese Chemical.'... He said he has made as many as one million pills in a week."[862] These fentanyl pills are sometimes brightly colored, appearing like candy, designed to specifically appeal to young people.[863] Other forms of the toxic fentanyl resemble sidewalk chalk, appearing virtually identical to the chalk many, including myself, use in playing with our young children.

Frighteningly, far too many teens are totally ignorant of the dangers they face. A Morning Consult poll found that just 27 percent of teenagers were aware of fentanyl being mixed with what seem like otherwise commonly used prescription drugs like Percocet or Adderall.[864] Ranking drugs like heroin and cocaine as "extremely dangerous," a small percentage of teenagers put fentanyl in this same category with many not even knowing what fentanyl was.[865] One bad decision—like ordering an Adderall ahead of exam time—combined with ignorance to the lethality it could hold is now claiming the lives of America's youth.

Social media is offering our youth a tornado of depression, toxicity, and even lethal drugs. When you combine the advent of twenty-first century platforms and smartphones with a decline in the traditional values of faith and family, we are left with a generation that is lost, alone, and dangerously at risk of becoming victims of society's worst maladies.

POLITICAL DIVISION

SOME OF MY earliest memories in life are political in nature. I explored my early years in detail in *For Such a Time as This*, so I will recount this time period briefly here. I had a peculiar, young love for politics, dating all the way back to the 1996 presidential race between Republican presidential nominee Bob Dole and President Bill Clinton. Though I was just eight years old at the time, I remember cheering for Bob Dole on the playground and lobbying my brother to vote for Dole in the school election.

My passion for politics blossomed into a love of debate, which I pursued at my all-girls Catholic high school with some success. I managed to win state championships and even participate in nationals one summer in Philadelphia. Naturally, as a young lover of politics, the place I wanted to be for college was Washington, DC, specifically Georgetown University. With a tremendous amount of hard work, I was accepted to Georgetown University School of Foreign Service, where I interned on Capitol Hill and in the Bush White House during my time there.

I spent my junior year abroad in Oxford, England, at St. Edmund Hall, Oxford University. In *For Such a Time as This*, I wrote fondly about my time at Oxford University and my discussions with a tutor—similar to an American professor—who had a very different view than my own but made me better as a student by challenging me in a respectful and productive manner.[866] My interactions with fellow students at Oxford mirrored my relationship with my professor.

The fall of 2008 was dominated by the presidential election between then-Senator Barack Obama and Senator John McCain. Although I was more than three thousand miles away from the United States, American politics still proliferated conversation in the charming little town of Oxford, England, also known as the "city of dreaming spires" for its castle-like architectural design.[867]

Without a doubt, I found Oxford students to be liberal leaning, in fact, more so than in the United States. Generally speaking, the United Kingdom tends to skew further left politically than America, especially on social issues. In Oxford, therefore, I was a rather rare breed—a Christian, conservative, and committedly pro-life. Despite a vast political chasm between my colleagues and me, I found my interactions to be pleasant, diplomatic, and amicable.

On several occasions leading up to the 2008 presidential election, and on the evening of President Obama's election, I recall having debates with my fellow students. They picked my brain, wanting to explore my reasons for supporting the Republican Party and for thinking the way that I do. My classmates, as I remember, applauded the election of Obama and were genuinely intrigued how their American peer could think differently. Our conversations were spirited and passionate but pleasant.

In fact, it is a bit sad to say, but I think my time abroad really represented the last time when I felt totally comfortable opening up about my views and expounding on them on a college campus. By the time I got to Harvard Law School years later, the environment among students was caustic, hostile, and narrow-minded. As I wrote in detail in my first book, *The New American Revolution*, it was not the faculty but the students who had become so intolerant of alternate viewpoints that you were ostracized as a conservative, effectively relegated to silence or submission.[868]

Unfortunately, the sets of CNN were no different. During the 2016 election, I worked as a political commentator at CNN, where I expressed support for then-candidate Donald J. Trump. CNN had become known for its enormous panels—eight commentators plus one host. From an ideological standpoint, the panels were stacked heavily in one direction—typically eight liberals on one conservative since the host was a leftist too. While many of my CNN colleagues were very kind off the set, asking about family and putting politics aside, others were not. As a friendly, good-natured person, I would try to engage in conversation off camera and was not always met with the kindest of reactions.

My time at the podium as President Donald Trump's press secretary in 2020 was really no different than my time at CNN. Far too many of the reporters in the White House press corps were leftists, posing as reporters, who screamed and interrupted with biting, hostile questions, sometimes personal in nature. There was, without a doubt, a left-wing agenda among the reporters. Sure, there were some great reporters, but the self-serving ones stole the spotlight and garnered the headlines.

When I look at the trajectory of my career—from Oxford to Harvard to CNN to the White House—and the trajectory of society over the course of more than a decade, there is simply no question that hostility, toxicity, and political division have increased exponentially. Data bears that out. In the wake of President Trump's 2016 election, a Reuters/Ipsos poll found that "16 percent of respondents said they had stopped communicating with a friend or family member because of the election."[869] An American Enterprise Institute study conducted after the 2020 election made a similar finding: "15 percent of adults have ended a friendship over politics."[870]

Though that number may seem small, it astounds me that a double-digit percentage of those surveyed decided to stop associating with a friend over an election. One of my best friends, a longtime friend dating back to middle school, told me openly that she had decided to vote for Hillary Clinton. While I obviously disagreed with her politically, it in no way interrupted our friendship or changed our feelings toward one another. To this day, she is still one of my very best friends.

For far too many, that thought is intolerable. According to a Generation Lab/Axios poll, a decently sized number of college students would not be friends with someone of an opposite political party.[871] Moreover, the polling reveals that Republicans seem to be more open-minded in associating with the other party than Democrats. For example, 37 percent of Democrats would not "be friends with" a Republican, whereas 5 percent of Republicans would not be friends with a Democrat.[872]

As *The Atlantic* points out, "Until a few decades ago, most Democrats did not hate Republicans, and most Republicans did not hate Democrats. Very few Americans thought the policies of the other side were a threat to the country...."[873] Now, it appears members of opposite political parties have a hard time even being friends. Taken together, as reflected in a Pew survey, the United States is one of the most politically divided countries in the developed world.[874] It is truly a shame.

I often say to young people during speeches that some of my best career mentors were polar opposite of me politically. As I recounted in *For Such a Time as This*, when I was a college student at Georgetown seeking an internship at Fox News, the late Alan Colmes helped me pursue my dream. A friend of mine at Georgetown had invited me to watch a taping of *Hannity & Colmes*. I was able to meet the liberal co-host of the show, Alan Colmes, in the greenroom, where we talked about politics and our differing views. I recall him saying that he appreciated my open-mindedness in listening to the other side of the political aisle. I ultimately received an internship with his show, *Hannity & Colmes*. Throughout my internship at Fox, my time as a producer at the network, and even my time as a CNN commentator, Alan would provide me with wise counsel about my next career step. Alan reached out to me while I was working at CNN with a word of wisdom after a hot and boisterous panel: "You don't fight fire with fire, you fight it with water," he shared.[875]

Liberal CNN host and former Obama administration official, Van Jones, likewise became a career mentor to me. As I shared previously, when I was just a nervous, young commentator preparing for my first CNN election night panel, Van Jones's first words to me were heart-warming: "I love your cross." Before we had even formally met, he took note of the cross necklace I was wearing. Throughout the night, he offered pro tips as a seasoned television commentator and helped me through the several hours that we were on air.[876]

These are the kinds of relationships that polling suggests have become regrettably rare in an age of hyper-partisan divide. Social media amplifies the hostility, allowing so-called "keyboard warriors" to attack people anonymously in crude and hateful ways. The media just exacerbates the problem, and so, too, do our politicians.

President Joe Biden promised to be different. He vowed to bridge the divide and unify the country. Just take a look at his Inauguration Day address, where he mentioned "unity" at least half a dozen times. Here is a reminder of his pledges to the American people on January 20, 2021:

"Every disagreement doesn't have to be a cause for total war," he said.[877]

"To overcome these challenges—to restore the soul and to secure the future of America—requires more than words. It requires that most elusive of things in a democracy: Unity. Unity."

"With unity we can do great things. Important things."

"I know speaking of unity can sound to some like a foolish fantasy."

"History, faith, and reason show the way, the way of unity. We can see each other not as adversaries but as neighbors. We can treat each other with dignity and respect. We can join forces, stop the shouting, and lower the temperature. For without unity, there is no peace, only bitterness and fury."

"This is our historic moment of crisis and challenge, and unity is the path forward."

"And together, we shall write an American story of hope, not fear. Of unity, not division."[878]

These were the promises that President Joe Biden made. He was "Mr. Unity." But, as it turns out, he was Mr. Unity in word, not action. There are many examples, including the time he gave a mafia-like speech announcing his vaccine mandate, which the Supreme Court eventually struck down in part. Here were President Biden's words then:

"This is not about freedom or personal choice."[879]

"For the vast majority of you who have gotten vaccinated, I understand your anger at those who haven't gotten vaccinated."

"If you break the rules, be prepared to pay."

"We've been patient, but our patience is wearing thin."[880]

Truly the words of a great unifier. Mr. Unity!

In Atlanta, Georgia, while promoting a federal takeover of elections and speaking in opposition to a Georgia bill that implemented voter integrity measures and actually expanded voting access, President Biden gave what I previously described as one of the most divisive speeches that I have ever heard, where he compared Republicans opposing him to segregationists. "At consequential moments in history, they present a choice," he said. "Do you want to be…on the side of Dr. King or George Wallace? Do you want to be on the side of John Lewis or Bull Connor? Do you want to be on the side of Abraham Lincoln or Jefferson Davis?"[881] Press Secretary Jen Psaki later insisted that Biden "was not comparing them as humans," defending a comment that was a rather direct human-to-human comparison between Republican opponents and segregationists.[882]

This speech came after Biden falsely dubbed the Georgia law "Jim Crow 2.0." As it turns out, early voting in Georgia actually increased following their election integrity bill, exceeding early vote numbers for the 2020 presidential election. According to WSB-TV, "The Secretary of State's office says these numbers show a 168% increase in early voting turnout from the last gubernatorial primary in 2018 and 212% increase from the last presidential primary in 2020."[883] Moreover, as the *National Review* pointed out, "Of the voting electorate, black voters make up 2.75 percent more of the total electorate than 2020. This is not the result that one would expect if the legislation was aimed at voter suppression, and 'makes Jim Crow look like Jim Eagle,' as President Biden put it."[884] But the facts are of no moment!

In August of 2022, President Biden echoed his unity vow, seeming to suggest that he had made good on it. "We're always being told that Democrats and Republicans can't work together," President Biden said, speaking at a legislative signing for veterans. "When I ran, I said one of the reasons I was running…was to unite the country, and I was roundly criticized for being naïve. 'That was the old days, Joe. You used to be able to do that.' There are a lot of issues we can disagree on, but there are issues we can work together on. And this is one of those issues."[885]

But then, the very next month, on September 1, 2022, President Biden gave a prime-time address that outdid any of his past divisiveness. Standing before an ominous, hellish, blood red background that was widely mocked, President Biden declared that MAGA Republicans "threaten the very foundations of our republic" as they embrace "anger" and "chaos" and see "carnage and darkness and despair."[886] Quoting a judge's words, Biden asserted that MAGA Republicans are "'a clear and present danger' to our democracy.... MAGA Republicans do not respect the Constitution. They do not believe in the rule of law," he declared.[887] In fact, he said the Republican party was "dominated" and "driven" by MAGA Republicans. Here was our president ferociously, in no uncertain terms, attacking half of the country.

Oddly, in the same breath, President Biden declared that he was "an American president, not a president of red America or blue America, but of all America."[888] He called for "honesty and decency and respect for others" and "the willingness to see each other not as enemies but as fellow Americans."[889] The president then urged us to "come together, unite" as he noted that "politics can be fierce and mean and nasty in America."[890] Perhaps he needed a mirror after the speech he had just given, decrying half of the country! As it turns out, President Biden's version of "unity" was indeed "elusive," to echo a word from his inaugural address.

After President Biden's address to a Joint Session of Congress in the beginning of 2021—the remarks a newly inaugurated president gives in lieu of a State of the Union Address—Senator Tim Scott of South Carolina delivered the Republican response. Responses to presidential addresses usually fall flat. The one-on-one camera shot—no matter the setting—simply cannot compare to the grandeur and pomp and circumstance of presidential remarks in the House Chamber. I would argue that Senator Scott's response stands out as the exception. His heartfelt words offered a faith-filled message that we all needed to hear.

He spoke of "redemption" and offered hope. "I won't waste your time tonight with finger-pointing or partisan bickering. You can get that on T.V. any time you want. I want to have an honest conversation," Senator Scott said. "About common sense and common ground. About this feeling that our nation is sliding off its shared foundation, and how we can move forward."[891]

"[W]hy do we feel so divided and anxious?" he asked. "A nation with so much cause for hope should not feel so heavy-laden. A President who promised to bring us together should not push agendas that tear us apart. The American family deserves better," he posited before listing off a litany of successes that America had achieved together over the last four years.[892]

Senator Scott said unequivocally: "America is not a racist country" before proclaiming that "we get to live in the greatest country on Earth. The country where my grandfather, in his 94 years, saw his family go from cotton to Congress in one lifetime."[893]

He closed by offering words taken from Scripture and then stating, "I am standing here because my mom has prayed me through some very tough times. I believe our nation has succeeded the same way. Because generations of Americans, in their own ways, have asked for grace—and God has supplied it."[894]

Hope. Faith. Family. These are the values that make America great.

In a telling moment, Senator Tim Scott's hope-filled rebuttal was met with all the rage and toxicity that Twitter and social media have to offer. For twelve hours, "Uncle Tim," a racial slur aimed at Senator Scott, trended on Twitter.[895] After the term trended for half a day, Twitter finally removed the slur from its site.[896]

The Twitter trend in response to what was an uplifting, optimistic, unifying rebuttal speaks to the state of our country's political discourse. Hate and ad hominem attacks proliferate across the airwaves, social media, and beyond. What our country needs is exactly what Senator Scott suggested—a return to "grace" and God who "supplied it."

CHAPTER 11

A PROVEN SAVIOR

What is your identity? I don't mean your name, your social security number, or some other identifying marker. What *defines* you as a person? What makes you, *you*? Merriam-Webster defines "identity" as "the distinguishing character or personality of an individual."[897] What is your distinguishing character? In the hierarchical pyramid of your life, which block rests at the very top, dictating how each of the other blocks beneath are organized? Which distinguishing character informs the way you interact with others, the way you view yourself, or the way you deal with the inevitable trials that life will bring? Everyone has one. What is yours?

Growing up in a Christian home, I was always taught that my identity was embedded in something far superior to my human self. There was something so much bigger, so much greater than "Kayleigh McEnany." I was a mere reflection of my creator, and my identity, my "distinguishing character," was found in Jesus Christ. My Christian upbringing kept me grounded. I did not find my identity in the lonely, critical abyss of social media. I did not chase pleasure or worldly objectives. Sure, at times, the things of this world crept up and tried to take center stage. The seemingly endless quest to find a boyfriend in my adolescence and challenges in pursuing my career as a young adult, for example, all took their turn in trying to become the block on the top of my life's pyramid. But when the going got tough, my faith put life into perspective. Despite the challenges, I have strived and will continue to strive to keep Christ at the center of my identity.

You don't have to look far to find that society has gone grievously astray. I postulate that the reason for that is quite simple. Increasingly, a God-centered identity has been replaced with a self-centered one. Gallup's June 2022 survey found that in the United States, belief in God has dipped to a new low, with 81 percent of those surveyed professing belief in God.[898] While this number may seem fairly high, Gallup notes that this is "down six percentage points from 2017 and is in the lowest in Gallup's trends" going back to the 1940s when belief in God used to register at 98 percent.[899] Moreover, Gallup observes that the trend toward disbelief has been most notable among two groups in particular: "Belief in God has fallen the most in recent years among young adults and people on the left of the political spectrum (liberals and Democrats)," Gallup writes, recording a double-digit drop for each group.[900]

In Tim Keller's book, *Walking with God through Pain and Suffering*, he writes that Western society has embraced a "secular frame" whereby "[w]e see ourselves as able to control our own destiny, able to discern for ourselves what is right and wrong, and we see God as obligated to arrange things for our benefit...."[901] This secular attitude, in turn, has affected not just whether one believes in God or not but also how a believer relates to God. Keller observes, "Many people today believe in God, and may go to church, but if you ask them whether they are certain of their salvation and acceptance with God, or whether the idea of Jesus' sacrificial death on the cross is real and profoundly moving to them, or whether they are convinced of the bodily resurrection of Jesus and believers—you are likely to get a negative answer, or just a stare. Western culture's immanent frame weakens intellectual belief in God, and it makes heart certainty even more difficult to come by."[902]

Gallup polling reflects this observation, showing that just 42 percent of Americans think "God hears prayers and can intervene on a person's behalf."[903] When did this trend start? Keller cites Andrew Delbanco, who wrote about the American dream and what this secular trend, which began in the late twentieth century, has meant for America's religious community and for society at large. Delbanco wrote that "something died," and that something was "any conception of a common destiny worth tears, sacrifice, and maybe even death."[904]

This move toward the secular self and away from the all-loving God has its roots in "nihilism," a term derived from the Latin word "nihil" meaning "nothing." Merriam-Webster defines nihilism as "a doctrine that denies any objective ground of truth and especially of moral truths."[905] The *Routledge Encyclopedia of Philosophy* describes moral nihilism as "reject[ing] any possibility of justifying or criticizing moral judgments, on grounds such as that morality is a cloak for egoistic self-seeking, and therefore a sham...."[906] The *Encyclopedia Britannica* goes a step further in its definition: "Nihilism represented a crude form of positivism and materialism, a revolt against the established social order; it negated all authority exercised by the state, by the church, or by the family. It based its belief on nothing but scientific truth; science would be the solution of all social problems. All evils, nihilists believed, derived from a single source—ignorance—which science alone would overcome."[907]

In the view of the nihilist, there is no place for objective truth and moral judgments; where, then, is the place for God? The famous nihilist philosopher Friedrich Nietzsche appears to answer that question. "Have you not heard of that madman who lit a lantern in the bright morning hours, ran to the market place, and cried incessantly: 'I seek God! I seek God!'" Nietzsche wrote.[908] "As many of those who did not believe in God were standing around just then, he provoked much laughter. Has he got lost? asked one. Did he lose his way like a child? asked another. Or is he hiding? Is he afraid of us? Has he gone on a voyage? emigrated?—Thus they yelled and laughed. The madman jumped into their midst and pierced them with his eyes. 'Whither is God?' he cried; 'I will tell you. *We have killed him*—you and I.'"[909] And such was the infamous proclamation of Nietzsche in "The Parable of the Madman" that God is dead.

You find antipathy toward religion similarly in the philosophy of Karl Marx who notoriously called religion "the opiate of the masses."[910] But as Dr. Francis Collins, a renowned scientist and the former head of the National Institute of Health (NIH), cautioned, "The great Marxist experiments in the Soviet Union and in Mao's China, aiming to establish societies explicitly based upon atheism, proved capable of committing at least as much, and probably more, human slaughter and raw abuse of power than the worst of all regimes in recent times."[911]

Author Josh McDowell states the repercussions of atheist regimes in startling terms: "[N]o other fundamental worldview has caused as much misery and bloodshed as atheism. Specifically, the number of people slaughtered by twentieth-century atheistic regimes, such as communist China, communist Russia, and Nazi Germany is more than one hundred million people."[912]

For the modern-day atheist, though, faith is the problem. Richard Dawkins, the well-known atheist philosopher, said, "Faith is the great cop-out, the great excuse to evade the need to think and evaluate evidence. Faith is belief in spite of, even perhaps because of, the lack of evidence."[913] And as I mentioned in the introduction, Dawkins goes even further in calling faith not just "the great cop-out, the great excuse" but also "one of the world's great evils" when he wrote, "It is fashionable to wax apocalyptic about the threat to humanity posed by the AIDS virus, 'mad cow' disease, and many others, but I think a case can be made that *faith* is one of the world's great evils, comparable to the smallpox virus but harder to eradicate."[914]

The secular, nihilist, and atheist worldview has become increasingly prevalent in American society, and with it has come an array of negative bedfellows. After church one Sunday, my husband, Sean, said to my parents and me, "You guys have to listen to this." It was a 1965 broadcast from the famous radio broadcaster, the late Paul Harvey. We all listened to Harvey's words with total bewilderment as he predicted the direction of American society with remarkable prescience.

Harvey said, "If I were the devil...If I were the Prince of Darkness, I'd want to engulf the whole world in darkness.... I would whisper to you as I whispered to Eve: 'Do as you please.' To the young, I would whisper that 'The Bible is a myth'.... And the old, I would teach to pray, after me, 'Our Father, which art in Washington.... And then I'd get organized."[915]

He goes on to say exactly what the Prince of Darkness would do to corrupt society—fill our televisions with filth, push drugs to our children, pit families against one other, cause conflict among churches, and take God out of schools. "I'd have mesmerizing media fanning the flames," he said. "I would encourage schools to refine young intellects, but neglect to discipline emotions—just let those run wild, until before you knew it, you'd have to have drug sniffing dogs and metal detectors at every schoolhouse door."[916]

How did Harvey state with such accurate precision in 1965 the cultural ills that would plague twenty-first century American society? Perhaps he was already seeing—even then—the trend toward man placing secularism within the so-called "God-shaped void" in the human heart that pastors so often speak of. The theologian and philosopher Saint Augustine put it this way: "You [God] stir man to take pleasure, because you have made us for yourself, and our heart is restless until it rests in you."[917] Similarly, Saint Thomas Aquinas wrote, "There is within every soul a thirst for happiness and meaning."[918]

And then there was Blaise Pascal, the seventeenth-century French intellectual, who concluded, "What else does this craving, and this helplessness, proclaim but that there was once in man a true happiness, of which all that now remains is the empty print and trace? This he tries in vain to fill with everything around him, seeking in things that are not there the help he cannot find in those that are, though none can help, since this infinite abyss can be filled only with an infinite and immutable object; in other words by God himself."[919]

IN CHAPTER FOUR on pain and suffering, I mentioned my great interest in Christian apologetics. It was my dad who introduced me to apologetics during my teenage years. Apologetics comes from the Latin "*apologia*" essentially meaning "speaking in defense" of a belief. Defined in its simplest form, apologetics is "the rational response against the objections" posed to Christianity.[920]

The concept of apologetics is rooted in scripture. 1 Peter 3:15 says, "But in your hearts revere Christ as Lord. Always be prepared to give an answer to everyone who asks you to give the reason for the hope that you have. But do this with gentleness and respect...."[921] We are instructed to have a "reason" for our hope, but the second part of this verse is key—"do this with gentleness and respect."

In other words, we must exhibit grace when we are under fire, a concept that comports with biblical truth. Proverbs 15:1 reads, "A gentle answer turns away wrath, but a harsh word stirs up anger."[922] Galatians 5:22–23 says, "But the fruit of the Spirit is love, joy, peace, forbearance, kindness, goodness, faithfulness, gentleness and self-control. Against such things there is no law."[923]

Thanks to my dad and his intellectual curiosity, I, too, developed a love for Christian apologetics. What was my reason for being a Christian? While the ultimate answer is found in the heart, it became clear to me that the mind also played an important role in my belief. Over the years—during my time in academia and in my personal studies—I have discovered a collection of great minds from science, journalism, philosophy, and other disciplines who have engaged in rigorous study of the Christian faith and found a compelling, intellectual, and rational basis for belief. Their work is inspiring, and I endeavor to share some of it with you in the remaining pages of this book. In the pain and suffering chapter, we briefly explored Christian philosophy. Here, I hope that you will find interest in additional subject areas of Christian apologetics.

By the world's secular standards, these scholars I will introduce you to are imminently qualified. Oxford mathematics professor John Lennox has an impressive array of letters behind his name (MA, PhD, DPhil, DSc) while renowned scientist Dr. Francis Collins was both the head of the Human Genome Project and the former head of the National Institutes of Health. Both men speak to how science can inform faith.[924] Meanwhile, Lee Strobel, the "award-winning legal editor of the *Chicago Tribune*," used his skills at a journalist to interview thirteen accomplished scholars on the authenticity of the Bible and the Christian faith.[925] C. S. Lewis, the highly acclaimed author and Oxford and Cambridge scholar, needs no introduction as his work forms a philosophical foundation for much of Christian apologetics today.

Though it was not necessarily my intent, coincidentally, most of the literature I surveyed—books by Francis Collins, Lee Strobel, C. S. Lewis, and Josh McDowell—were all by former skeptics who set out to either disprove or thoroughly investigate Christianity, only to find themselves as believers in the end. I think you will find their work compelling.

SCIENCE

TAKE A BASIC biology class, and you can't help but walk away in utter bewilderment at the complexity of the human body. Or perhaps an even more intimate experience is going through the journey of pregnancy—an awe-inspiring phenomenon both for a pregnant woman and her spouse. As I sit here writing this, almost seven months pregnant, I routinely feel my son kick or adjust his tiny two-pound body. At twenty-six weeks of pregnancy, my pregnancy app tells me that "[w]hile listening to music, you might notice that your baby moves 'rhythmically' in response to the sounds…. The lungs are developing air sacks (alveoli) and the membrane that allows for the exchange of carbon dioxide and oxygen is now thin enough to let your baby take a breath by the end of the week."[926]

Amazing!

To a student of science, I imagine this complexity is even more bewildering, especially in the way that it is a form of "ordered" or working complexity that allows our universe to continue functioning and humanity to exist within it. In *God's Undertaker: Has Science Buried God?*, John Lennox cites philosopher Richard Swinburne on "the explanatory power of science itself."[927] Swinburne writes, "I am postulating a God to explain why science explains; I do not deny that science explains, but I postulate God to explain why science explains. The very success of science in showing us how deeply ordered the natural world is provides strong grounds for believing that there is an even deeper cause for that order."[928]

Swinburne makes a key point: our human bodies are ordered, remarkably so. Dr. Francis Collins, as mentioned previously, led the Human Genome Project, which sequenced the entire human genome. Describing the task, Collins wrote, "The human genome consists of all the DNA of our species, the hereditary code of life. This newly revealed text was 3 billion letters long, and written in a strange and cryptographic four-letter code. Such is the amazing complexity of the information carried within each cell of the human body, that a live reading of that code at a rate of three letters per second would take thirty-one years, even if reading continued day and night. Printing these letters out in regular font size on normal bond paper and binding them all together would result in a tower the height of the Washington Monument."[929]

Josh McDowell is a well-known theologian who wrote *More Than a Carpenter*, which sold more than fifteen million copies in print.[930] My dad introduced me to this tiny, almost pocket-sized book growing up. He would keep several copies of the book in his truck and routinely hand out the piece of literature, which impressively walks through science, archaeology, philosophy, and prophecy in a concise fashion. In discussing the complexity of human DNA, McDowell notes that DNA doesn't just store information, but it processes it as well.[931] As Bill Gates observed, "DNA is more advanced than any software ever created."[932] McDowell writes, "The informational content of DNA was one of the primary reasons former atheist Antony Flew changed his mind about God. He concluded: 'The only satisfactory explanation for the origin of such 'end-directed, self-replicating' life as we see on earth is an infinitely intelligent Mind.'"[933]

Over the course of several pages in his book, Collins wrote about discovering the recessive gene for cystic fibrosis—a genetic disorder that can cause a debilitating mucus buildup affecting organs.[934] Collins described how enormous the task before him and his research team was: "All we knew was that somewhere in the 3 billion letters of the DNA code, at least one letter had gone wrong in a vulnerable location."[935] He analogized the intricacy of the search to "looking for a single burned-out lightbulb in the basement of a house somewhere in the United States.... A house-to-house search, lightbulb by lightbulb was required."[936] And he described the remarkable joy in finding this recessive gene after a decade of work, $50 million of investment, and "two dozen teams worldwide"—"[a]nd cystic fibrosis was supposed to be one of the easiest," he wrote.[937] For Collins, his work had an evident spiritual lens, especially after the enormity of sequencing the entirety of the human genome: "For me, as a believer, the uncovering of the human genome sequence held additional significance. This book was written in the DNA language by which God spoke life into being."[938]

In looking at the complexity of just one strand of human DNA, you must consider the probability of creation and, therefore, the probability of a creator. As Collins observed, "The existence of a universe as we know it rests upon a knife edge of improbability."[939] McDowell cited "renowned physicist" Paul Davies, who puts it in even starker terms: "The cliché that 'life is balanced on a knife-edge' is a staggering understatement in this case: no knife in the universe could have an edge that fine."[940]

Collins expounded upon the improbability of the universe by noting that there are "fifteen physical constants" for a functioning physical universe—constants like the speed of light, the force of gravity, and so on. "The chance that all of these constants would take on the values necessary to result in a stable universe capable of sustaining complex life forms is almost infinitesimal," Collins said. "And yet those are exactly the parameters that we observe. In sum, our universe is wildly improbable."[941] McDowell put the number of constants or universal constraints at nineteen, noting that "Oxford physicist Roger Penrose concluded that if we jointly considered all the laws of nature that must be fine-tuned, we would be unable to write down such an enormous number, since the necessary digits would be greater than the number of elementary particles in the universe."[942]

When you consider all of this together, you are left with the common-sense conclusion reached by physicist Freeman Dyson, as quoted by John Lennox: "As we look out into the universe and identify the many accidents of physics and astronomy that have worked together to our benefit, it almost seems as if the universe must in some sense have known we were coming."[943] In other words, a creator crafted a universe working in perfect harmony for His creature. It would take a great and extraordinary amount of faith to believe otherwise.

In considering the relationship between faith and science, any student of science must acknowledge the limitations of their discipline. Thomas Nagel, described by Lennox as "a prominent atheist professor of philosophy" wrote that "[t]he purposes and intentions of God, if there is a god, and the nature of his will, are not possible subjects of scientific theory or scientific explanation."[944]

S. Lewis describes a similar limitation in discussing the "materialist" view that the universe came about by chance versus the "religious" view that there was a creator: "You cannot find out which view is the right one by science in the ordinary sense," he concluded.[945] According to Lewis, the question becomes "whether there is anything behind the things science observes—something of a different kind—this is not a scientific question."[946]

Taken together, science reaches an end where the inquiry to explain complexity begins. How did the human cell come about with intricate, detailed information—as mapped out in Collins's

Human Genome Project—that would take thirty-one years to read out loud? What about the entirety of the human body? And how is one to explain the existence of the universe, with nearly twenty universal constants necessary, the likelihood of all existing in unison being a number so large that it is unable to be written down? Indeed, if the law of gravity "varied just slightly," according to McDowell, "the universe would not be habitable for life."[947] And that is just one of the many universal constants necessary to sustain life!

What a remarkable amount of faith it would take to believe this all came about randomly, just by chance with no creator at the helm. The scientific theories available to us regarding the creation of the universe and the complexity of humanity inevitably all collide into one overarching, all-encompassing question. What explains science? For those of us who simply do not have the extraordinary faith to say "nothing," the logical conclusion is God.

THE BIBLE

ANY DISCUSSION OF Christian apologetics would not be complete without a brief look at the historical reliability of the Bible. The Bible is the most read book in human history. A recent analysis of just the last fifty years found that 3.9 *billion* copies of the Bible have been sold.[948] The second most-sold book, *Quotations from Chairman Mao Tse-tung*, did not even come close in selling just 820 *million* copies.[949]

The popularity of the Bible is equally matched by its reliability as a historical source. In the first portion of Lee Strobel's *The Case for Christ*, he interviews several academics on the historical and archaeological underpinnings of the Bible.[950] Craig L. Blomberg, PhD, a senior research fellow at Cambridge who is described as "one of the country's foremost authorities on the biographies of

Jesus," described the dates in which the Gospels (Matthew, Mark, Luke, and John) were written: "The standard scholarly dating, even in very liberal circles, is Mark in the 70s [AD], Matthew and Luke in the 80s [AD], John in the 90s [AD]. But listen: that's still within the lifetimes of various eyewitnesses of the life of Jesus, including hostile eyewitnesses who would have served as a corrective if false teachings about Jesus were going around."[951] As a point of comparison, Blomberg noted, Alexander the Great's earliest biographies— deemed reliable by scholars—were written more than four centuries after Alexander's death.[952]

Ancient manuscripts from the decades after the Gospel accounts were written continue to confirm their accuracy.[953] Scholar Bruce Metzger, cited by McDowell, observed, "The quantity of New Testament material is almost embarrassing in comparison with other works of integrity."[954] For example, while the classical text, *The Iliad*, has 643 confirming manuscripts, McDowell wrote that—at the time he wrote *More Than a Carpenter*'s updated version—there were 5,600 confirming Greek manuscripts for the Bible![955]

The discovered manuscripts not only prove remarkably consistent with the Gospels in their text, but in several cases, they have actually corroborated biblical details previously challenged or provided answers to lingering questions about certain aspects of the text.[956] While there are many examples explored by Strobel and McDowell, here is one provided in the discovery of the Dead Sea Scrolls, Hebrew manuscripts found near the Qumran caves in the late 1940s.

One of these manuscripts, labeled 4Q521, clarifies a question in scripture raised by the eleventh chapter of Matthew.[957] In Matthew 11, John the Baptist is in prison and sends disciples to ask Christ, "Are you the one who is to come, or should we expect someone else?"[958] In this passage, you have John the Baptist trying to learn if Christ is indeed the promised Messiah. Jesus replies, "Go back and report to John what you hear and see: The blind receive sight, the lame walk, those who have leprosy are cleansed, the deaf hear, the dead are raised, and the good news is proclaimed to the poor."[959]

Biblical scholar John McRay, PhD, points out that, in this passage, Jesus is making an allusion to the Old Testament book of Isaiah in confirming that he is the Messiah. Curiously, Jesus added the words "the dead are raised," which appears to be a departure from Isaiah's text.[960] That is, until 4Q251 was found, "contain[ing] a version of Isaiah 61 that does include the missing phrase, 'the dead are raised.'"[961] Taking in this new information McRay provided, Strobel said, "I sat back in my chair. To me…[this] discovery was a remarkable confirmation of Jesus' self-identity. It was staggering to me how modern archaeology could finally unlock the significance of a statement in which Jesus boldly asserted nearly two thousand years ago that he was indeed the anointed one of God."[962]

PROPHESY

IN LEE STROBEL'S *The Case for Christ*, Strobel recounts his interview with scholar Louis S. Lapides, MDiv, ThM, who made a personal journey from Judaism to Eastern religions, when he battled with depression and drugs, before eventually becoming a Christian.[963] One day, a pastor challenged him: "Just read the Old Testament and ask the God of Abraham, Isaac, and Jacob—the God of Israel—to show you if Jesus is the Messiah."[964] Lapides obliged and began reading the Old Testament, where he was immediately struck by the number of prophesies he found that were fulfilled in the person of Jesus Christ.

For instance, when Lapides read Isaiah—believed to be written more than seven hundred years before the birth of Christ—he discovered a stunningly accurate portrayal of a savior who would die for our sins.[965] In Isaiah 53, we learn of a savior "despised and rejected by men"; "a man of sorrows and acquainted with grief"; and who was "like a lamb that is led to the slaughter" and "was pierced for our transgressions...crushed for our iniquities."[966] As the Jeremiah Study Bible explains, "Isaiah prophetically spoke of the unjust trial of Jesus before Pilate, of His silence before His accusers, of His shameful treatment by the rulers, and of His slaughter as a lamb on the cross for all of us."[967]

Strobel writes, "Over and over Lapides would come upon prophecies in the Old Testament—more than four dozen major predictions in all. Isaiah revealed the manner of the Messiah's birth (of a virgin); Micah pinpointed the place of his birth (Bethlehem); Genesis and Jeremiah specified his ancestry (a descendent of Abraham, Isaac, and Jacob, from the tribe of Judah, the house of David); the Psalms foretold his betrayal, his accusation by false witnesses, his manner of death (pierced in the hands and feet, although crucifixion hadn't been invented yet), and his resurrection (he would not decay but would ascend on high); and on and on."[968]

I remember having this experience myself as a young Christian girl when I discovered Psalm 22—a Psalm written one thousand years before Christ.[969] Though Psalm 22 was written many hundreds of years before crucifixion was invented, it seems to perfectly describe Christ's death by crucifixion: "They pierce my hands and feet," the Psalm reads.[970] "I am poured out like water, and all my bones are out of joint...and my tongue sticks to the roof of my mouth...." Psalm 22 depicts Christ's manner of death in what Christian Broadcasting Network (CBN) calls a "description of the agony caused by crucifixion [that] is eerily accurate."[971]

Not only does Psalm 22 accurately portray the death of the Messiah, it also predicts the actions of third-party actors. Psalm

22:18 reads, "[t]hey divide my clothes among them and cast lots for my garment," foreshadowing the actions of the Roman soldiers, who "...took his clothes, dividing them into four shares...."[972] And then Psalm 22:7–8 depicts the mocking of the crowd: "All who see me mock me; they hurl insults, shaking their heads. 'He trusts in the Lord,' they say, 'let the Lord rescue him. Let him deliver him, since he delights in him.'"[973] As CBN points out, this describes the crowd with precision as Matthew 27:39, 41–43 reads, in part, "Those who passed by hurled insults at him, shaking their heads" while "...elders mocked him. 'He trusts in God. Let God rescue him.'"[974]

In my teenage years, when I discovered Psalm 22, and still today, as a young adult, I read it with bewilderment. How could King David, who wrote these words hundreds of years before Christ and crucifixion, have spoken in a manner so accurate and so foretelling? How could he have predicted the actions, not just of third parties, but of hostile third parties with no interest in conforming their behavior to an Old Testament prophesy? This ancient scripture, like so many others, had to be divinely inspired.

There are dozens and dozens of messianic prophecies just like these, as Lapides discovered. Many scholars have endeavored to calculate the odds of the Old Testament prophesies being fulfilled in the person of Jesus Christ. Peter Stoner, a writer and a professor in mathematics and astronomy, calculated that the chances of one man fulfilling just eight of the Old Testament prophesies was one in ten to the seventeenth power![975] To put this into perspective, Stoner says that these odds would be the equivalent of marking one silver dollar, covering the state of Texas with two feet of silver dollars, and having a blindfolded man pick out the one that happened to be the marked silver dollar. The ominous odds for the blindfolded man in picking the silver dollar are the equivalent of just eight of these prophesies being fulfilled in Jesus Christ. Even more daunting, Strobel writes, "Stoner also computed that the probability of fulfilling forty-eight prophecies was one chance in a trillion, trillion, trillion, trillion, trillion, trillion, trillion, trillion, trillion, trillion, trillion, trillion, trillion."[976]

Long odds indeed!

This brief synopsis in no way does justice to the study of Old Testament prophesy. The conversation between Strobel and Lapides is illuminating, and very much worth a read as they dismiss the assertion that Christ could have intentionally fulfilled the prophesies. Christ had no control over many prophesies—like His place of birth, the exact time of His birth, that He would be betrayed for thirty pieces of silver, or that His legs would not be broken during His crucifixion, among others.[977]

Yet, each of these prophecies—one by one—were fulfilled. How could the life of Jesus so perfectly conform to ancient writings, in some cases written many centuries before He even walked the earth? While the study of Christian prophecy is often discussed from the perspective of yet-to-be fulfilled prophecies and what the Bible says about the future, of great intrigue and amazement is the backward look at the prophecies already confirmed in the person of Jesus Christ. To cavalierly dismiss the abundance of prophecies in the Old Testament is to dismiss once again odds and probabilities so great as to defy logic. And, like in our scientific inquiry, which converged on one answer (the existence of a creator), our prophetic inquiry comes together in the name of one person: Jesus Christ.

MORALITY

ONE OF THE most compelling intellectual arguments for belief in God is the law of morality. Since we explored this concept in chapter five, I will only briefly recount it here. C. S. Lewis opens his book *Mere Christianity*—one of the most famous apologetic texts ever written—with a section entitled "Right and Wrong as a Clue to the Meaning of the Universe."[978] The argument is really a very simple one, and it is difficult for the skeptic to answer. How is it that humanity generally agrees on basic concepts of morality? Humanity has indeed coalesced around several basic truths pertaining to morality. For the most part, societies across the globe and throughout time agree that it is wrong to murder, wrong to steal, wrong to lie, and admirable to engage in charity, sacrifice for fellow man, and exhibit basic kindness and generosity. Sure, there are many people who break these rules, but that does not change the fact that humanity basically agrees on these tenants.[979]

C. S. Lewis calls this basic code of morality the "law of human nature."[980] If there is no such "law of human nature," then on what basis can we say that the abhorrent actions of those who breach human morality are wrong? As Lewis goes on to observe, how can we indict the actions of the murderous atheistic regimes in human history in the absence of a universal "law of human nature"?[981]

What separates us from the animals and what gives us the capacity to say the atrocities in human history were unquestionably immoral is the fact that we have a moral law—a compass of sorts in the human heart that discerns between basic tenants of good and evil. And to have a moral law, there must be a moral law giver.

This survey of Christian apologetics does not even begin to touch the surface of the deep, rich, and illuminating study of the intellectual rationale for Christianity. But the inquiry of Christian apologetics can never be an end in itself. While Christian apologetics can be useful in opening the mind of the skeptic, it is merely a segue to the heart, where the beautiful, radical, and life-transforming work of Christ truly happens. For the remedy to society's ills lies not in the head but in the heart.

CHAPTER 12

THE HEART CONVERSION

In Lee Strobel's final interview—interview number thirteen with philosopher J. P. Moreland, PhD—Moreland tells Strobel, an inquisitive and thorough journalist, "There's one category of evidence you haven't asked about.... It's the ongoing encounter with the resurrected Christ that happens all over the world, in every culture, to people from all kinds of backgrounds and personalities—well educated and not, rich and poor, thinkers and feelers, men and women. They all will testify that more than any single thing in their lives, Jesus Christ has changed them."[982]

Moreland is onto something. Beyond all of the science, history, philosophy, and prophesy available—and there is much of it—the encounters of men and women with the risen savior are astounding. The story of Christianity is the story of broken marriages healed, drug addicts fully recovered, hardened hearts softened, the most violent of prisoners completely reformed, and life-transforming rehabilitation beyond anything that psychology or self-help could offer.

In my interview with Asmaan in chapter two, recall how she marveled at the two Afghan brothers, one with murderous tendencies, both of whom were inexplicably transformed by the love and power of Jesus Christ. In addition, I found ample evidence of these heart transformations, as I will call them, in the various books I referenced from Christian apologetics. As I mentioned, several of the authors I cited—Collins, McDowell, Strobel, Lewis, and Lapides—were all atheists who eventually came to the truth of Christianity. While they began the journey with their minds, they concluded with their hearts.

Dr. Francis Collins, the head of the Human Genome Project, wrote, "On a beautiful fall day, as I was hiking in the Cascade Mountains during my first trip west of the Mississippi, the majesty and beauty of God's creation overwhelmed my resistance. As I rounded a corner and saw a beautiful and unexpected frozen waterfall, hundreds of feet high, I knew the search was over. The next morning, I knelt in the dewy grass as the sun rose and surrendered to Jesus Christ."[983]

Louis Lapides told Lee Strobel about a trip he took to the Mojave Desert with friends, where he prayed for God to give him assurance that Christ is savior. Speaking of his experience, Lapides said, "The best I can put together out of that experience is that God objectively spoke to my heart. He convinced me, experientially, that he exists. And at that point, out in the desert, in my heart I said, 'God, I accept Jesus into my life. I don't understand what I'm supposed to do with him. But I want him. I've pretty much made a mess of my life; I need you to change me.... My friends knew my life had changed, and they couldn't understand it. They'd say, 'Something happened to you in the desert. You don't want to do drugs anymore. There's something different about you.'"[984]

Meanwhile, journalist Lee Strobel wrote, "After a personal investigation that spanned more than six hundred days and countless hours, my own verdict in the case for Christ was clear. However, as I sat at my desk, I realized that I needed more than an intellectual decision."[985] He decided to commit his life fully to Christ. Reflecting on that decision, he said, "Looking back all these years later, I can see with clarity that the day I personally made a decision in the case for Christ was nothing less than the pivotal event of my entire life."[986]

And McDowell, who began as a skeptic, also had a life-transforming encounter with Christ. "Christianity. Ha!" he used to say. "That's for unthinking weaklings, not intellectuals.... Jesus Christ? Oh, for God's sake, don't give me that kind of garbage...."[987] But after months of studying and discovering mounds of evidence in support of Christianity, something else happened. "On December 19, 1959, at 8:30 p.m., during my second year at the university, I became a Christian. Someone asked me, 'How do you know you became a Christian?' One of several answers was simple: 'It has changed my life.'"[988]

I know exactly the kind of heart transformation each of these authors speak of because I have experienced it myself. As a young girl, I walked down the aisle of my Southern Baptist church and gave my life to Christ. That Sunday evening, I knelt beside my bed my with my father and acknowledged my sins, professed my belief in Christ, and committed my life to Him. In that moment, I know that I became a Christian.

As a teenager, I was devoted to my faith. I prayed by my bedside and regularly journaled to my savior. I became inspired by Rachel Joy Scott, the first victim of the Columbine shooting, who was a young woman of great faith. Rachel regularly wrote journals to Christ, and they were published in the aftermath of her death. She spoke to God like she was talking to a friend, and her conversations with her Savior showed a remarkable premonition of her death. On May 2, 1998, she wrote these words: "This will be my last Lord, I have gotten what I can, thank you."[989] Less than a year later, on April 20, 1999, Rachel was killed in the Columbine High School shooting.

In another journal entry, Rachel traced her hands and inscribed these words in the middle of her left hand: "These hands belong to Rachel Joy Scott and will someday touch millions of people's hearts." I wonder if she knew just how true those words were when she wrote them, because she was exactly right. Rachel's tragic death was only the beginning of her impact on the world. The *Daily Mail* reported, "Rachel's funeral was broadcast on CNN and drew the highest viewing figures the network had received at that point, more than Princess Diana's funeral."[990]

Following her death, Rachel's father, Darrell, created the organization Rachel's Challenge, which spreads Rachel's message of love and compassion throughout our nation's schools. In total, Rachel's Challenge has reached thirty million students, parents, and educators; stopped approximately 150 suicides per year; and even, according to law enforcement, averted eight school shootings.[991] Darrell explained the power of Rachel's story to Denver ABC 7 like this, "The inmates are in tears. We have gang [members]...I mean tough murderers, stand up bawling like a baby and say, 'I'm calling my daughter. I haven't talked to her in 20 years.' I personally believe there is a divine touch to her story, because otherwise I can't explain it."[992] Rachel's story has changed countless hearts, including mine. I learned, through Rachel, that God could be as much a friend and a partner in life as He is a father.

After college, I moved to New York City to take a job as a production assistant with the show *Huckabee* at Fox News. I lived alone in an apartment in Manhattan, and I discovered a city that was much different than my home state of Florida. I attended The Journey church in New York one Sunday, and I remember the pastor saying that even though New York City is full of millions of people, it can feel like one of the loneliest places. He was right.

At one point during my three years in the city, I remember feeling so lonely. I left work and went back to my small, basically windowless apartment. I tried calling my mom, but she wasn't by her phone. I laid in my bed and prayed to God: "If you're out there, I need to hear from you right now." I kid you not. In that *very* moment, my phone lit up. It was a number I didn't recognize with a New York area code. And while I typically don't pick up numbers I don't know, in that moment, I was happy to talk to anyone—even a telemarketer!

I answered the phone, "Hello."

I will never forget the first words that I heard in reply: "Hi Kayleigh. This is The Journey church. How can we pray for you today?"

Completely stunned, I sat in silence for a moment before replying to The Journey churchgoer who had decided to call me in that moment. After speaking with them briefly, I hung up the phone and began to cry tears of joy. I knew, without a doubt, I had just had a divine moment of outreach from the risen Savior.

I do not know who it was that called my phone that day. I don't even remember if the caller was a man or a woman, but I do know that person was used by Christ in that specific moment. As I wrote in *For Such a Time as This*, "God has for you a plan, a purpose. No one can stop his plan for your life. He will lead you to victory and carry you through the trials if you only let Him. What my dad told me in the wake of my fears is true for you as well. Indeed, you are here 'for such a time as this.' This is my story. But, rest assured, He has already written yours."[993]

I believe the person who called my phone that day was used "for such a time as this." Their call changed my life forever. It occurred to me a few months ago that I have had a few life-defining calls. I wrote about two of them in my last book. There was the call I received at the start of the COVID-19 outbreak. I was riding in the car with my mom and my daughter, just a few months old, when I received a call from the president of the

United States, Donald J. Trump, asking me to be the White House press secretary. It was a call that defined my career.

Then, there was the call I got on Christmas Eve during my senior year of college. It was an unwanted and emotional call from my doctor informing me that I had tested positive for the BRCA2 genetic mutation, which as I noted earlier in this book put me at about an 84 percent chance of breast cancer and 27 percent chance of ovarian cancer over my lifetime. After a decade of aggressive surveillance—mammograms, MRIs, and ultrasounds—I made the difficult decision to have a preventative double mastectomy, taking my breast cancer chances to close to zero. But that call on Christmas Eve morning set in motion a decade of worry and a lot of tough medical choices.

But then there was that call from The Journey church, more important and consequential in my life than a call from the president of the United States or a call with life-changing medical news from my healthcare provider. For it was a call, through a human being, sent directly from my Lord and Savior Jesus Christ. I can say, without hesitation, that call changed my life, taking my Christian faith from my head to my heart, where it will live forever.

As I was writing this book, and as I considered what it means to have serenity in the storm, one New Testament anecdote about the life of Jesus stood out to me. It is recounted in the gospels of Matthew, Mark, and John.[994] In Matthew 14, we learn about one of the great miracles of Jesus. With just five loaves of bread and two fish, Jesus fed a crowd of about five thousand people.[995] After this miracle, as Jesus dismissed the multitudes, He told his disciples to "get into the boat and go before him to the other side" of the sea to Capernaum while Jesus "went up on the mountain by himself to pray."[996] By evening, the disciples were "a long way from the land," and the boat was "beaten by the waves, for the wind was against them."[997] But then something happened during "the fourth watch of the night," which the Jeremiah Study Bible (JSB) says was "between 3 and 6 AM."[998] At this time, "[H]e came to them, walking on the sea."[999]

Imagine that—Christ Jesus walking on the tumultuous waters of the sea in the dead of night. What that must have been like!

But rather than expressing joy, the disciples were "terrified, and said, 'It is a ghost!'" as they "cried out in fear."[1000] With this reaction, the gospel of Mark describes Jesus's followers as having "hardened" hearts.[1001] As the JSB notes, "Even though they had just witnessed the miraculous feeding of a multitude, they failed to apply that experience of Jesus' power to this situation."[1002] Matthew 14:27 says, "But immediately Jesus spoke to them, saying, 'Take heart; it is I. Do not be afraid.'"[1003]

According to the JSB, this means that the disciples were alone in the boat, where they were eventually thrashed by the waves, likely for hours![1004] The JSB then asks an important question and provides an enlightening answer. "Why did Jesus allow His followers to struggle in isolation for seven or eight hours?"[1005] The JSB continues, "If He had rescued them immediately, the disciples might have forgotten His intervention or perhaps assumed that, given enough time, they could have saved themselves. The Lord sometimes waits until His followers have exhausted their resources before He steps in."[1006]

And when He did step in, one disciple, Peter, stepped out in faith—at least for a moment. When Jesus told his followers not to be afraid, Peter responded, "'Lord, if it is you, command me to come to you on the water.'"[1007] Jesus replied, "'Come,'" prompting Peter to step out in faith onto the water.[1008] The JSB observes, "Peter was not acting foolishly, and this was not a daring stunt; it was obedience. When Jesus beckoned him to come, Peter willingly went. He had enough faith to get out of the boat and walk toward Jesus—something no prophet had ever done."[1009]

But then something instructive happened: "…when he saw the wind, he was afraid, and beginning to sink he cried out, 'Lord, save me.'"[1010] Even as Peter doubted, though, Christ intervened: "Jesus immediately reached out his hand and took hold of him, saying to him, 'O you of little faith, why did you doubt?' And when they got into the boat, the wind ceased. And those in the boat worshipped him, saying, 'Truly you are the Son of God.'"[1011]

Peter's actions demonstrated a remarkable level of faith, stepping onto the roaring waters on the verge of consuming his vessel. But his faith only lasted a moment because he took his eyes away from Christ and looked instead to the thrashing waves. In that moment, Peter looked at the storm and not at the savior. And that is only human. As an innate worrier, I find myself doing just the same. There is a tendency in us all to focus on and sometimes get lost in the storms of life. Indeed, sometimes the storm may be more like an all-consuming, life-threatening hurricane that we cannot escape.

But rest assured that we find the answers to the treacherous waters in life and the unexplainable weather patterns that can ravage us in the person of Christ Jesus. Whatever you may be going through—marital turmoil, loneliness, depression, heartbreaking loss—know that there is someone who will heal your wounds and mend your broken heart.

If you doubt it, take the same challenge that was issued to the doubting Louis Lapides: "Just read the Old Testament and ask the God of Abraham, Isaac, and Jacob—the God of Israel—to show you if Jesus is the Messiah."[1012] I did. My challenge came, not in reading the Old Testament, but in asking the all-living God during a moment of loneliness: "If you're out there, I need to hear from you right now."

Miraculously, He answered my call.

He will answer yours too.

Only here—only in Him—will you find serenity in the storm.

ENDNOTES

1　Alex B. Berezow, "Richard Dawkins Is Wrong About Religion," Real Clear Science, September 28, 2013 (https://tinyurl.com/5d5tcbuv).

2　*Kennedy v. Bremerton School District*, 597 U.S. (2022) (https://tinyurl.com/5c3pjcb8).

3　*Calvary Chapel Dayton Valley v. Steve Sisolak, Governor of Nevada, et al.*, 591 U.S. (2020) (Alito, J., dissenting at 2) (https://tinyurl.com/t7jau3kc).

4　*On Fire Christian Center, Inc. v. Fischer et al,* Temporary Restraining Order and Memorandum Opinion, (W.D. Ky. 2020) (https://tinyurl.com/46panx35).

5　*Engel v. Vitale*, 370 U.S. 421, 450 (1962) (Stewart, J., dissenting) (https://tinyurl.com/53sshv4y).

6　*Elk Grove Unified School District v. Newdow*, 542 U.S. (2004) (Rehnquist, C. J., concurring) (https://tinyurl.com/zpvx7fnw).

7　Mahita Gajanan, "These Are the Bible Verses Past Presidents Have Turned to on Inauguration Day," *Time*, January 19, 2017 (https://tinyurl.com/2u76msx4).

8　Isaac Schorr, "*New York Times* Editorial Board Member 'Disturbed' by Sight of American Flags," *National Review*, June 8, 2021 (https://tinyurl.com/4rty7dfj).

9   Alex Noble, "Macy Gray Trashed for Suggesting 'Divisive' American Flag Be Updated: 'Find a New Country,'" The Wrap, June 19, 2021 (https://tinyurl.com/5859f3yu).

10 *Ibid.*

11 Christopher Rufo, "Racism in the Cradle," ChristopherRufo.com, March 2, 2021 (https://tinyurl.com/yc8xucdt).

12 Mary Kay Linge & Jon Levine, "Over $200K being spent on drag queen shows at NYC schools, records show," *New York Post*, June 11, 2022 (https://tinyurl.com/2p8uh5n3).

13 "Fentanyl overdoses become No. 1 cause of death among US adults, ages 18-45: 'A national emergency," Fox29, December 16, 2021 (https://tinyurl.com/yc584564).

14 Troy Closson & Andy Newman, "Woman Dies After Being Pushed Onto Subway Tracks in Times Square," *New York Times*, January 15, 2022 (https://tinyurl.com/4v7sr553).

15 Alyssa Paolicelli & Ruschell Boone, "NYPD: 1-Year-Old Boy Shot Dead at Brooklyn BBQ," Spectrum News NY1, July 13, 2020 (https://tinyurl.com/28utcwu6).

16 Tina Moore, Amanda Woods & Bruce Golding, "Summer 2022 crime surged in nearly every major category, NYPD stats reveal," *New York Post*, September 4, 2022 (https://tinyurl.com/yzthkmnu).

17 Carla K. Johnson, "US abortions rise: 1 in 5 pregnancies terminated in 2020," Associated Press, June 14, 2022 (https://tinyurl.com/y55vty58).

18 Kyle Morris & Sam Dorman, "Over 63 million abortions have occurred in the US since Roe v. Wade decision in 1973," Fox News, May 4, 2022 (https://tinyurl.com/yeymynaj).

19 Caitlin Burke, "Seeds of Revival in Afghanistan: Taliban's Oppressive Islamic Governance Creating 'Ripe Soil for Church to Grow,'" September 8, 2021 (https://tinyurl.com/4rwtfh7r).

20 Rick Warren, "We Know How the Story Ends," PastorRick. com, June 29, 2021 (https://tinyurl.com/3cj3wsuh).

21 Terri Moon Cronk, "Biden Announces Full U.S. Troop Withdrawal From Afghanistan by Sept. 11," U.S. Department of Defense, April 14, 2021 (https://tinyurl. com/3fxty4eh).

22 Eugene Kiely & Robert Farley, "Timeline of U.S. With-drawal from Afghanistan," FactCheck.org, August 17, 2021 (https://tinyurl.com/4ybmee84).

23 Lucas Y. Tomlinson & Edmund DeMarche, "Taliban insurgents take Kandahar, Herat as US plans to evacuate Americans from embassy in Kabul," Fox News, August 13, 2021 (https://tinyurl.com/yckfvm7z).

24 *Ibid.*

25 "Remarks by President Biden on the Drawdown of U.S. Forces in Afghanistan," WhiteHouse.gov, July 8, 2021 (https://tinyurl.com/am77kwkr).

26 "Secretary Antony J. Blinken With Chuck Todd of Meet the Press on NBC," The State Department, August 15, 2021 (https://tinyurl.com/eyt4j39v).

27 Rachel Pannett, "U.S. to probe allegations former Afghan president Ghani fled Taliban with millions in cash," *The Washington Post*, October 7, 2021 (https://tinyurl.com/ ycktsdwk).

28 Paul Sperry, "Taliban leader was freed from Guantanamo Bay in 2014 swap by Obama," *New York Post*, August 16, 2021 (https://tinyurl.com/5wjpwb4v).

29 Richard Engel, Twitter, August 15, 2021 (https://tinyurl. com/4c7m2ykj).

30 Kathy Gannon, "Taliban flag rises over seat of power on fateful anniversary," Associated Press, September 11, 2021 (https://tinyurl.com/2fz82dhe); Ellen Knickmeyer, "Costs of the Afghanistan war, in lives and dollars," Associated Press, August 16, 2021 (https://tinyurl. com/3bhmnhhv).

31 Fox Butterfield & Kari Haskell, "Getting it Wrong in a Photo," *New York Times*, April 23, 2000 (https://tinyurl.com/yua339zd).

32 Glenn Kessler, "Biden, Trump, and Afghanistan: Statements that haven't aged well," *The Washington Post*, August 17, 2021 (https://tinyurl.com/5a3redwz).

33 Katelyn Caralle, "Biden's words haunt him: President said a month ago there's 'no circumstance where Americans will be lifted out of the U.S. embassy in Kabul by helicopter,'" *The Daily Mail*, August 15, 2021 (https://tinyurl.com/4khd4bvx).

34 Deirdre Shesgreen & Tom Vanden Brook, "US Embassy in Kabul shelters staff at airport after evacuation," *USA Today*, August 15, 2021 (https://tinyurl.com/335ptatr).

35 Brian Ross et al., "ISIS 2 Years Later: From 'JV Team' to International Killers," ABC News, June 29, 2016 (https://tinyurl.com/2p98nvvy).

36 Miranda Devine, "Damning pic of a weak leader: Devine," *New York Post*, August 18, 2021 (https://tinyurl.com/mr3xek43).

37 Bryan Bender et al., "'This Is Actually Happening,'" *Politico*, August 20, 2021 (https://tinyurl.com/yvr5hcj8).

38 *Ibid.*

39 Rob Crilly, "Biden BEGS Taliban to spare US embassy as he sends US troops to Kabul: Heads back to Wilmington after TWO DAYS in DC," *Daily Mail*, August 12, 2021 (https://tinyurl.com/3vzxss5d).

40 Bender, "This Is Actually Happening."

41 Crilly, "Biden BEGS Taliban."

42 Steven Hendrix, "From JFK to Omarosa: The White House Situation Room's history-making moments," *The Washington Post*, August 13, 2018 (https://tinyurl.com/mr3vumts).

43 "Camp David," The White House, (https://tinyurl.com/5fu9r4st).

44 Ashley Parker et al., "72 hours at Camp David: Inside Biden's lagging response to the fall of Afghanistan," *Washington Post*, August 17, 2021 (https://tinyurl.com/459c89ex).

45 Michael Lee, "Jen Psaki 'out of the office' as Biden remains silent on Taliban takeover of Afghanistan," Fox News, August 15, 2021 (https://tinyurl.com/33p4mh5h).

46 "Press Briefing by Press Secretary Jen Psaki and National Security Advisor Jake Sullivan, August 17, 2021," The White House, August 17, 2021 (https://tinyurl.com/34d-jxkb4).

47 President Biden, Twitter, August 16, 2021 (https://tinyurl.com/yc48yttn).

48 Julie Tsirkin et al., "Up to 15,000 Americans remain in Afghanistan after Taliban takeover," NBC News, August 17, 2021 (https://tinyurl.com/4n8rbary).

49 Jennifer Smith et al., "Overloaded but airborne: Incredible photo shows 640 Afghans inside a US C-17 cargo jet—designed to carry 150—after they ran on before soldiers could close ramp and pilot decided to take off from Kabul and save them all," *Daily Mail*, August 16, 2021 (https://tinyurl.com/ymryawvd).

50 Kathy Gannon, "After Afghans fell from plane, families live with horror," Associated Press, September 21, 2021 (https://tinyurl.com/4stv62y9).

51 Emily Crane, "Body of Afghan found in US military plane's landing gear," *New York Post*, August 17, 2021 (https://tinyurl.com/5t4wf8zj).

52 "Remarks by President Biden on Afghanistan," The White House, August 16, 2021 (https://tinyurl.com/5n8hba47).

53 *Ibid.*

54 *Ibid.*

55 Joe Biden, Twitter, June 4, 2020 (https://tinyurl.com/25c9etxw).

56 Joseph A. Wulfsohn, "MSNBC's Nicolle Wallace praises Biden Afghan address, claims '95%' of Americans will 'agree with everything,'" Fox News, August 16, 2021 (https://tinyurl.com/ju9bum44).

57 Kayleigh McEnany, Twitter, August 17, 2021 (https://tinyurl.com/ytp3965m).

58 The Editorial Board, "The debacle in Afghanistan is the worst kind: Avoidable," *The Washington Post*, August 16, 2021 (https://tinyurl.com/2p96v3p9).

59 George Packer, "Biden's Betrayal of Afghans Will Live in Infamy," *The Atlantic*, August 15, 2021 (https://tinyurl.com/474kv9px).

60 David E. Sanger, "For Biden, Images of Defeat He Wanted to Avoid," *The New York Times*, August 31, 2021 (https://tinyurl.com/ru75kkrj).

61 Kayleigh McEnany, Twitter, August 17, 2021 (https://tinyurl.com/ymj7jmud).

62 Houston Keene, "Obama-era Afghanistan ambassador has 'grave questions' about Biden's 'ability to lead' US," Fox News, August 16, 2021 (https://tinyurl.com/4nnh6rv9).

63 "Obama CIA Director John Brennan: Biden Administration 'Caught Off Guard' in Afghanistan," GOP War Room, YouTube, August 16, 2021 (https://tinyurl.com/2twbmfzk).

64 Samuel Chamberlain, "Ex-CIA chief Panetta: Afghan debacle is Bay of Pigs moment for Biden," *New York Post*, August 16, 2021 (https://tinyurl.com/ycxxk7fv).

65 "Pelosi Statement Following President Biden's Remarks on Afghanistan," Speaker of the House, August 16, 2021 (https://tinyurl.com/c4f3cxfh).

66 Alexandra Hutzler, "Pentagon Spokesperson John Kirby Says There Are Thousands of Americans Still in Afghanistan," *Newsweek*, August 17, 2021 (https://tinyurl.com/yv6tt4ah).

67 "Press Briefing by Press Secretary Jen Psaki and National Security Advisor Jake Sullivan, August 17, 2021," The White House, August 17, 2021 (https://tinyurl.com/34djxkb4); Aaron Mehta, "Pentagon Leaders: Not Enough Capacity For Rescue Operations In Kabul," Breaking Defense, August 18, 2021 (https://tinyurl.com/2p923wwj).

68 Kayleigh McEnany, Twitter, August 18, 2021 (https://tinyurl.com/yjpkbaud).

69 John Cooper, Twitter, August 19, 2021 (https://tinyurl.com/48sncbns).

70 Chris Pleasance & James Fielding, "US troops fire shots into the air and use teargas on desperate crowds as chaos at Kabul airport enters fifth day: Taliban block Westerners from reaching flights and Afghan mothers give their BABIES to soldiers," Daily Mail, August 19, 2021 (https://tinyurl.com/2p8cumfd).

71 Ibid.

72 Kim Sengupta, "Afghanistan: Mothers throw babies over airport barbed wire to British soldiers as they are beaten by Taliban," The Independent, August 19, 2021 (https://tinyurl.com/2rm5wetf).

73 "Full transcript of ABC News' George Stephanopoulos' interview with President Joe Biden," ABC News, August 19, 2021 (https://tinyurl.com/mr2yem3f).

74 Ibid.

75 "Press Briefing by Press Secretary Jen Psaki, January 20, 2021," The White House, January 20, 2021 (https://tinyurl.com/4bf8dtc3).

76 Joe Concha, Twitter, August 19, 2021 (https://tinyurl.com/5yzuwrfw).

77 Kathryn Watson, Twitter, August 19, 2021 (https://tinyurl.com/bdftnbb8); Kathryn Watson, Twitter, August 19, 2021 (https://tinyurl.com/3rn6aaam).

78 "Department Press Briefing—August 19, 2021," U.S. Department of State, August 19, 2021 (https://tinyurl.com/3tmnjz4k).

79 *Ibid.*

80 "Afghanistan: Taliban says August 31 deadline for troop withdrawals a 'red line,'" Euronews, August 23, 2021 (https://tinyurl.com/5dfa2ra5).

81 Brigid Kennedy, "Biden says he's heard of 'no circumstance' in which an American is unable to access Kabul airport. ABC's Ian Pannell begs to differ," *The Week*, August 20, 2021 (https://tinyurl.com/2p9yb7ap).

82 Steven Nelson & Juliegrace Brufke, "Psaki claims it's 'irresponsible' to say Americans 'are stranded' in Afghanistan," *New York Post*, August 23, 2021 (https://tinyurl.com/57mrpn96).

83 Barbara Starr et al., "ISIS terror threat forces US military to establish alternate routes to Kabul airport," CNN, August 22, 2021 (https://tinyurl.com/mryk8sp8); Graison Dangor, "U.S. Embassy Tells Americans To Stay Away From Airport Due To 'Potential Security Threats'—Reportedly Islamic State," *Forbes*, August 21, 2021 (https://tinyurl.com/4eyam99f).

84 Roger Cohen, "Chaos Persists at Kabul Airport as Taliban Discuss New Government," *New York Post*, August 22, 2021 (https://tinyurl.com/msjjhhyj).

85 Jerry Dunleavy, "Biden raises specter of ISIS-K attack at Kabul airport," Yahoo! News, August 22, 2021 (https://tinyurl.com/4k4mbpym).

86 Jennifer Griffin, Twitter, August 26, 2021 (https://tinyurl.com/bdeebuwu).

87 Yaroslav Trofimov, Nancy A. Youssef & Sune Engel Rasmussen, "Kabul Airport Attack Kills 13 U.S. Service Members, at Least 90 Afghans," *The Wall Street Journal*, August 27, 2021 (https://tinyurl.com/2p8b97k2).

88   Bret Baier, Twitter, August 26, 2021 (https://tinyurl.com/22vb6mcx).

89   "Remarks by President Biden on the Terror Attack at Hamid Karzai International Airport," The White House, August 26, 2021 (https://tinyurl.com/ejdpdsym).

90   *Ibid.*

91   Kash Patel, "I ran Team Trump's Afghan withdrawal—Biden's attempt to blame us is just sad," *New York Post*, August 19, 2021 (https://tinyurl.com/my57aahd).

92   Julian Borger, "Trump reportedly tells Taliban official 'you are a tough people' in first phone call," *The Guardian*, March 3, 2020 (https://tinyurl.com/5796t78b).

93   "John Ratcliffe: Afghanistan 'debacle' is not an intelligence failure, it's a failure to listen to intelligence," Fox Business, August 18, 2021 (https://tinyurl.com/2pmd2pfu).

94   Natasha Turak, "'The puppet master is dead': Iranian Gen. Qasem Soleimani's power, and why his death is such a big deal," CNBC, January 3, 2020 (https://tinyurl.com/4wzv22kd).

95   Rebecca Kheel, "US goes full year without combat death in Afghanistan," *The Hill*, February 8, 2021 (https://tinyurl.com/2p8nuy8c).

96   Tom Bowman, "U.S. Military Has Withdrawn From Largest Base In Afghanistan, Handed Over Control," NPR, July 2, 2021 (https://tinyurl.com/rm9z75bm).

97   Kathy Gannon, "US left Afghan airfield at night, didn't tell new commander," Associated Press, July 5, 2021 (https://tinyurl.com/5c4un79b).

98   *Ibid.*

99   Angelica Stabile, "Grenell: Disaster in Afghanistan a DC politican failure, not an intelligence failure," Fox News, August 26, 2021 (https://tinyurl.com/582555d6).

100 Cal Thomas, "Biden has been wrong on every major foreign policy decision in last 4 decades," *The Washington Times*, August 16, 2021 (https://tinyurl.com/yptuts9e).

101 Ratcliffe, "Afghanistan 'debacle.'"

102 Stabile, "Grenell: Disaster."

103 "Full transcript of ABC News' George Stephanopoulos' interview with President Joe Biden," ABC News, August 19, 2021 (https://tinyurl.com/mr2yem3f).

104 Mark Mazzetti et al., "Intelligence Warned of Afghan Military Collapse, Despite Biden's Assurances," *The New York Times*, September 8, 2021 (https://tinyurl.com/24jmxwpm).

105 Vivian Salama, "Internal State Department Cable Warned of Kabul Collapse," *The Wall Street Journal*, August 19, 2021 (https://tinyurl.com/3nssjhbp).

106 Robert Burns & Lolita Baldor, "Joint Chiefs chairman calls Afghan war a 'strategic failure,' Associated Press, September 28, 2021 (https://tinyurl.com/47emy38f).

107 Gabrielle Fonrouge, Samuel Chamberlain & Mary Kay Linge, "These are the US service members killed in the Kabul airport attack," *New York Post*, August 27, 2021 (https://tinyurl.com/2p89hjkm).

108 "Daughter of fallen US Marine born Monday," Local News 8, September 14, 2021 (https://tinyurl.com/26d-bhbz2).

109 John 15:13, New International Version, Bible Gateway (https://tinyurl.com/4atz558s).

110 Arianna Poindexter, "99-year-old Mississippi WWII veteran, former POW reflects on his years of service," Action News 5, November 11, 2021 (https://tinyurl.com/2ejbf5r9).

111 Poindexter, "99-year-old Mississippi WWII veteran."

112 *See* Genesis 39:3–4, New International Version, Bible Gateway (https://tinyurl.com/y9r6rrnb); Genesis 39:21–23, New International Version, Bible Gateway (https://tinyurl.com/ckvuuufb).

113 Genesis 50:15, New International Version, Bible Gateway (https://tinyurl.com/3hurn79c).

114 Genesis 50:18, New International Version, Bible Gateway (https://tinyurl.com/2s4aha89).

115 Genesis 50:19–20, New International Version, Bible Gateway (https://tinyurl.com/2wv6jr6b).

116 Matthias Gebauer, "A Community of Faith and Fear," *Spiegel International*, March, 30, 2006 (https://tinyurl.com/4twrretc).

117 *Ibid.*

118 Mindy Belz, "The Taliban seizes power while taking names," *World*, August 16, 2021 (https://tinyurl.com/5n7kwzzy).

119 "Afghanistan," Open Doors (https://tinyurl.com/2hk-c2rfx).

120 "GCM and the Underground Church's Official Statement from Boots on the Ground in Afghanistan," Global Catalytic Ministries, August 17, 2021 (https://tinyurl.com/47wwwv3v).

121 Lindy Lowry, "A secret message from Christians in Afghanistan," Open Doors, September 29, 2021 (https://tinyurl.com/5annv95m).

122 Jim Denison, "The Taliban are killing Christians with Bibles on their cellphones," Denison Forum, August 20, 2021 (https://tinyurl.com/mudrtdtn).

123 Mark Kellner, "Afghanistan's Christians, small in number, have gone underground, expert says," *Washington Times*, August 19, 2021 (https://tinyurl.com/2p85k4eb).

124 *See* chapter 8 for more.

125 Kelsey Zorzi, "Afghanistan's Christians are turning off phones and going into hiding," *The Hill*, August 23, 2021 (https://tinyurl.com/ut5stsb2).

126 Fionn Shiner, "For Afghan Christians, the Taliban takeover is a nightmare," *The Spectator*, August 18, 2021 (https://tinyurl.com/4bxjke92).

127 Global Catalytic Ministries.

128 Psalms 2: 1–4, New International Version, Bible Gateway (https://tinyurl.com/4fmvj98w).

129   Global Catalytic Ministries.

130   Global Catalytic Ministries.

131   Global Catalytic Ministries.

132   Global Catalytic Ministries.

133   Global Catalytic Ministries.

134   Romans 5: 20–21, English Standard Version, Bible-Gateway.com (https://tinyurl.com/4hy256fr).

135   The Jeremiah Study Bible, 1504, English Standard Version (2019).

136   *Ibid*, 1455, Acts 8:1; Acts 8:3.

137   *Ibid*.

138   *Ibid*.

139   *Ibid*, 1457, Acts 9:1.

140   *Ibid*, 1455.

141   *Ibid,* 1543–44, 1 Corinthians 13: 4–7

142   Caitlin Burke, "Seeds of Revival in Afghanistan: Taliban's Oppressive Islamic Governance Creating 'Ripe Soil for Church to Grow,'" September 8, 2021 (https://tinyurl.com/4rwtfh7r).

143   "Taliban Say No Christians Live in Afghanistan; US Groups Concerned," *Voice of America*, May 16, 2022 (https://tinyurl.com/3nn4dud6).

144   Burke, "Seeds of Revival."

145   DC Talk, *Jesus Freak* 3 (May 1, 1997).

146   *Ibid*, 19.

147   Ken Curtis, "Whatever Happened to the Twelve Apostles?," Christianity.com, April 28, 2010 (https://tinyurl.com/3xfccu78).

148   DC Talk, *Jesus Freak*, 15.

149   Peter Walker, "900,000 Christians were 'martyred' over last decade, says Christian research," *The Independent*, January 13, 2017 (https://tinyurl.com/bdfxjduv).

150   *Ibid*.

151   "Pray For: Iran," Operation World (https://tinyurl.com/4n8623as).

152 *Ibid.*

153 *Ibid.*

154 Mark Howard, "God is Transforming the Tiny Church in Iran into One of the Fastest-Growing," Open Doors, April 17, 2017 (https://tinyurl.com/y6p3p8y9).

155 John Davison, "Christianity grows in Syrian town once besieged by Islamic State," Reuters, April 16, 2019 (https://tinyurl.com/bd6c537k).

156 "China," Open Doors (https://tinyurl.com/2jsyrrmp).

157 *Ibid.*

158 "Pray For: People's Republic of China," Operation World (https://tinyurl.com/5c3dep9w).

159 Eleanor Albert, "Christianity in China," Council on Foreign Relations, October 11, 2018 (https://tinyurl.com/2s4bxecu).

160 *Ibid.*

161 "In U.S., Decline of Christianity Continues at Rapid Pace," Pew Research Center, October 17, 2019 (https://tinyurl.com/m3ce37av); "You'll Be Surprised Where Christianity Is Growing—And Where It Is Not," Missions Box, April 26, 2019 (https://tinyurl.com/4hpza248).

162 *Ibid.*

163 Hebrews 13:3, New International Version, Bible Gateway (https://tinyurl.com/5n6fc3wf).

164 *See* Isaiah 61:3 (https://tinyurl.com/5n8fjhy).

165 Lowry, "A secret message."

166 *Ibid.*

167 *Ibid.*

168 Steve Portnoy, Twitter, January 9, 2022 (https://tinyurl.com/48vsxeh2).

169 Kelly O'Donnell, Twitter, January 13, 2022 (https://tinyurl.com/4shw2byj).

170 "Press Briefing by Press Secretary Jen Psaki and FEMA Administrator Deanne Criswell, January 14, 2022," The

White House, January 14, 2022 (https://tinyurl.com/4c-ceve7h).

171 "The East Room," The White House Historical Association (https://tinyurl.com/bdhnwh3s).

172 *Ibid.*

173 *Ibid.*

174 Thomas Moore, "Here are the reporters who were called on at Biden's first presser," *The Hill*, March 25, 2021 (https://tinyurl.com/mu4km4d6).

175 Mark Moore, "Most Americans say Biden not focused enough on inflation, the economy: poll," *New York Post*, January 16, 2022 (https://tinyurl.com/28427efu).

176 Matthew Chance et al., "Ukraine warns Russia has 'almost completed' build-up of forces near border," CNN, January 19, 2022 (https://tinyurl.com/yz6rw4hy).

177 Paul Sonne, Missy Ryan & John Hudson, "Russia planning potential sabotage operation in Ukraine, U.S. says," *The Washington Post*, January 14, 2022 (https://tinyurl.com/pusyj94p).

178 "Remarks by President Biden in Press Conference," The White House, January 19, 2022 (https://tinyurl.com/34nrz453).

179 *Ibid.*

180 *Ibid.*

181 *Ibid.*

182 Seung Min Kim, Twitter, January 19, 2022 (https://tinyurl.com/3hyssx22).

183 John L. Dorman, "White House press secretary Jen Psaki says she advises Biden not to take spontaneous questions from reporters," *Business Insider*, May 8, 2021 (https://tinyurl.com/jvt8cwy9).

184 "NBC's Richard Engel: Many Wonder If Biden Just Give Putin 'A Greenlight To Launch An Invasion," GOP War Room, YouTube, January 19, 2022 (https://tinyurl.com/5n8fajw8).

185 "CBS' Margaret Brennan Blasts Biden's Comment: 'Russia Is Going To Pounce On That,'" GOP War Room, YouTube, January 19, 2022 (https://tinyurl.com/mr24csum).

186 "CNN: Ukrainians 'Watched In Shock' As Biden Gave 'Green Light' To Putin To Invade Ukraine," GOP War Room, YouTube, January 19, 2022 (https://tinyurl.com/3xje84s8).

187 "CNN's Dana Bash On Joe Biden's Disastrous Press Conference, 'Clean Up On Aisle State Department,'" GOP War Room, YouTube, January 19, 2022 (https://tinyurl.com/yc59uh7t).

188 Shane Harris et al., "Road to war: U.S. struggled to convince allies, and Zelensky, of risk of invasion," *Washington Post*, August 16, 2022 (https://tinyurl.com/yvuyt89k).

189 *Ibid.*

190 Jacob Pramuk, "Trump: I don't give a specific ISIS plan because I don't want enemies to know it," CNBC, September 7, 2016 (https://tinyurl.com/bdhprpxv).

191 Kevin Liptak, "Biden says US troops in Ukraine are off the table but promises withering sanctions if Russia invades," CNN, December 8, 2021 (https://tinyurl.com/2p8ha4ad).

192 David E Sanger & Eric Schmitt, "U.S. Details Costs of a Russian Invasion of Ukraine," *The New York Times*, January 8, 2022 (https://tinyurl.com/yx6bknya).

193 *Ibid.*

194 "Remarks by President Biden in Press Conference," The White House, January 19, 2022 (https://tinyurl.com/34nrz453).

195 *Ibid.*

196 "Republican Party Platform of 1980," The American Presidency Project, July 15, 1980 (https://tinyurl.com/2p8mbnau).

197 Mark Landler & Gardiner Harris, "In Retaliation, U.S. Orders Russia to Close Consulate in San Francisco," *The New York Times*, August 31, 2017 (https://tinyurl.com/29cb77bj).

198 "U.S. Expels 60 Russian Officials, Closes Consulate In Seattle," NPR, March 26, 2018 (https://tinyurl.com/5n8f74xf); Michael R. Pompeo, "U.S. Withdrawal from the INF Treaty on August 2, 2019," U.S. Department of State, August 2, 2019 (https://tinyurl.com/yckzd5fu).

199 "Transcript: Robert O'Brien on 'Face the Nation,' August 9, 2020," CBS News, August 9, 2020 (https://tinyurl.com/yc8dvauc).

200 Thomas Colson, "Trump was slammed for cozying up to Putin, but Biden handed him a greater gift by waiving sanctions on a gas pipeline that could destabilize Europe," *Business Insider*, October 20, 2021 (https://tinyurl.com/ycy55rm5).

201 Josh Hammer, "Joe Biden Has Given Vladimir Putin a Huge Win on the Nord Stream 2 Pipeline," *Newsweek*, July 23, 2021 (https://tinyurl.com/2p82nccw).

202 Andrew Roth, "Biden says he won't send US troops to Ukraine to deter Russian threat," *The Guardian*, December 8, 2021 (https://tinyurl.com/zx2kncd3); Paul D. Shinkman, "Putin Signals Change of Tone on Ukraine After Biden Call," *US News*, December 8, 2021 (https://tinyurl.com/2p84n753).

203 "'This Week' Transcript 12-12-21: FEMA Administrator Deanne Criswell & Dr. Anthony Fauci," ABC News, December 12, 2021 (https://tinyurl.com/yckm42v2).

204 "Russia's military build-up enters a more dangerous phase," *The Economist*, February 11, 2022 (https://tinyurl.com/yy85hdna).

205 Olivier Knox, "Four escalating foreign problems test Biden's reaction speed," *The Washington Post*, January 25, 2022 (https://tinyurl.com/32kyked5).

206 *Ibid.*

207 Geoff Earle et al., "Joe goes SHOPPING and buys a Kamala mug while world holds it [*sic*] breath over Ukraine-Russia conflict: President threatens Putin with 'severe consequences' if he 'changes the world' with invasion," *Daily Mail*, January 25, 2022 (https://tinyurl.com/bddp2hhs).

208 "Remarks by President Biden in Press Gaggle," The White House, January 25, 2022 (https://tinyurl.com/4dsw8tn4).

209 Earle, "Joe goes SHOPPING."

210 Aamer Madhani et al., "Biden's 'Armageddon' talk edges beyond bounds of US intel," Associated Press, October 7, 2022 (https://tinyurl.com/fn3xb2wh).

211 Brad Dress, "US officials say Russia at 70 percent of buildup needed for invasion: reports," *The Hill*, February 5, 2022 (https://tinyurl.com/3m6k5vpx).

212 Matthew Lee, "US evacuating most Ukraine embassy staff over invasion fears," Associated Press, February 12, 2022 (https://tinyurl.com/4484snnx).

213 Kayleigh McEnany, Twitter, February 18, 2022 (https://tinyurl.com/3r89y5tt).

214 Sarah Kolinovsky & Justin Gomez, "Biden 'convinced' Putin has made decision to invade Ukraine as crisis with Russia escalates," ABC News, February 18, 2022 (https://tinyurl.com/ms4m23cj).

215 David Martin & Melissa Quinn, "U.S. has intel that Russian commanders have orders to proceed with Ukraine invasion," CBS News, February 20, 2022 (https://tinyurl.com/3xp4rt5b).

216 Courtney Subramanian, Matthew Brown & Joey Garrison, "Putin orders troops to two Ukraine regions after declaring their independence," *USA Today*, February 21, 2022 (https://tinyurl.com/mr48d9e4).

217 Tommy Wilkes & John Mccrank, "Explainer: Western sanctions on banks only scratch surface of Fortress Russia," Reuters, February 23, 2022 (https://tinyurl.com/bd8sm6v2).

218 CPAC (https://tinyurl.com/45vvr87h).

219 "Explosions mark beginning of Russian invasion of Ukraine, NATO official says | Special Report," CBS News, YouTube, February 23, 2022 (https://tinyurl.com/3b7hc7ta).

220 *Ibid.*

221 "Ukrainian TV broadcasts instructions for how to make Molotov cocktails," CNN, February 25, 2022 (https://tinyurl.com/4zybak6n).

222 Taylor Simone Mitchell, "Ukrainian parents brace their children for a Russian invasion, sending them to school with strickers identifying their blood type," *Business Insider*, February 22, 2022 (https://tinyurl.com/yyxf9y5e).

223 Patrick Reilly, "Viral video allegedly shows broken Ukrainian father saying goodbye to daughter fleeing to safety," *New York Post*, February 24, 2022 (https://tinyurl.com/mru9eyn9).

224 Mstyslav Chernov, "A shelling, a young girl, and hopeless moments in a hospital," Associated Press, February 27, 2022 (https://tinyurl.com/4uruvzrs).

225 "'Show this to Putin': A 6-year-old girl killed in Ukraine," CNN, February 28, 2022 (https://tinyurl.com/2xw-f7xbk).

226 Jim Sciutto & Katie Bo Williams, "US concerned Kyiv could fall to Russia within days, sources familiar with intel say," CNN, February 25, 2022 (https://tinyurl.com/36k69era).

227 Mark Mazzetti et al., "Intelligence Warned of Afghan Military Collapse, Despite Biden's Assurances," *The*

New York Times, August 17, 2021 (https://tinyurl.com/24jmxwpm).

228 Harris, "Road to war."

229 Julian Vierlinger, "UN: Ukraine refugee crisis is Europe's biggest since WWII," Atlantic Council, April 20, 2022 (https://tinyurl.com/2p89cxyw).

230 "Kyiv prepares for a gruelling siege," *The Economist*, March 1, 2022 (https://tinyurl.com/muvm5v7d).

231 *Ibid.*

232 Mark Puleo, "Ukrainian refugees face frigid wintry conditions as they flee war," AccuWeather, March 2, 2022 (https://tinyurl.com/mrxzpkdu).

233 "A new refugee crisis has come to Europe," *The Economist*, March 5, 2022 (https://tinyurl.com/y4h9etr6).

234 "Operational Data Portal Ukraine Refugee Situation," UNHCR (https://tinyurl.com/54bkxhfv).

235 Evgeniy Maloletka, "In pictures: Maternity hospital bombed in Ukraine," CNN, March 14, 2022 (https://tinyurl.com/4vbashw6).

236 Mstyslav Chernov, "Pregnant woman, baby die after Russian bombing in Mariupol," Associated Press, March 14, 2022 (https://tinyurl.com/yxwb259f).

237 *Ibid.*

238 *Ibid.*

239 *Ibid.*

240 "Faces of the Fallen," *Washington Post* (https://tinyurl.com/2p9drxxm).

241 Steve Warren, "'Nothing Sacred': Russia Destroys One of Orthodox Christianity's Holiest Sites—113 Ukrainian Churches Reported Damaged," CBN News, June 6, 2022 (https://tinyurl.com/ybykwfa9).

242 Steve Warren, "'Jesus. He Died for Us': Nine-Year-Old TX Shooting Victim Shared Gospel to Social Media Before She Died," CBN News, May 27, 2022 (https://tinyurl.com/77t3yu69).

243   *Ibid.*

244   *Ibid.*

245   Jasmine Aguilera, "Uvalde Community Worships Together on First Sunday Since School Shooting Claimed 21 Lives," *Time*, June 6, 2022 (https://tinyurl.com/4ry4dbde).

246   The Jeremiah Study Bible, 231, Deuteronomy 6:18.

247   Aguilera, "Uvalde Community Worships Together."

248   Chris Harris, "Family of Uvalde Victim Eliahna Garcia Holds Funeral Days After She Would Have Turned 10," *People*, June 6, 2022, (https://tinyurl.com/4ww5fy3h).

249   "Logical Problem of Evil," Internet Encyclopedia of Philosophy (https://tinyurl.com/29r7jycm).

250   *Ibid.*

251   C. S. Lewis, *The Problem of Pain*, HarperCollins (1940).

252   *Ibid*, 3.

253   *Ibid*, 16.

254   Benjamin Morrison, "Bomb Shelter Ministry in My Ukrainian Town," *Christianity Today*, March 3, 2022 (https://tinyurl.com/5n8xxckr).

255   Aguilera, "Uvalde Community Worships."

256   Francis S. Collins, *The Language of God*, Simon & Schuster (2006).

257   *Ibid.* 19–20.

258   *Ibid.*

259   Timothy Keller, *Walking with God through Pain and Suffering*, 65, Penguin Books (2013).

260   Samuel G. Freedman, "In a Crisis, Humanists Seem Absent," *New York Times*, December 28, 2012 (https://tinyurl.com/42ru3spx).

261   Keller, *Walking with God*, 65.

262   "Views on human suffering and God's role in it," Pew Research Center, November 23, 2021 (https://tinyurl.com/bdrtykvf).

263   *Ibid.*

264 *Ibid.*

265 Freedman, "In a Crisis."

266 *Ibid.*

267 Bob Abernethy, "Hurricane Katrina Faith-Based Relief Efforts," PBS, September 2, 2005 (https://tinyurl.com/2p9fjyne).

268 Keller, *Walking with God*, 41.

269 Takanori Inoue, "The Early Church's Approach to the Poor in Society and Its Significance to the Church's Social Engagement Today," Asbury Theological Seminary (https://tinyurl.com/murp7kvr).

270 John Stonestreet, "How Christianity Created the Hospital," *Daily Citizen*, August 17, 2022 (https://tinyurl.com/4kez2vfz); "Christian History Timeline: Healthcare and Hospitals in the Mission of the Church," Christian History Institute (https://tinyurl.com/2t-w6hrhe).

271 Keller, *Walking with God*, 21.

272 Lewis, *Problem of Pain*, 38.

273 Lewis, *Problem of Pain*, 38–39.

274 Keller, *Walking with God*, 104.

275 Keller, *Walking with God*, 105.

276 Keller, *Walking with God*, 105.

277 "Apologia," Blue Letter Bible (https://tinyurl.com/y3tb7rdy).

278 "Alvin Plantinga—Does Evil Disprove God?," YouTube, November 10, 2014 (https://tinyurl.com/2p9yfdyu).

279 Isaiah 55:9, New International Version, Bible Gateway (https://tinyurl.com/3sr9cnrj).

280 Proverbs 3:5–6, New International Version, Bible Gateway (https://tinyurl.com/4cxu923e).

281 Alvin Plantinga, *God, Freedom, and Evil*, 28, Eerdmans (March 21, 1989).

282 *Ibid*, 30.

283 Lewis, *Problem of Pain*, 48.

284 *Ibid*, 19.
285 Keller, *Walking with God,* 136.
286 Kayleigh McEnany, *The New American Revolution*, Simon & Schuster (January 9, 2018).
287 *Ibid*, 14, 22, 29.
288 *Ibid*, 30.
289 *Ibid*.
290 *See Ibid*, chapter 1.
291 *Ibid*, 91.
292 The Jeremiah Study Bible, 1452, Acts 6:8.
293 *Ibid*, 1452, Acts 6:10.
294 *Ibid*, 1452, Acts 6:15.
295 *Ibid*, 1452–1455, Acts 7:1–53.
296 *Ibid*, 1455, Acts 7:54.
297 *Ibid*, 1455, Acts 7:56–58.
298 *Ibid*, 1455, Acts 7:59–60.
299 *Ibid*, 1455, Acts 8:1.
300 *Ibid*, 1455.
301 *Ibid*, 1455, Acts 7:58.
302 *Ibid*, 1455.
303 *Ibid,* 637, Job 1:1.
304 *Ibid,* 637, Job 1:2.
305 *Ibid,* 639, Job 1:20–22.
306 *Ibid,* 640, Job 3:11.
307 *Ibid,* 640, Job 3:16.
308 *Ibid,* 640, Job 3:20–22.
309 *Ibid,* 663, Job 29:21.
310 *Ibid,* 663, Job 30:1.
311 *Ibid,* 648, Job 12:4.
312 *Ibid,* 663 Job 30:9–10.
313 *Ibid,* 639, Job 1:22.
314 *Ibid,* 675, 677, Job 42:10.
315 *Ibid,* 671.
316 Keller, *Walking with God,* 119.
317 The Jeremiah Study Bible, 646–47, Job 9:32–33.

318 *Ibid*, 655, Job 19:25.
319 *Ibid*; Clarence L. Hayes Jr., "What Is the Oldest Book in the Bible?," Crosswalk.com, January 11, 2022 (https://tinyurl.com/yzwzxpnf).
320 The Jeremiah Study Bible, 655.
321 *Ibid*, 1293, Matthew 26:36.
322 "Jerusalem olive trees among oldest in world," Australian Broadcasting Corporation, October 19, 2012 (https://tinyurl.com/48bfbfbr).
323 *Ibid*.
324 The Jeremiah Study Bible, 1293, Matthew 26:37.
325 *Ibid*, 1293, Matthew 26:38.
326 *Ibid*, 1293.
327 *Ibid*, 1293, Matthew 26:39.
328 *Ibid*, 1388, Luke 22:43
329 *Ibid*, 1388, Luke 22:44.
330 Lee Strobel, *The Case for Christ: A Journalist's Personal Investigation of the Evidence for Jesus*, 211, Zondervan (1998).
331 Saugato Biswas et al., "A Curious Case of Sweating Blood," Indian Journal of Dermatology, November–December 2013 (https://tinyurl.com/4w6we73u).
332 Strobel, *The Case for Christ*, 214.
333 The Jeremiah Study Bible, 1293, Matthew 26:42.
334 *Ibid*, 1333, Mark 14:36
335 Steve Rogers, "When we say 'Father,'" Billy Graham Evangelistic Association of Canada, June 2, 2021 (https://tinyurl.com/5hfwa8n4).
336 Strobel, *The Case for Christ*, 144, 149.
337 *Ibid*, 149.
338 *Ibid*.
339 Keller, *Walking with God*, 51.
340 *Ibid*, 119.
341 The Jeremiah Study Bible, 1298, Matthew 27:46

342   Billy Graham, "Did God Abandon Jesus on the Cross? Billy Graham Answers," Billy Graham Evangelistic Association, March 24, 2016 (https://tinyurl.com/ynpfep9j).

343   "What the Bible Says About Christ's Second Coming," David Jeremiah blog, (https://tinyurl.com/25h5r9y6).

344   *Ibid.*

345   18 USC Section 1531(b)(1) (https://tinyurl.com/4sn-8pzvz); Julie Rovner, "'Partial-Birth Abortion': Separating Fact From Spin," NPR, February 21, 2006 (https://tinyurl.com/2p9f2ctm).

346   Rovner, "Partial-Birth Abortion"; *Stenberg v. Carhart,* 530 U.S. 914 (2000) (https://tinyurl.com/yupt6f5m).

347   Conor Friedersdorf, "Why Dr. Kermit Gosnell's Trial Should Be a Front-Page Story," *The Atlantic,* April 12, 2013 (https://tinyurl.com/mr3d4e8c).

348   Shannen W. Coffin, "Kermit Gosnell Is Not an Outlier," *National Review,* April 12, 2013 (https://tinyurl.com/2p-8wxybe).

349   *Stenberg,* 922.

350   *Ibid,* 973.

351   *Ibid,* 922.

352   *Ibid,* 923.

353   *Ibid.*

354   *Ibid,* 924.

355   *Ibid,* 925.

356   Mayo Clinic Staff, "Fetal development: The 2nd trimester," Mayo Clinic (https://tinyurl.com/35pcc3t6).

357   *Ibid.*

358   Pregnancy +, Philips (https://tinyurl.com/3fxrbmwa).

359   *Stenberg,* 925.

360   *Ibid.*

361   *Ibid,* 926.

362   *Stenberg,* (Kennedy, J., dissenting, 958).

363   *Ibid.*

364   *Ibid.*

365   *Ibid*, 959.

366   *Ibid.*

367   *Ibid.*

368   *Stenberg*, 927.

369   *Ibid.*

370   *Ibid*, 927, 936.

371   Mayo Clinic Staff, "Fetal development."

372   Stuart WG Derbyshire, "Reconsidering fetal pain," 4, Journal of Medical Ethics, November 14, 2019 (https://tinyurl.com/ybwjab27); *See* Charlotte Lozier Institute, "Fact Sheet: Science of Fetal Pain," Charlotte Lozier Institute, September 13, 2022 (https://tinyurl.com/2s45nna7).

373   *Stenberg*, (Kennedy, J., dissenting, 960).

374   *Ibid*, 963.

375   *Stenberg*, (Thomas, J., dissenting, 1007).

376   *Stenberg*, (Scalia, J., dissenting, 953).

377   *Ibid.*

378   "President Bush Signs Partial Birth Abortion Ban Act of 2003," The White House, November 5, 2003 (https://tinyurl.com/4bw52yeh).

379   Richard W. Stevenson, "Bush Signs Ban on a Procedure For Abortions," November 6, 2003 (https://tinyurl.com/ms26499p).

380   "President Bush Signs."

381   *Gonzales v. Carhart*, 550 U.S. 124 (2007) (https://tinyurl.com/mrxm6mrm).

382   Adam Liptak, "The New 5-to-4 Supreme Court," *The New York Times*, April 22, 2007 (https://tinyurl.com/573bbw88).

383   William Davis, "Virginia Del. Kathy Tran Submitted Bill To Save Caterpillars On Same Day As Late-Stage Abortion Bill," *Daily Caller*, January 31, 2019 (https://tinyurl.com/yufarv5r).

384   Alexandra DeSanctis, "Virginia Governor Defends Letting Infants Die," *National Review*, January 30, 2019 (https://tinyurl.com/29msfm4k).

385   "S.311—116th Congress (2019-2020)" (https://tinyurl.com/4b4v93w5).

386   Alexandra DeSanctis, "House Democrats Refuse 75 Times to Vote on Born-Alive Bill," *National Review*, July 24, 2019 (https://tinyurl.com/44rxhh3h).

387   *Ibid.*

388   Peter Kasperowicz, "210 Democrats vote against bill requiring medical care for babies born alive after abortion attempt," Fox News, January 11, 2023 (https://tinyurl.com/4w353p32).

389   "Jill Stanek Testimony," U.S. Senate Judiciary Committee, 1, February 11, 2020 (https://tinyurl.com/9wtyr35y).

390   *Ibid.*

391   *Ibid*, 1–2.

392   *Ibid*, 2.

393   *Ibid.*

394   *Ibid*, 3.

395   *Ibid.*

396   *Ibid*, 2.

397   *Ibid.*

398   Andrew C. McCarthy, "When Obama Voted For Infanticide," *National Review*, February 9, 2012 (https://tinyurl.com/yt7945r2).

399   *Ibid.*

400   *Ibid.*

401   "H.R.3755—117th Congress (2021-2022)" (https://tinyurl.com/mtdsbfmn).

402   Katie Yoder, "US Senate's vote on radical abortion bill: Here's what to know," Catholic News Agency, May 11, 2022 (https://tinyurl.com/3853bbjz).

403   *Ibid.*

404 Virginia Allen, "Democrats Seek to Pass What Could Be World's Most Permissive Abortion Bill," *The Daily Signal*, May 10, 2022 (https://tinyurl.com/3pb9kace).

405 Michelle Ye Hee Lee, "Is the United States one of seven countries that 'allow elective abortions after 20 weeks of pregnancy?,'" *The Washington Post*, October 9, 2017 (https://tinyurl.com/54rpuce5).

406 Allen, "Democrats Seek."

407 *Ibid.*

408 *Dobbs v. Jackson Women's Health Organization,* Oral Arguments 54, December 1, 2021 (https://tinyurl.com/rc4trbtj).

409 "Remarks by President Biden on the Supreme Court Decision to Overturn Roe v. Wade," The White House, June 24, 2022 (https://tinyurl.com/yjwphf85).

410 Kristan Hawkins, "Remove statues of Margaret Sanger, Planned Parenthood founder tied to eugenics and racism," *USA Today*, July 23, 2020 (https://tinyurl.com/4ejt6tcc).

411 *Ibid.*

412 *Ibid.*

413 *Ibid.*

414 "Opposition Claims About Margaret Sanger," Planned Parenthood, April 2021 (https://tinyurl.com/2rj5u869).

415 *Ibid.*

416 Susan A. Cohen, "Abortion and Women of Color: The Bigger Picture," Guttmacher Institute, August 6, 2008 (https://tinyurl.com/4e5u7j5v).

417 Michael R. Pompeo, "Determination of the Secretary of State on Atrocities in Xinjiang," U.S. Department of State, January 19, 2021 (https://tinyurl.com/mszr8ewc).

418 Jen Kirby, "Concentration camps and forced labor: China's repression of the Uighurs, explained," *Vox*, September 25, 2020 (https://tinyurl.com/5bemvphm).

419　"China cuts Uighur births with IUDs, abortion, sterilization," Associated Press, June 28, 2020 (https://tinyurl.com/2p8ptf9s).

420　*Ibid.*

421　*Ibid.*

422　*Ibid.*

423　*Ibid.*

424　*Ibid.*

425　*Ibid.*

426　Hawkins, "Remove statues."

427　Sarah Zhang, "The Last Children of Down Syndrome," *The Atlantic*, December 2020 (https://tinyurl.com/5n7w359k).

428　*Ibid.*

429　*Ibid.*

430　Julian Quinones & Arijeta Lajka, "'What kind of society do you want to live in?': Inside the country where Down syndrome is disappearing," CBS News, August 15, 2017 (https://tinyurl.com/mwavpvjw).

431　Lois Rogers, "Could this be the last generation of Down's syndrome children?," *The Telegraph*, October 1, 2021 (https://tinyurl.com/3pwr97fy).

432　*Ibid.*

433　 Psalm 139:13–14, New International Version, Bible Gateway (https://tinyurl.com/y4ej7atw).

434　Zhang, "The Last Children."

435　*Ibid.*

436　*Ibid.*

437　 Kayleigh McEnany, *For Such a Time as This*, Post Hill Press (2021).

438　Nancie Petrucelli, MS, Mary B Daily, MD, PhD, and Tuya Pal, MD, "BRCA1- and BRCA2-Associated Hereditary Breast and Ovarian Cancer," GeneReviews, December 15, 2016 (https://tinyurl.com/22xhz3pd).

439 Mark Batterson, *Draw the Circle: The 40 Day Prayer Challenge*, Zondervan (2012).

440 *Ibid*, 2.

441 *Ibid*, 22.

442 *Ibid*, 82.

443 *Ibid*, 84.

444 "Way Maker," Sinach, May 30, 2015.

445 Matthew 18:20, New International Version, Bible Gateway (https://tinyurl.com/34m7dyue).

446 Philippians 4:6–7, New International Version, Bible Gateway (https://tinyurl.com/f8av2zp7).

447 Politico Staff, "Read Justice Alito's initial draft abortion opinion which would overturn Roe v. Wade," *Politico*, May 2, 2022 (https://tinyurl.com/yr9pru3n).

448 *Ibid*.

449 Kipp Jones, "'They'll Go After Gay Marriage and Maybe Brown v. Board of Education': Joy Behar Worries Supreme Court Might Allow Racial Segregation Again," Mediaite, May 3, 2022 (https://tinyurl.com/3sd26x4a).

450 "Press Briefing by Press Secretary Jen Psaki, May 10, 2022," The White House, May 10, 2022 (https://tinyurl.com/4n2vykk9).

451 *Ibid*.

452 18 U.S.C. § 1507 (https://tinyurl.com/32r2nkmc).

453 Maria Cramer & Jesus Jimenez, "Armed Man Traveled to Justice Kavanaugh's Home to Kill Him, Officials Say," June 8, 2022 (https://tinyurl.com/286ewu2z).

454 Ellie Silverman et al., "Man with gun is arrested near Brett Kavanaugh's home, officials say," June 8, 2022 (https://tinyurl.com/ear6rcms).

455 "California Man Facing Federal Charges in Maryland for Attempted Murder of a United States Judge," The United States Attorney's Office District of Maryland, June 8, 2022 (https://tinyurl.com/22wjmj5k).

456   Timothy H. J. Nerozzi, "'Ruth Sent Us' group hinted at targeting Supreme Court Justice Barrett's children, church," Fox News, June 10, 2022 (https://tinyurl.com/598bvynw).

457   Emma Colton, "Pro-choice protesters descend on Coney Barrett's home with blood and doll props," Fox News, June 19, 2022 (https://tinyurl.com/3t8yka3s).

458   "White House condemns pro-abortion violence after new Jane's Revenge threats," Catholic News Agency, June 15, 2022 (https://tinyurl.com/552eb8kj).

459   *Ibid.*

460   Liz Wolfe, "Elizabeth Warren Wants To Shut Down All of the Country's Crisis Pregnancy Centers," Reason, July 14, 2022 (https://tinyurl.com/yeyt2ksd).

461   Caroline Downey, "FBI Investigations into Wave of Vandalism against Pro-Life Pregnancy Centers Stall," *National Review*, August 8, 2022 (https://tinyurl.com/96ewb2ks).

462   *Ibid.*

463   "Memorandum for Director, Federal Bureau of Investigation; Director, Executive Office for U.S. Attorneys; Assistant Attorney General, Criminal Division; United States Attorneys," Department of Justice, October 4, 2021 (https://tinyurl.com/4mffpb3b).

464   Nicole Ault, "The Attacks on Crisis-Pregnancy Centers," *The Wall Street Journal*, June 20, 2022 (https://tinyurl.com/2ckmaps5).

465   *Ibid.*

466   Life International (https://tinyurl.com/ykuduwh7).

467   *Dobbs v. Jackson Women's Health Organization*, 597 U.S. (2022) 3, 35 (https://tinyurl.com/j4xuj48v).

468   *Ibid*, 1.

469   *Ibid,* 3, footnote 4.

470 Timothy P. Carney, "The pervading dishonesty of Roe v. Wade," *Washington Examiner*, January 23, 2012 (https://tinyurl.com/mpfbxrwf).

471 *Dobbs,* 54.

472 *Ibid.*

473 *Ibid,* 46.

474 *Ibid,* 2.

475 *Ibid,* 7.

476 *Ibid.*

477 *Outnumbered*, Fox News, June 24, 2022.

478 Michelle Boorstein, "As DC shuts down for a blizzard, a small, faithful crowd still joins the March for Life," *The Washington Post*, January 22, 2016 (https://tinyurl.com/ycy9prpf).

479 McEnany, *The New American Revolution.*

480 Evie Fordham, "Jen Psaki dodges question on whether Biden thinks 15-week-old unborn baby is a person," Fox News, June 21, 2021 (https://tinyurl.com/3c4d2ub6).

481 Jack Butler, "Joe Biden is Wrong about Catholic Teaching on Abortion," National Review, September 23, 2022 (https://tinyurl.com/2p95crpd).

482 *Ibid.*

483 "Respect for Unborn Human Life: The Church's Constant Teaching," United States Conference of Catholic Bishops (https://tinyurl.com/2bzkztkm).

484 Brittany Bernstein, "Newsom Campaign Runs Billboard Ads in Red States Advertising California Abortions," National Review, September 16, 2022 (https://tinyurl.com/3td5r7m4).

485 *Ibid.*

486 Matt Hadro, "Pelosi defends her support for legal abortion: 'God has given us a free will,'" Catholic News Agency, September 23, 2021 (https://tinyurl.com/hxa3n35p).

487   Katie Yoder, "Nancy Pelosi Says It's 'Sinful' to Protect Babies from Abortions," Life News, August 30, 2022 (https://tinyurl.com/fesn55n7).

488   Marquise Francis, "Stacey Abrams says her faith in God guides her abortion-rights stance," Yahoo! News, August 3, 2022 (https://tinyurl.com/353jva2f).

489   Ben Johnson, "Fact Check: 'There Is No Such Thing as a Heartbeat at 6 Weeks,' Says Stacey Abrams," *The Daily Signal*, September 23, 2022 (https://tinyurl.com/yww64x4j).

490   Timothy H. J. Nerozzi, "Planned Parenthood edits fact sheet to say no heartbeat at 6 weeks of fetal development," Fox News, September 22, 2022 (https://tinyurl.com/ycken6h2).

491   *Ibid*.

492   "Slide show: Fetal ultrasound," Mayo Clinic (https://tinyurl.com/ceu5cunf).

493   Nerozzi, "Planned Parenthood edits fact sheet."

494   *Ibid*.

495   Josephine Harvey, "Stacey Abrams Enrages Republicans By Citing Science On 'Fetal Heartbeats,'" HuffPost, September 22, 2022 (https://tinyurl.com/mrxjmy62).

496   Glenn Kessler, Twitter, September 22, 2022 (https://tinyurl.com/23bwsu9c).

497   *Ibid*.

498   "Your 6-Week Ultrasound: What to Expect," Healthline (https://tinyurl.com/5n6d2s68).

499   Guy Benson, Twitter, September 22, 2022 (https://tinyurl.com/2z7wjkhb).

500   "Pregnant and Recently pregnant People," March 3, 2022 (https://tinyurl.com/yc2y5spj).

501   Focus on the Family, Advocacy Team, "Scriptures Advocating for the Pre-Born," Focus on the Family, February 19, 2021 (https://tinyurl.com/5dmwrj73).

502 Jeremiah 1:5, New International Version, Bible Hub (https://tinyurl.com/2p88hv9p).

503 Isaiah 49:1, New International Version, Bible Gateway (https://tinyurl.com/4u7tvc9f); Jess Ford, "What Does the Bible Say About Abortion?," Focus on the Family, March 4, 2021 (https://tinyurl.com/3jhr83p9).

504 "Scriptures Advocating for the Pre-Born."

505 Luke 12:7, New International Version, Bible Hub (https://tinyurl.com/2p9hdwet).

506 Genesis 1:27, New International Version, Bible Hub (https://tinyurl.com/mr34efzp).

507 Job 31:15, New International Version, Bible Hub (https://tinyurl.com/mryesaf8).

508 Psalm 22:10, New International Version, Bible Hub (https://tinyurl.com/ywce6jy9).

509 "Scriptures Advocating for the Pre-Born."

510 *Ibid.*

511 Luke 1:41, New International Version, Bible Hub (https://tinyurl.com/29f9hry2).

512 Psalm 127:3, New International Version, Bible Hub (https://tinyurl.com/mv37cfzh).

513 "Scriptures Advocating for the Pre-Born."

514 *Ibid.*

515 *Konen v. Caldiera*, Plaintiff "Statement of Facts and Claims," LibertyCenter.org (https://tinyurl.com/4f-bh7fwm).

516 *Ibid,* 6.

517 *Ibid.*

518 *Ibid,* 7.

519 *Ibid.*

520 *Ibid.*

521 Nikolas Lanum, "California mom, attorney accuse teachers of 'predatory behavior' for telling 11-year-old she was transgender," Fox News, January 25, 2022 (https://tinyurl.com/yv533fzt).

522 *Konen*, 10.

523 *Ibid*, 11.

524 Danielle Echeverria, "2 California teachers attacked over LGBTQ outreach are cleared of wrongdoing," *San Francisco Chronicle*, July 9, 2022 (https://tinyurl.com/bdeve5fh).

525 Lanum, "California mom."

526 "BREAKING: Firm sues Florida public school district for hiding gender counseling from parents," GenSpect. org, January 25, 2022 (https://tinyurl.com/2npuvmw5).

527 Natasha Anderson, "EXCLUSIVE: 'They created a double life for my daughter,'" *Daily Mail*, January 27, 2022 (https://tinyurl.com/bdpvde23).

528 "Transgender Student Guidance for School Districts," State of New Jersey Department of Education (https://tinyurl.com/8ebd2trj).

529 Zachary Mettler, "New Jersey to Require 1st Graders to Learn About Gender Identity Starting This Fall," Daily Citizen, April 8, 2022 (https://tinyurl.com/2p8ktd7t).

530 "2020 New Jersey Student Learning Standards—Comprehensive Health and Physical Education," State of New Jersey Department of Education (https://tinyurl.com/bdz2crsj).

531 Houston Keene, "New Jersey to require 2nd graders learn about gender identity in fall, alarming parents," April 7, 2022 (https://tinyurl.com/4bw2nmx7).

532 *Ibid*.

533 *Ibid*.

534 Dana Kennedy, "Dalton parents enraged over 'masturbation' videos for first-graders," *New York Post*, May 29, 2021 (https://tinyurl.com/2vf6pv5s); Dana Kennedy, "Columbia Prep students and parents reel after class on 'porn literacy,'" *New York Post*, May 22, 2021 (https://tinyurl.com/4aja5x3p).

535 Kennedy, "Dalton parents."

536 *Ibid.*

537 *Ibid.*

538 *Ibid.*

539 *Ibid.*

540 *Ibid.*

541 *Ibid.*

542 Kennedy, "Columbia Prep."

543 *Ibid.*

544 *Ibid.*

545 *Ibid.*

546 *Ibid.*

547 *Ibid.*

548 *Ibid.*

549 *Ibid.*

550 *Ibid.*

551 *Ibid.*

552 Hannah Natanson, "Fairfax school system pulls two books from libraries after complaints over sexual content," *The Washington Post*, September 28, 2021 (https://tinyurl.com/haxczp6h).

553 *Ibid.*

554 *Ibid.*

555 *Ibid.*

556 Nicole Asbury, "Fairfax schools will return 2 books to shelves after reviewing complaints over content," *Washington Post*, November 23, 2021 (https://tinyurl.com/595eect8).

557 Brian Lopez, "Keller school officials order 41 books—including the Bible and an Anne Frank adaptation—off of library shelves," *The Texas Tribune*, August 16, 2022 (https://tinyurl.com/sdv9v26f).

558 HB 1557, Florida House of Representatives, 2022 (https://tinyurl.com/5ay8ucwa).

559 Alison Durkee, "Disney Says Striking Down 'Don't Say Gay' Law Is Company's 'Goal' After DeSantis Signs Bill," *Forbes*, April 14, 2022 (https://tinyurl.com/yc6r63b9).

560 Andrew Mark Miller, "Psaki fights back tears over Florida's parental rights bill, says it's hurting children's 'lives,'" Fox News, April 19, 2022 (https://tinyurl.com/3xhzsf88).

561 "Kayleigh McEnany: Jen Psaki should cry over 62M aborted children," *Daily Mail* (https://tinyurl.com/3p-5d9vdb).

562 Gary Fineout, "Poll: Americans split over Florida's controversial bills on gender identity and race," Politico, March 16, 2022 (https://tinyurl.com/52ny4say).

563 Ben Johnson, "New Poll Finds What Most Americans Think About Teaching K-3 Children About Sexual Orientation, Transgender Issues," *The Daily Wire*, April 18, 2022 (https://tinyurl.com/4ccz8pa9).

564 *Ibid.*

565 Jonathan Butcher, "New Jersey Schools Want To Talk to Kids About Sex—And Keep It a Secret," Heritage Foundation, April 19, 2022 (https://tinyurl.com/4r7ws2bb).

566 Caitlin O'Kane, "Head of teachers union says critical race theory isn't taught in schools, vows to defend 'honest history,'" CBS News, July 8, 2021 (https://tinyurl.com/4bn4x34h).

567 Christopher F. Rufo, Twitter (https://tinyurl.com/2c-j96ptj).

568 Christopher F. Rufo, "Critical Race Theory in Education," ChristopherRufo.com, April 27, 2021 (https://tinyurl.com/m899k2xx).

569 Sam Dorman, "At least 25 public schools, districts pushing kids' book featuring 'Whiteness' contract with devil: report," Fox News, July 8, 2021 (https://tinyurl.com/3mt5b6ad); Christopher F. Rufo, Twitter, July 8, 2021 (https://tinyurl.com/4xxy9xjb).

570 *Stacy Deemar v. Board of Education of the City of Evanston/Skokie*, "Complaint for Declaratory and Injunctive Relief," June 29, 2021 (https://tinyurl.com/36abyvp5).

571 Rufo, "Racism in the Cradle."

572 *Ibid.*

573 Haley Strack, "Atlanta Mom Exposes Elementary School's Racist Segregation Policy," *The Federalist*, August 11, 2021 (https://tinyurl.com/2jn3p5f2).

574 *Ibid.*

575 *Ibid.*

576 *Ibid.*

577 Emily Crane, "Atlanta mom says school 'segregated' daughter into black-only classes: lawsuit," *New York Post*, August 11, 2021 (https://tinyurl.com/54bkw97b).

578 Sean Salai, "Report: More universities holding segregated graduation events," *Washington Times*, April 18, 2022 (https://tinyurl.com/ypc2pw8t).

579 *Brown v. Board of Education*, 347 U.S. 483 (1954) (https://tinyurl.com/2s35uu4s).

580 "Ethnic Studies Model Curriculum - Chapter 3: Instructional Guidance for K–12 Education, SBE-Approved Draft," April 2021, California Department of Education (https://tinyurl.com/5cn2wbr9).

581 Kenny Xu, "California's 'Ethnic Studies' Gold Rush," *The Wall Street Journal*, July 12, 2021 (https://tinyurl.com/3xx7j59h).

582 "Ethnic Studies Model Curriculum."

583 Christopher F. Rufo, "Revenge of the Gods," *City Journal*, March 10, 2021 (https://tinyurl.com/3c46xndj).

584 *Ibid.*

585 *Ibid.*

586 Evan Symon, "Lawsuit Forces California Department of Education to Remove Aztec God Chants From Ethnic Studies Curriculum," *California Globe*, January 18, 2022 (https://tinyurl.com/47j9cevt).

587 Christopher F. Rufo, "Woke Elementary," *City Journal*, January 13, 2021 (https://tinyurl.com/57vk2h8p).

588 *Ibid.*

589 "Teacher Tells Loudoun School Board 'I Quit' After School Bashes 'White, Christian, Able-Bodied Females,'" CBN News, August 11, 2021 (https://tinyurl.com/3jue-muuh).

590 Christopher F. Rufo, "'Antiracism' Comes to the Heartland,'" ChristopherRufo.com, January 19, 2021 (https://tinyurl.com/4fh8twep).

591 Rufo, "Critical Race Theory."

592 Rufo, "'Antiracism' Comes to the Heartland"; Christopher F. Rufo, "'Antiracism' Comes to the Heartland," *City Journal*, January 19, 2021 (https://tinyurl.com/4cn-fzhtm).

593 Aimee Cho, "'Privilege Bingo' in Fairfax Co. Class Meets Controversy for Including Being a Military Kid," News4, January 21, 2022 (https://tinyurl.com/zz3dztne).

594 *Ibid.*

595 *Ibid.*

596 "Remarks by President Trump at the White House Conference on American History," The White House, September 17, 2020 (https://tinyurl.com/4uaj8re4).

597 Jessie Kratz, "Masterpieces of Freedom: The Faulkner Murals," National Archives, June 30, 2017 (https://tinyurl.com/3nmcz84n).

598 "Remarks by President Trump."

599 Nick Niedzwiadek, "Trump goes after Black Lives Matter 'toxic propaganda' in schools," *Politico*, September 17, 2020 (https://tinyurl.com/2t29f94f).

600 Erwin Chemerinsky, "President Trump's attack on the Critical Race Theory is sad," *The Sacramento Bee*, September 18, 2020 (https://tinyurl.com/2hamwtx7).

601   Aaron Rupar, "Trump's dark National Archives speech was white resentment run amok," *Vox*, September 18, 2020 (https://tinyurl.com/fyvy6yy5).

602   "Remarks by President Biden at the 2022 National and State Teachers of the Year Event," The White House, April 27, 2022 (https://tinyurl.com/4rhvuhez).

603   *Ibid.*

604   "Ed COVID-19 Handbook," Department of Education, April 2021 (https://tinyurl.com/mrysj6cs).

605   Jessica Chasmar, "Psaki insists Biden not pushing critical race theory, says curriculum left to local schools," Fox News, July 22, 2021 (https://tinyurl.com/2p8u2z7t).

606   Jessica Chasmar, "Biden admin walks back ties to group pushing critical race theory in schools," Fox News, July 21, 2021 (https://tinyurl.com/ez7afc62).

607   Chasmar, "Psaki insists."

608   "Press Briefing by Press Secretary Jen Psaki, July 9, 2021," The White House, July 9, 2021 (https://tinyurl.com/3rvkarxj).

609   Philip Wegmann, "White House Backs Teachers Unions, CRT Curricula," Real Clear Politics, July 10, 2021 (https://tinyurl.com/2p8krry2).

610   The Editorial Board, "The Center for Politics and Unions," *The Wall Street Journal*, May 4, 2021 (https://tinyurl.com/ttjxhj93).

611   Jon Levine, "Powerful teachers union influenced CDC on school reopenings, emails show," *New York Post*, May 1, 2021 (https://tinyurl.com/7bpaxzmk).

612   Ben Chapman & Douglas Belkin, "Reading and Math Scores Plummeted During Pandemic, New Data Show," *The Wall Street Journal*, September 1, 2022 (https://tinyurl.com/2p8txjdp).

613   "Press Briefing by Press Secretary Karine Jean-Pierre," The White House, September 1, 2022 (https://tinyurl.com/mwr3zu44).

614 "Press Briefing by Press Secretary Kayleigh McEnany," The White House, July 24, 2020 (https://tinyurl. com/9z352udb).

615 "Final Report on the Events Surrounding the National School Boards Association's September 29, 2021, Letter to the President," National School Boards Association (https://tinyurl.com/y9t6wmpy).

616 *Ibid.*

617 *Ibid.*

618 "Memorandum for Director."

619 *Ibid.*

620 *Ibid.*

621 "Final Report on the Events."

622 "NSBA Apologizes for Letter to President Biden," National School Boards Association, October 22, 2021 (https://tinyurl.com/448z38kx).

623 Tyler O'Neil, "NSBA coordinated with White House, DOJ before sending notorious 'domestic terrorists' letter: emails," Fox News, November 12, 2021 (https://tinyurl. com/59xrsace).

624 "Final Report on the Events."

625 *Ibid.*

626 "Remarks by President Trump."

627 Christopher F. Rufo, Twitter, October 13, 2021 (https:// tinyurl.com/2p9vdkd8).

628 *Ibid.*

629 Andrew Mark Miller, "Virginia Dept. of Education website promotes CRT despite McAuliffe claims it's 'never been taught' there," Fox News, October 30, 2021 (https://tinyurl.com/2p8s8dwf).

630 Emma Colton, "Loudoun County mom says 6-year-old asked her if she was 'born evil' because she's White," Fox News, October 31, 2021 (https://tinyurl.com/ mr442sn9).

631   The Editors, "Terry McAuliffe's War on Parents," *National Review*, October 1, 2021 (https://tinyurl.com/bdfz5prv).

632   *Ibid.*

633   "McAuliffe: 'Our School Boards Were Fine...These People Started Showing Up Creating Such A Ruckus," YouTube, GOP War Room, October 31, 2021 (https://tinyurl.com/2p9esv5a).

634   Joshua Rhett Miller, "Critics blast Randi Weingarten-Terry McAuliffe rally ahead of Virginia election," *New York Post*, November 2, 2021 (https://tinyurl.com/2zd9tytu).

635   Evan Johnson, "Poll: Education is the most important issue facing Virginia voters," WFXR, October 26, 2021 (https://tinyurl.com/2nhccbnx).

636   "Enthusiasm gap and shift in voter priorities boost Youngkin," Monmouth University, October 20, 2021 (https://tinyurl.com/ymnajv7n).

637   *Ibid.*

638   *Ibid.*

639   Breck Dumas, "Virginia governor's race now hinges on education, and one candidate has a clear edge: poll," Fox News, October 29, 2021 (https://tinyurl.com/2h22yc5v).

640   Anya Kamenetz, "Why education was a top voter priority this election," NPR, November 4, 2021 (https://tinyurl.com/2p8wnxh4).

641   Andrew Schwartz, "Fox News Voter Analysis: How Virginia voters decided between Youngkin, McAuliffe," Fox News, November 3, 2021 (https://tinyurl.com/3pkwpvjv).

642   *Ibid.*

643   Andrew Rice, "New Jersey's Education Rebellion Was a Long Time Coming But Democrats didn't heed the signs," *New Yorker*, November 5, 2021 (https://tinyurl.com/3maeduhz); Matt Friedman, "Murphy reelected

New Jersey governor by razor-thin margin," *Politico*, November 3, 2021 (https://tinyurl.com/2za68es2).

644 Rice, "New Jersey's Education."

645 Jeremy B. White & Chris Ramirez, "San Francisco school board members ousted in parental backlash," *Politico*, February 16, 2022 (https://tinyurl.com/4mu58pbs).

646 Joe McLean, "In 'unprecedented' move, Gov. DeSantis gets involved in school board races, backs 3 local candidates," News4Jax, June 21, 2022 (https://tinyurl.com/yb2es5yf).

647 Zac Anderson & Kathryn Varn, "DeSantis scores big school board victories as most of his endorsed candidates win or advance," *Tallahassee Democrat*, August 24, 2022 (https://tinyurl.com/484uprvd).

648 William J. Murray, *Let Us Pray*, William Morrow and Company, Inc. (1995).

649 *Ibid*, 4.

650 *Ibid*.

651 *Ibid,* 5.

652 *Ibid*, 4.

653 *Ibid,* 5.

654 *Ibid*.

655 *Ibid,* 7.

656 *Ibid,* 8.

657 *Ibid,* 9.

658 *Ibid*.

659 *Ibid*, 10.

660 *Ibid*.

661 *Ibid*.

662 *Ibid*, 11.

663 *Ibid*.

664 *Murray v. Curlett*, 179 A.2d 698 (1962) (https://tinyurl.com/36h67smb).

665 *Engel*, 422.

666 *Ibid*.

667   *Ibid,* 424.

668   *Ibid,* (Stewart, J., dissenting 445).

669   *Engel,* 425.

670   *Ibid,* (Stewart, J., dissenting 445).

671   *Ibid,* 439.

672   *Ibid,* 446.

673   *Ibid.*

674   *Ibid,* 449.

675   *Ibid,* 450.

676   *Abington School District v. Schempp,* 374 U.S. 203, 213 (1963) (https://tinyurl.com/mr33w3pd).

677   *Ibid,* 226.

678   Murray, *Let Us Pray,* 49.

679   *Ibid,* 27.

680   "O'Hair, Madalyn Murray (1919–1995)," Texas State Historical Association, July 14, 2021 (https://tinyurl.com/2p8u29vp).

681   Collins, *The Language of God,* 160.

682   W. David Woods & Frank O'Brien, "Apollo 8," Apollo Flight Journal, (2001) (https://tinyurl.com/mrysw92s).

683   "O'Hair, Madalyn Murray."

684   *Ibid.*

685   Frank P. L. Somerville, "After 30 years, participants recall school-prayer ruling O'Hair keeps 'faith'; son gets religion," *Baltimore Sun,* June 13, 1993 (https://tinyurl.com/yc6s95e7).

686   Pat Gilliland, "Famed Atheist's Baptist Son To Speak at Bethany Church," *The Oklahoman,* September 6, 1998 (https://tinyurl.com/354hc24z).

687   *Ibid.*

688   Ted Dracos, *Ungodly: The Passions, Torments, and Murder of Atheist Madalyn Murray O'Hair,* 138, New York: Free Press, Internet Archive (2003) (https://tinyurl.com/2p86382z5).

689   *Ibid*; Jonathan V. Last, "The Most Hated Woman in America," *Washington Examiner*, March 30, 2017 (https://tinyurl.com/3w3pssje).

690   *Wallace v. Jaffree*, 472 U.S. 38 (1985) (https://tinyurl.com/j7e4b866).

691   *Santa Fe Independent School District v. Doe*, 530 U.S. 290 (2000) (https://tinyurl.com/3udp9rk3).

692   *Lee v. Weisman*, 505 U.S. 577 (1992) (https://tinyurl.com/2p829rzr).

693   *Mellen v. Bunting*, 181 F. Supp. 2d 619 (W.D. Va. 2002) (https://tinyurl.com/yddufdk5).

694   *Edwards v. Aguillard*, 482 U.S. 578 (1987) (https://tinyurl.com/554sjfhd).

695   "Religion in the Public Schools," Pew Research Center, October 3, 2019 (https://tinyurl.com/yc2kjvkh).

696   *Ibid*; "Supreme Court will not review policy banning nativity scenes in NY schools," Baptist News Global, February 19, 2007 (https://tinyurl.com/5f7esrr7).

697   *Roberts v. Madigan*, 921 F.2d 1047 (10th Cir. 1990) (https://tinyurl.com/4mne9tpx).

698   *Ibid*, 1055.

699   *Ibid*, 1049.

700   *Schempp*, 255.

701   *Elk Grove Unified School District v. Newdow*, 542 U.S. 1 (2004) (https://tinyurl.com/2ufwznpn).

702   *Ibid*.; Maura Dolan, "Pledge of Allegiance Violates Constitution, Court Declares," *Los Angeles Times*, June 27, 2002 (https://tinyurl.com/5n7tn9uf); Carol J. Williams, "Pledge of Allegiance's God reference now upheld by court," *Los Angeles Times*, March 12, 2010 (https://tinyurl.com/59u4aftk).

703   "Religion in the Public Schools."

704   *Elk Grove*, (Rehnquist, J., concurring, 9).

705   *Ibid*.

706   *Ibid*, 10.

707 *Ibid.*

708 *Ibid.*

709 *Ibid,* 11.

710 *Ibid.*

711 *Ibid,* 11–12.

712 *Ibid,* 12.

713 *Ibid.*

714 *Ibid,* 13.

715 *Ibid,* 16.

716 Murray, *Let Us Pray,* 88.

717 *Ibid,* 90.

718 *Ibid.*

719 *Ibid,* 95.

720 *Ibid,* 94.

721 Somerville, "After 30 years."

722 *Kennedy,* 2.

723 *Ibid,* 3.

724 *Ibid,* 5.

725 *Ibid,* 13.

726 McEnany, *New American.*

727 *Ibid.*

728 *Kennedy,* 15.

729 *Ibid,* 22.

730 *Ibid,* 28.

731 *Ibid,* 18.

732 *Ibid,* 28, 29.

733 Lindsay Kornick, "Sports Illustrated hit for article claiming Supreme Court ruling on prayer could erode 'American democracy,'" Fox News, June 13, 2022 (https://tinyurl.com/yc826h39).

734 Lee Lawrence, "School prayer: 50 years after the ban, God and faith more present than ever," *The Christian Science Monitor,* June 16, 2013 (https://tinyurl.com/4jzwdjs6).

735 *Ibid.*

736 *Ibid.*

737 *Widmar v. Vincent*, 454 US 263 (1981) (https://tinyurl.com/2p8recxp).

738 Jane G. Rainey, "Equal Access Act of 1984 (1984)," The First Amendment Encyclopedia (https://tinyurl.com/2j2jjzhx).

739 "Religion in the Public Schools." *See Board of Education of Westside Community Schools v. Mergens*, 496 US 226 (1990) (https://tinyurl.com/bdhhsnpc); *Rosenberger v. Rector*, 515 US 819 (1995) (https://tinyurl.com/ym6evcaf); *Good News Club v. Milford*, 533 US 98 (2001) (https://tinyurl.com/2z8m2c25).

740 *Carson v. Makin*, 596 U.S. (2022) (https://tinyurl.com/yvm48kea).

741 Mark J. Perry, "Ronald Reagan: Some Thoughts for Memorial Day," American Enterprise Institute, May 25, 2015 (https://tinyurl.com/47deynby).

742 "George Washington's Farewell Address (1796)," Bill of Rights Institute (https://tinyurl.com/2s43y6bh).

743 "Press Briefing by Press Secretary Kayleigh McEnany," The White House, May 23, 2020 (https://tinyurl.com/bdz6665f).

744 *Ibid.*

745 *Ibid.*

746 Andrew Mark Miller, "Psaki dodges questions on past dismissal of Hunter Biden laptop as 'Russian disinformation,'" Fox News, March 17, 2022 (https://tinyurl.com/2p8ymn8k).

747 Steven Nelson, "Karine Jean-Pierre won't discuss Biden voicemail on Hunter's laptop," *New York Post*, July 5, 2022 (https://tinyurl.com/5ckfrtw6).

748 "Press Briefing by Press Secretary Kayleigh McEnany."

749 The Editorial Board, "Minnesota's 'Essential' Churches," *The Wall Street Journal*, May 24, 2020 (https://tinyurl.com/mwtm3je5).

750 *Ibid.*

751 *Ibid.*

752 Bill Chappell, "Justice Alito: Pandemic Has Brought 'Unimaginable Restrictions' On Freedoms," NPR, November 13, 2020 (https://tinyurl.com/msdxnnxm).

753 Kelly Shackelford, "Religious Freedom Is Under Attack Like Never Before," *Newsweek*, August 5, 2020 (https://tinyurl.com/mrysxbbv).

754 *South Bay v. Newsom*, 590 U.S. (Kavanaugh, J., dissenting, 1) (2020) (https://tinyurl.com/kknrh4pw).

755 *Calvary Chapel v. Sisolak*, 591 U.S. (Alito, J., dissenting, 2) (2020) (https://tinyurl.com/336aterv).

756 *Ibid*, 1.

757 *Ibid*, (Gorsuch, J., dissenting, 1).

758 *Ibid*, (Alito, J., dissenting, 8); Kelsey Penrose, "Gov. Sisolak makes appearance at Black Lives Matter Protest in Carson City," Carson NOW, June 19, 2020 (https://tinyurl.com/4dxppxwm).

759 *Calvary Chapel v. Sisolak,* "Emergency Application for an Injunction Pending Appellate Review," (https://tinyurl.com/29ekptaz).

760 *Ibid.*

761 Douglas Ernst, "Bill de Blasio: NYC churches caught holding services during coronavirus may be 'permanently' closed," *Washington Times*, March 30, 2020 (https://tinyurl.com/yda4xbt2).

762 *On Fire Christian Center, Inc. v. Fischer et al*, Temporary Restraining Order, April 11, 2020 (https://tinyurl.com/2p8d5r5c).

763 Chris Otts, "Fischer: Police will collect license plates of Easter churchgoers," WDRB, April 10, 2020 (https://tinyurl.com/4ndxtr8t).

764 *Ibid.*

765 *On Fire,* Temporary.

766   *Temple Baptist Church v. City of Greenville*, The United States' Statement of Interest in Support of Plaintiffs, 2–3, April 14, 2020 (https://tinyurl.com/ya4y3x7b).

767   *Ibid.*

768   *Ibid.*

769   *Calvary Chapel,* 3–4.

770   *Capitol Hill Baptist Church v. Bowser,* Plaintiff's Original Complaint, 7, September 22, 2020 (https://tinyurl.com/mppb7p43).

771   *Ibid,* 9.

772   *Ibid,* 10.

773   *Ibid,* 2.

774   *Ibid,* 11.

775   *Ibid,* 2–3.

776   *Capitol Hill Baptist Church v. Bowser,* Memorandum Opinion, 17–18, October 9, 2020 (https://tinyurl.com/2p9baaa5).

777   Marty Johnson, "Bowser addresses record crowd at Black Lives Matter Plaza," *The Hill,* June 6, 2020 (https://tinyurl.com/5ewcpujj).

778   *Capitol Hill,* Memorandum, 2.

779   *Capitol Hill,* Plaintiff's.

780   *Ibid,* 3.

781   *Capitol Hill,* Memorandum, 26.

782   *Roman Catholic Diocese of Brooklyn, New York v. Cuomo,* 592 U.S. (Per Curiam, 2) (2020) (https://tinyurl.com/mwdzz2f6).

783   *Ibid,* 2–3.

784   *Ibid,* 3.

785   *Ibid,* 2.

786   *Ibid,* 5.

787   *Ibid,* 8.

788   *Ibid,* 2.

789   *Ibid,* (Gorsuch, J., concurring, 2).

790   *Ibid.*

791   *Ibid*, 3.
792   "South Bay United Pentecostal Church v. Newsom; Harvest Rock Church v. Newsom," Becket, February 5, 2021 (https://tinyurl.com/bdfy6jv5).
793   *Ibid*.
794   Tom Goldstein, "Counting votes in the *South Bay* decision," Scotus Blog, February 9, 2021 (https://tinyurl.com/2vueffwj).
795   *South Bay v. Newsom*, 592 U.S. (Statement of Gorsuch, J., 1) (2021) (https://tinyurl.com/r2vppjbr).
796   *Ibid*, 4–5.
797   *Ibid*, 6.
798   John R. Vile, "Tandon v. Newsom (2021)," The First Amendment Encyclopedia (https://tinyurl.com/24cd3pa9).
799   *Tandon v. Newsom*, 593 U.S. (Per Curiam, 3) (2021) (https://tinyurl.com/3te6mjda).
800   Bill Melugin & Shelly Insheiwat, "Fox 11 obtains exclusive photos of Gov. Newsom at French restaurant allegedly not following COVID-19 protocols," Fox 11, November 18, 2020 (https://tinyurl.com/4pnwkam3).
801   *Tandon*, Per Curiam, 5, *supra* note XX.
802   Chappell, "Justice Alito."
803   *Ibid*.
804   Editor Judith Resnik, "Urgency and Legitimacy," Global Constitutionalism 2021, Yale Law School (2021) (https://tinyurl.com/3jzrpbpm).
805   Brendan Pierson, "How COVID and shadow docket exploded SCOTUS' scope of religious freedom," Reuters, June 17, 2021 (https://tinyurl.com/bdzhzy3a).
806   Joan Biskupic, "How the Supreme Court is dismantling the separation of church and state," CNN, June 27, 2022 (https://tinyurl.com/3ed22zvu).

807 Ian Millhiser, "The Supreme Court is leading a Christian conservative revolution, *Vox*, January 30, 2022 (https://tinyurl.com/2p996uy9).

808 Christian Farias, "'No Victory for Religious Liberty': In Ruling for Praying Football Coach, the Supreme Court Smashes What's Left of Separation between Church and State," *Vanity Fair*, June 28, 2022 (https://tinyurl.com/msvne5a5).

809 David Smith, "Alarm as US supreme court takes a hatchet to church-state separation," *The Guardian*, July 2, 2022 (https://tinyurl.com/2t44jsdx).

810 *Ibid.*

811 *Ibid.*

812 Ian Prasad Philbrick, "A Pro-Religion Court," *New York Times*, June 22, 2022 (https://tinyurl.com/5n8a6bu2).

813 *Ibid.*

814 Lee Brown, "Child hits and swears at cop in 'heartbreaking' video from Minnesota," *New York Post*, July 12, 2022 (https://tinyurl.com/mtvcxfbe); Matthew Impelli, "Transgender Athlete Chelsea Wolfe Says Goal Is To 'Burn a US Flag' at Olympic Podium," *Newsweek*, June 21, 2021 (https://tinyurl.com/rjsbw7t3); Jeremiah Poff, "Story hour: How drag queen shows for minors have become increasingly common," *Washington Examiner*, June 11, 2022 (https://tinyurl.com/mry72dp6).

815 Shirin Ghaffary, "It's getting harder for people to believe that Facebook is a net good for society," *Vox*, September 16, 2021 (https://tinyurl.com/4xkjakyz).

816 "Opening Statement of the Republican Leader Cathy McMorris Rodgers," March 25, 2021 (https://tinyurl.com/ycysn2zs).

817 Miles Parks, "Facebook Calls links To Depression Inconclusive. These Researchers Disagree," NPR, May 18, 2021 (https://tinyurl.com/27h9k2ha).

818   Georgia Wells, Jeff Horowitz & Deepa Seetharaman, "Facebook Knows Instagram Is Toxic for Teen Girls, Company Documents Show," *The Wall Street Journal*, September 14, 2021 (https://tinyurl.com/yzubws9h).

819   *Ibid.*

820   *Ibid.*

821   *Ibid.*

822   *Ibid.*

823   *Ibid.*

824   *Ibid.*

825   *Ibid.*

826   *Ibid.*

827   Theo Wayt, "Instagram curates anorexia images to teen girls who have eating disorders: docs," *New York Post*, October 26, 2021 (https://tinyurl.com/4j5ymyh2).

828   *Ibid.*

829   *Ibid.*

830   *Ibid.*

831   Wells, "Facebook Knows Instagram."

832   Matt Grossman, "States Urge Facebook to Abandon Plan for Children's Instagram," *The Wall Street Journal*, May 10, 2021 (https://tinyurl.com/3nk2a4md).

833   Jeff Horwitz, "Instagram's Plan for Kids Met With Hostile Response," *The Wall Street Journal*, April 7, 2021 (https://tinyurl.com/2p8ffh7b).

834   *Ibid.*

835   Deepa Seetharaman, "Senators Seek Answers From Facebook After WSJ Report on Instagram's Impact on Young Users," *The Wall Street Journal*, September 14, 2021 (https://tinyurl.com/y29jwdc8).

836   "Attorneys General Urge Facebook to Abandon Launch of Instagram Kids," National Association of Attorneys General, May 10, 2021 (https://tinyurl.com/2y7p35u9).

837   *Ibid.*

838 Aaron Gregg & Elizabeth Dwoskin, "Facebook hits pause on Instagram Kids app amid growing scrutiny," *The Washington Post*, September 27, 2021 (https://tinyurl.com/2v6697u7).

839 Eleanor Klibanoff, "In pandemic's isolation, an alarming number of teenage girls are attempting suicide," *The Texas Tribune*, February 1, 2022 (https://tinyurl.com/2vbc5rn6).

840 Kristen Rogers, "Adolescent suicides increased in 5 US states during the pandemic. Why parents should be concerned," CNN, April 25, 2022 (https://tinyurl.com/bd77mabn).

841 "A declaration from the American Academy of Pediatrics, American Academy of Child and Adolescent Psychiatry and Children's Hospital Association," American Academy of Pediatrics, October 19, 2021 (https://tinyurl.com/35yuwzyj).

842 *Ibid.*

843 *Ibid.*

844 Jon Kamp, "Drug overdose deaths, fueled by fentanyl, hit record high in US," Fox News, November 17, 2021 (https://tinyurl.com/3uhay4tw).

845 *Ibid.*

846 Julie Appleby, "Overdose deaths declined in 2018. But there's more to the story," PolitiFact, August 26, 2020 (https://tinyurl.com/2jmtfct9).

847 Kamp, "Drug overdose deaths."

848 Jon Kamp, José de Córdoba & Julie Wernau, "How Two Mexican Drug Cartels Came to Dominate America's Fentanyl Supply," *The Wall Street Journal*, August 30, 2022 (https://tinyurl.com/vdupztwf).

849 Jan Hoffman, "Fentanyl Tainted Pills Bought on Social Media Case Youth Drug Deaths to Soar," *The New York Times*, May 19, 2022 (https://tinyurl.com/2hvx2wj8).

850   *Ibid.*

851   Erin McCormick, "US teen overdose deaths double in three years amid fentanyl crisis," *The Guardian,* April 12, 2022 (https://tinyurl.com/2p47vjvt).

852   Hoffman, "Fentanyl Tainted Pills."

853   *Ibid.*

854   *Ibid.*

855   "Emoji Drug Code | Decoded," Drug Enforcement Administration (https://tinyurl.com/2p8ku9h2).

856   *Ibid.*

857   *Ibid.*

858   *Ibid.*

859   Hoffman, "Fentanyl Tainted Pills."

860   *Ibid.*

861   Kamp, "How Two Mexican Drug Cartels."

862   *Ibid.*

863   Sydney Murphy, "Deadly 'Rainbow Fentanyl' Looks Like Candy, Could Entice Kids," *U.S. News & World Report,* September 1, 2022 (https://tinyurl.com/5dm467wx).

864   Hoffman, "Fentanyl Tainted Pills."

865   *Ibid.*

866   McEnany, *For Such a Time as This.*

867   Ben Johnson, "Oxford, City of Dreaming Spires," Historic UK, (https://tinyurl.com/2p85pd7y).

868   McEnany, *The New American Revolution.*

869   Joe Pinsker, "Trump's Presidency Is Over. So Are Many Relationships," *The Atlantic,* March 30, 2021 (https://tinyurl.com/y22e7dru).

870   Lisa Bonos, "Republicans have more friends across the political divide than Democrats, study finds," *The Washington Post,* July 3, 2021 (https://tinyurl.com/2u7uw4w2).

871   Neal Rothschild, "Young Dems more likely to despise the other party," *Axios,* December 7, 2021 (https://tinyurl.com/2p8w9d7h).

872 *Ibid.*

873 Yascha Mounk, "The Doom Spiral of Pernicious Polarization," *The Atlantic*, May 21, 2022 (https://tinyurl.com/3tu4866e).

874 David Lauter, "Researchers asked people worldwide about divisiveness. Guess where U.S. ranked," *Los Angeles Times*, October 15, 2021 (https://tinyurl.com/ycx76827).

875 McEnany, *For Such a Time as This.*

876 McEnany, *For Such a Time as This.*

877 "Inaugural Address by President Joseph R. Biden, Jr.," The White House, January 20, 2021 (https://tinyurl.com/3hmbskfd).

878 *Ibid.*

879 "Remarks by President Biden on Fighting the COVID-19 Pandemic," The White House, September 9, 2021 (https://tinyurl.com/yc827c3d).

880 *Ibid.*

881 "Remarks by President Biden on Protecting the Right to Vote," The White House, January 11, 2022 (https://tinyurl.com/5dvzt4dp).

882 Joseph A. Wulfsohn, "Psaki mocked for saying Biden wasn't making 'human' comparison between GOP, segregationists in Atlanta speech," Fox News, January 14, 2022 (https://tinyurl.com/ywc2n6a8).

883 "Georgia sees record early voting turnout during primary elections," WSBTV, May 22, 2022 (https://tinyurl.com/2np6huz9).

884 Jim Geraghty, "Much Higher Minority Early Voting in Georgia's Upcoming Primaries," *National Review*, May 19, 2022 (https://tinyurl.com/39vpuvx7).

885 "Remarks by President Biden at Signing of S. 3373, 'The Sergeant First Class Heath Robinson Honoring Our Promises to Address Comprehensive Toxics (PACT) Act of 2022,'" The White House, August 10, 2022 (https://tinyurl.com/4et7ch3s).

886 "Full Transcript of President Biden's Speech in Phila-delphia," *New York Times*, September 1, 2022 (https://tinyurl.com/3spnbxpa).

887 *Ibid.*

888 *Ibid.*

889 *Ibid.*

890 *Ibid.*

891 "Read Republican Sen. Tim Scott's response to Biden's address to Congress," CNN, April 28, 2021 (https://tinyurl.com/mpb7y3xj).

892 *Ibid.*

893 *Ibid.*

894 *Ibid.*

895 Mark Moore, "Twitter allows 'Uncle Tim' to trend for hours after Sen. Tim Scott's rebuttal, and then took action," *New York Post*, April 29, 2021 (https://tinyurl.com/2uytechx).

896 *Ibid.*

897 "Identity," Merriam-Webster (https://tinyurl.com/yswvv6fe).

898 Jeffrey M. Jones, "Belief in God in U.S. Dips to 81%, a New Low," Gallup, June 17, 2022 (https://tinyurl.com/mas56m7f).

899 *Ibid.*

900 *Ibid.*

901 Keller, *Walking with God*, 57.

902 *Ibid*, 59.

903 Jones, "Belief in God."

904 Keller, *Walking with God*, 76.

905 "Nihilism," Merriam-Webster (https://tinyurl.com/2p9a4u5n).

906 Donald A. Crosby, "Nihilism," Routledge Encyclopedia of Philosophy (https://tinyurl.com/4k7y385m).

907 "Nihilism," Britannica (https://tinyurl.com/y638e5t6).

908 "Friedrich Nietzsche, *The Parable of the Madman* (1882)," History Guide (https://tinyurl.com/mryz8bvw).

909 *Ibid.*

910 Kate Blackwood, "Religion: less 'opiate,' more suppressant, study finds," Cornell Chronicle, October 19, 2020 (https://tinyurl.com/4hd9rbc5).

911 Collins, *The Language of God*, 42.

912 Josh McDowell & Sean McDowell, *More Than a Carpenter*, 60, Tyndale House Publishers (2009).

913 Collins, *The Language of God*, 4.

914 Alex B. Berezow, "Richard Dawkins Is Wrong About Religion," Real Clear Science, September 28, 2013 (https://tinyurl.com/52x82zte).

915 "'If I Were the Devil' by Paul Harvey | Illinois Fraternal Order Of Police," Illinois Fraternal Order Of Police (https://tinyurl.com/33crrzbs).

916 *Ibid.*

917 Collins, *The Language of God*, 161.

918 McDowell, *More Than a Carpenter*, 1.

919 Nick Nowalk, "Pascal's God-Shaped Hole," ichthus, May 2, 2011 (https://tinyurl.com/yb5btdmf).

920 "What is Apologetics?," Grace Theological Seminary, August 27, 2021 (https://tinyurl.com/57yk5c79).

921 1 Peter 3:15, New International Version, Bible Gateway (https://tinyurl.com/2kcj6v8n).

922 Proverbs 15:1, New International Version, Bible Gateway (https://tinyurl.com/ypscuw5u).

923 Galatians 5:22–23, New International Version, YouVersion (https://tinyurl.com/3zyfbjnz).

924 Collins, *The Language of God*; John C. Lennox, *God's Undertaker: Has Science Buried God?*, Lion (2009).

925 Strobel, *The Case for Christ*.

926 Pregnancy +.

927 Lennox, *God's Undertaker*, 48.

928 *Ibid.*

929 Collins, *The Language of God*, 1.

930 McDowell, *More Than a Carpenter.*

931 *Ibid*, 54.

932 *Ibid*; Bill Gates, Twitter, July 30, 2016 (https://tinyurl. com/2p8pyuv7).

933 McDowell, *More Than a Carpenter*, 54.

934 Cystic Fibrosis Foundation (https://tinyurl. com/4u4hfrk7).

935 Collins, *The Language of God,* 112–13.

936 *Ibid*, 114.

937 *Ibid*, 116.

938 *Ibid*, 123.

939 *Ibid*, 73.

940 McDowell, *More Than a Carpenter*, 56.

941 Collins, *The Language of God*, 74.

942 McDowell, *More Than a Carpenter*, 56.

943 Lennox, *God's Undertaker*, 59.

944 *Ibid*, 12.

945 C. S. Lewis, *Mere Christianity*, 22, HarperCollins (1952).

946 *Ibid*, 23.

947 McDowell, *More Than a Carpenter*, 56.

948 Jennifer Polland, "The 10 Most Read Books In The World," *Business Insider*, December 27, 2012 (https:// tinyurl.com/2x5x845v).

949 *Ibid.*

950 Strobel, *The Case for Christ.*

951 *Ibid*, 34.

952 *Ibid.*

953 McDowell, *More Than a Carpenter*, 64.

954 *Ibid*, 72.

955 *Ibid*, 73–4.

956 *See* Strobel, *The Case for Christ,* 48, 97, 106; McDowell, *More Than a Carpenter,* 64.

957 Strobel, *The Case for Christ,* 101.

958 Matthew 11:3, New International Version, Bible Hub (https://tinyurl.com/2jchkzna).

959 Matthew 11:4–5, New International Version, Bible Gateway (https://tinyurl.com/ycku8rss).

960 Strobel, *The Case for Christ,* 116.

961 *Ibid.*

962 *Ibid.*

963 *Ibid*, 188–191.

964 *Ibid*, 192.

965 *Ibid*, 193; Harold Willmington, "A Timeline Countdown Leading to the Incarnation and Birth of Jesus Christ (Part A)," Liberty University (2017) (https://tinyurl.com/y62dhzv8).

966 The Jeremiah Study Bible, 913, Isaiah 53:3, 5, 7.

967 *Ibid*, 913.

968 Strobel, *The Case for Christ,* 195.

969 Paul Strand, "Psalm 22: An Amazingly Accurate, Faith-Building Prophecy of Christ's Death on the Cross," CBN, April 14, 2022 (https://tinyurl.com/r5xfmeyy).

970 *Ibid*; Psalm 22:16, New International Version, Bible Hub (https://tinyurl.com/59s2pn8k).

971 *Ibid*; Psalm 22:14, 15, Bible Gateway (https://tinyurl.com/3yv9ymds).

972 Psalm 22:18, New International Version, Bible Gateway (https://tinyurl.com/mrax46rr); John 19:23, New International Version, Bible Gateway (https://tinyurl.com/msth78tk).

973 Psalm 22:7–8, New International Version, Bible Gateway (https://tinyurl.com/2vtwjkz3).

974 Strand, "Psalm 22."

975 McDowell, *More Than a Carpenter,* 148.

976 Strobel, *The Case for Christ,* 199.

977 *Ibid*, 200.

978 Lewis, *Mere Christianity*.

979 *See Ibid*, 5–6.

980 *Ibid*, 4.

981 *See Ibid*, 5–6.

982 Strobel, *The Case for Christ*, 266, 267.

983 Collins, *The Language of God*, 225.

984 Strobel, *The Case for Christ*, 196.

985 *Ibid*, 289.

986 *Ibid*, 291.

987 McDowell, *More Than a Carpenter*, 4–5.

988 *Ibid*, 160.

989 Anne Trujillo, "The inspiring writings of Rachel Scott uncovered in 'Rachel's Story: Triumph Over Tragedy,'" Denver ABC 7, January 24, 2017 (https://tinyurl.com/yc6seurr).

990 Laura Collins, "EXCLUSIVE: The Columbine shooters killed my daughter for her Christian faith. Now I have forgiven them—and formed a bond with one of their moms, reveals mother of massacre's first victim," *Daily Mail*, October 5, 2016 (https://tinyurl.com/yckwvjkn).

991 Rachel's Challenge (https://tinyurl.com/2z2rymct).

992 Trujillo, "The Inspiring Writings."

993 McEnany, *For Such a Time as This*.

994 Matthew 14:22–33; Mark 6:45–52; John 6:16–21.

995 The Jeremiah Study Bible, 1273, Matthew 14:19–21.

996 *Ibid*, 1273, Matthew 14:22–23.

997 *Ibid*, 1273, Matthew 14:24.

998 *Ibid*, 1273, Matthew 14:25.

999 *Ibid*.

1000 *Ibid*, 1273, Matthew 14:26.

1001 *Ibid*, 1318, Mark 6:52.

1002 *Ibid*, 1273.

1003 *Ibid*, 1273, Matthew 14:27.

1004 *Ibid*, 1273.

1005 *Ibid.*
1006 *Ibid.*
1007 *Ibid,* 1274, Matthew 14:28.
1008 *Ibid,* 1274, Matthew 14:29.
1009 *Ibid,* 1274.
1010 *Ibid,* 1274, Matthew 14:30.
1011 *Ibid,* 1274, Matthew 14:31–33.
1012 Strobel, *The Case for Christ*, 192.

ACKNOWLEDGMENTS

Nash—As I write these acknowledgments, I am seven months pregnant. I cannot believe that you will be here in less than three months! Each day, your kicks and movements grow stronger, and it has been such a joy to feel and see you grow as I wrote these pages. Your father and I can't wait for you to be here so that we can give you all of our love!

Blake—You are growing up to be a beautiful young woman, full of love, exuberance, and radiant joy. Even at this young age, I see such a fire and spark of passion within you. Without a doubt, you are going to leave your mark on this world. You light up every single room you walk into, and you fill Sean's and my hearts with so much love!

Sean—It is an understatement to say that I could not have finished this project without you. Your support and selflessness know no bounds. You are the best husband I could ask for, and it has been a tremendous joy to see what an incredible father you are to Blake and now Nash. I love you, and I am immensely blessed to walk through this life with you.

Dad, Mike McEnany, and Mom, Leanne McEnany—You gave me the best possible chance in this world for one simple reason: you instilled the love of Christ in me from a young age. Thanks to you, I knew my identity from the earliest days, and the words that fill these pages are a testament to you both. You are the most supportive and loving parents, and I thank God for you often. Dad, I must say to you specifically, that you have become quite the Instagram star—haha! When I give speeches, I routinely have "young eagles" say that they would love to meet my father. Let's do an Instagram live soon!

My brother, Michael McEnany, and my sister, Ryann McEnany—I am so proud of you both! Michael, you physically save lives as an emergency medicine doctor. Your work inspires me! Ryann, it has been an incredible experience working in the world of politics and media alongside of you. It is so fun to watch you soar!

Paul, JoAnna, and Michael Gilmartin—Thank you for being such supportive in-laws! You went above and beyond in helping with Blake and made this writing process so much easier. I am truly appreciative of you all!

Uncle Smoke and Aunt Linda—Thank you both for always being there for me. Aunt Linda, from hosting book parties to sending me so many pictures from my journey, you have been so supportive in all my endeavors!

Uncle George and Aunt Andie—Your love and support have been ever-present, and you never fail to make me laugh. See you in the Keys!

Uncle Bill, Aunt Donna, Will, Nicki, and William—Love you all! Will and Nicki, it has been so special to grow my young family alongside yours!

Angelina Oliva—You did a phenomenal job taking the photographs for this book. Thank you for your hard work and diligence!

Anthony Ziccardi and the Post Hill Press Team—I have thoroughly enjoyed partnering with you all on not just one, but now two books! Your editing, design, and publicity teams have all gone above and beyond, and I could not have completed this work without them.